Coal Towns

Coal Towns

Life, Work, and Culture
in Company Towns
of Southern Appalachia,
1880–1960

Crandall A. Shifflett

**The University of
Tennessee Press**
KNOXVILLE

The paper in this book meets the minimum requirements
of the American National Standard for Permanence
of Paper for Printed Library Materials.
∞
The binding materials have been chosen for strength
and durability.

Library of Congress Cataloging in Publication Data

Shifflett, Crandall A.
   Coal towns : life, work, and culture in company towns
   of Southern Appalachia, 1880-1960 / Crandall A. Shifflett.
   — 1st ed.
      p.   cm.
   Includes bibliographical references and index.
   ISBN 0-87049-678-6 (cloth: alk. paper)
   1. Appalachian Region, Southern – Social life and customs.
   2. Company towns – Appalachian Region, Southern – History.
   3. Coal miners – Appalachian Region, Southern – Social life
   and customs.   I. Title.
F217.A65S54   1991
974 – dc20   90-41458   CIP

Contents

Illustrations

Preface

Of all forms of industrial labor, coal mining is most clearly associated with the southern Appalachian Mountains of the United States. In the last decade of the nineteenth century, the Industrial Revolution dug into the steep mountain hillsides, and soon the lodes of rich bituminous coal filled the railroad cars bound for the boilers, furnaces, and hearths of America. Even more important was the production of industrial fuel in the form of coke, the distilled by-product of coal baked at high temperatures in sealed ovens. In the post-Civil War industrial age, America had a tremendous need for fossil fuel for locomotives and boilers, especially in the heavy industries of iron, steel, and railroads.

Not all regions of the southern Appalachians contained deposits of the black gold. Generally, the largest and richest veins lay in the mountain fastnesses of southwestern Virginia (confined mostly to the counties of Lee, Wise, Dickenson, Buchanan, Russell, and Tazewell), a large part of West Virginia (especially the southern and easternmost counties), eastern Kentucky, and as far south as the Birmingham, Alabama, industrial district. Beginning in the 1880s, capitalist investors from the nation's financial centers in New York and Philadelphia, with the assistance of local and state government officials, land agents, lawyers, and other retainers, grabbed huge acreages of mountain land at bargain prices, built railroad lines to their underground fortunes, and opened the Appalachian coalfields. Coal towns quickly sprang up, over five hundred of them altogether by 1925 when the boom ended.

The focus of this book is upon white working culture in the coal towns. Native-born white farmers and their families left shrinking, hilly, infertile mountain farms in Virginia, West Virginia, Kentucky, and Tennessee. Poor whites left the agriculturally depressed areas of the rural South in search of a better life. White culture dominated the mining towns, where blacks and immigrants lived in segregated areas commonly called "Niggertown" or "Hunktown." Black miners peaked as a percentage of the labor force in 1900 and declined every decade thereafter. Mechanization of the mines took a great toll of black labor.[1] Immigrants, primarily Italians, Poles, and Hungarians, left the coalfields in large numbers during World War I and never returned.

Although white mining families are the focus of the book, the emphasis upon them is by no means exclusive. Black and immigrant miners were important sources of labor; an entire chapter is devoted to their recruitment. Black tenants and sharecroppers fled the poverty and peonage of southern agriculture. Foreign immigrants, some new arrivals and others from the anthracite fields of Pennsylvania, came to the burgeoning coal camps on trains. Black labor made up 38 percent of the labor force before the percentage of black miners began to decline.[2] Some oral histories refer to entire towns in West Virginia using black or immigrant labor. Together, immigrants and blacks had an enormous impact upon life in the coal towns.

Geographically, the emphasis is upon the coal towns of southwestern Virginia, especially those planned by Stonega Coke and Coal, now the Westmoreland Coal Company. Stonega employed three-fourths of all of Virginia's miners; they lived in nine company towns in Wise County. Virginia's miners have been neglected in the history of mining studies; West Virginia has received most of the attention in southern Appalachia. In 1983, a massive collection of company records, previously stored in old bathhouses of abandoned mines, was opened to the public at Hagley Museum and Library in Wilmington, Delaware. Largely as a result of these records becoming available, along with those I became familiar with during my graduate study at the University of Virginia, did this study begin to take shape.

But the study is certainly not limited to Virginia. Other towns that figure prominently in the book are Borderland, a company town on the Tug Fork of the Big Sandy River in Mingo County, West Virginia, and Pike County, Kentucky. Kaymoor, West Virginia, located in the New River Gorge, is another town that looms large. Full data on these towns were available in both company records and oral histories. On Wheelwright, Kentucky, oral histories proved useful in making up for inadequacies of the company records. A rich oral-history collection housed at Samford University in Birmingham, Alabama, gave remarkably detailed accounts of life in Docena, a town on the outskirts of Birmingham. I know little about the many company towns mentioned in the Appalachian Oral History Project beyond what the informants have revealed in their valuable recollections. The worth of these many different accounts lies in the broad familiarity they provide with coal-town life in general.

The social and cultural history of coal-mining towns in southern Appalachia is the subject of this book. The building of company towns began in the 1880s and peaked in the early 1920s. Following closely on the heels of the great age of town-building, the mid-1920s through the 1950s were years of decline hastened by the Great Depression, market changes, and mechanization. It is an indication of the volatility of the energy industry that growth and decline could follow so closely one upon the other. After World War II, coal towns began to close. In the 1950s they disappeared, not entirely, but certainly as central features of Appalachian mining. To a far greater extent than coalfields in the northern United States, coal towns in southern Appalachia were largely the creations of the companies that secured the leases, founded the towns, and hired the miners, i.e., they were "company towns." It was the coal company that built and owned the houses and provided for all the other facilities—whether schools, churches, commissaries, theaters, dance halls, bowling alleys, soda fountains, or even graveyards.

The structure of the study is both chronological and topical. The book begins with a critical introduction to the controversies about Appalachian history and culture. The introduction lays bare the argumentative framework of the book. Part 1 consists of two chapters. The first examines conditions in preindustrial Appalachia and challenges the idea of a bucolic and changeless society. It stresses instead the fundamental importance of mobility as a means to achieve a stable society, as many families were led to migrate to the nearby centers of rural industry. The second chapter functions as an interlude, giving the factual details necessary to link the population crisis and agricultural collapse, which threatened local communities throughout the nineteenth century, with the migration to the southern Appalachian coalfields at the turn of the century. The agrarian crisis and the opening of the coalfields coincided, providing an explanation of the miners' willing hearts for a day's work and a day's pay, in spite of the crude and exploitative conditions of the pioneer years.

Part 2 analyzes the plans and designs of the coal operators who created company mining towns in the Appalachian wilderness between 1880 and 1930. The development from camp to coal town, the recruitment of labor—immigrants and blacks—from outside the region, and the impact of World War I are topics of chapters in this section. Company towns developed in three phases: the pioneer days of laying out and building the town, roughly the 1880s to 1915, the paternalistic period from World War I until the Great Depression, and the years of decline from the 1930s to the 1960s. The backgrounds of the major companies of the study and an identification of the towns these companies built are included here.

The world of mine work dominated every aspect of life in the coal towns. Working in the dark underground was a man's world. Women did not go into the mines. In fact, many miners considered it bad luck for women to enter a mine. Rigid work segregation gave to mine culture an ambience of maleness which was one of its most salient features. Social and cultural life mirrored this workingman's culture.

The context of industrial relations, including the process of mining coal, the organization of work, the dangers and occupational diseases and their impact on worker identity and solidarity are all topics of part 3. Also of interest are worker associations and the interconnections between work and culture in an urban, industrial setting. Here I analyze the saga of unionization, classically portrayed in the severe reactions of the Borderland Coal Company and its employment of labor spies, firings, evictions, yellow-dog contracts, and violent confrontations, which terminated in the closed shop and the total unionization of mine labor. Nonunionism remained strong to the end. The use of violence by pro and antiunion forces in the 1920s and 1930s and the closed shop of 1939 are forgotten legacies which may have sown the seeds of modern anti-unionism.

In Part 4, I am interested in coal towns as social and cultural communities. Indeed, mining towns were communities: births, baptisms, marriages, anniversaries, and deaths formed the life cycle of thousands of families in coal towns. Children were reared in this environment, and all the moments of life, big and small, which give to every family, great and ordinary, a cherishable history, likewise grew into a collective experience. The perspectives of former miners on life in the company town sometimes contrast sharply with conventional images of company towns.

Oral histories provide the context of everyday life: shopping at the company store, playing baseball, visiting neighbors, or listening to the radio. Viewed superficially, these activities seem trivial. At a deeper level, they reveal a process of assimilation. As elements of the rural folk culture blended with the demands of industrial labor, old values and ideals perdured, changed, or were renounced. A chapter on the company store analyzes the convergence of two creations — the company's town and the miner's town. The role of the company church in the miners' lives indicates the impact of industrialization and modernization upon rural habits of religion.

Finally, in the Conclusion, I discuss the sweeping changes that affected company towns beginning in the 1930s and leading to their closing in the 1950s. Changes in the fuel industry, along with the Great Depression and World War II, the automobile, and mechanization in the coalfields, were some of the major economic and historical forces that reshaped relationships between miners and their bosses and destroyed the company town.

Culture and paternalism are two major themes throughout this study. Miners, of course, had a culture, although it was not entirely homogeneous. Ideals of family, community, class, race, and gender were not identical. Nor were they immutable. Yet there was general agreement in the area of social relationships. More significantly, the coal-town experience changed some ideals and left others intact. For example, white mining families brought with them to the company town a set of racial and ethnic beliefs common to nineteenth-century Americans. There is little evidence that mine work mitigated social prejudice against immigrants and blacks. On the other hand, gender differences, which existed in rural society but were less sharply drawn, seem to have intensified in the coal town.

What precisely was the underlying relationship between cultural history on the one hand and economics, demography, and social structure on the other? In raising the issue, I do not presume to "prove" a relationship so much as to pursue it (without, I hope, enslaving the study to the digging). The history and culture of the rural white mountaineer can be brought face-to-face with the ambient urban, industrial society of the coal town, and some measure can then be taken of the miner's understanding of his new circumstances. I invite the reader to join the search for how mining families thought about family, community, work, and relationships of gender, class, or race.[3]

Paternalism is what the Stonega Coke and Coal Company called "contentment sociology." The work of Eugene Genovese especially has shown the fallacy of defining paternalism solely as a means of social control, or merely as an instrument of exploitation and oppression in the hands of bosses who might provide certain benefits unrelated to the productive process in order to buy labor stability. As Genovese has demonstrated, the problem in this monolithic understanding of paternalism is that it renders its subjects hapless victims with no hand in shaping their own destinies.[4]

Paternalism in the company town was dualistic; it had not only a controlling but a beneficent side. It benefited miners who lived under it. Many miners readily understood the difference between paternalistic management and operators who took little interest in the towns. Of course, they preferred operators who took an interest. Mining families were capable of accepting the benefits of paternalism without compromising their independence entirely.

To argue that paternalism had its beneficent side does not mean that it was benevolent. It exacted its price, most notably in the miners' freedom. Operators catered to the miners' social needs out of a desire to attract and retain adequate labor. The most formidable restriction on the miner's freedom as well as the greatest source of power and authority over the miner was the company house, which gave operators the right to evict any worker at a moment's notice. With eviction came the simul-

taneous loss of job and of home; nothing could have been more trau-
matic. The company store also provided ample opportunity for exploitation through its scrip system and, insofar as it provided the only outlet
for essential items mining families needed for life and work, it could
charge whatever the traffic would bear. In addition, coal operators assisted in the development of schools and churches and the hiring of
preachers and teachers, which presented them with the power to control
public opinion.

In spite of the limits the company-town setting and paternalism imposed on the freedom and autonomy of mining families, town residents
found or realized the means to circumvent the hegemony of the operators and preserve their independence. Sometimes they did so in small
ways, as when mining families avoided high prices and the entrapment
of indebtedness at the company store. The union provided some protection against arbitrary decisions in the workplace, although some miners
may have felt later that they had exchanged one master for another. Labor mobility was an important source of independence. Such features as
generation, marital status, gender, and race structured the towns during
their stages of development and often altered the contest of life in ways
that operators could not control. Social and cultural life in the towns also became a source of communal identity, mutual assistance, and
solidarity.

Acknowledgments

The sources for this study are the records of coal companies, oral-history collections, and government reports on the coal industry. The richest and largest collection of company records were those of the Stonega Coke and Coal Company (now the Westmoreland Coal Company) housed at the Hagley Library in Wilmington, Delaware, and opened to public use in 1983. Stonega employed the majority of miners in Virginia, and this study provides the first published work on Virginia miners. The company towns of the Stonega Company were Andover, Arno, Derby, Dunbar, Exeter, Imboden, Keokee, Osaka, Pine Branch, Roda, and Stonega.

The Low Moor Iron Company, which had its headquarters at Clifton Forge, Virginia, was primarily a producer of pig iron. But it was also the founder of Kaymoor, its company coal town located in the New River coal district of West Virginia. The Borderland Coal Company, under Edward L. Stone of Roanoke, Virginia, founded the company town of Borderland. It derived its name from its dual location in Mingo County, West Virginia, and Pike County, Kentucky. Borderland was incorporated in 1903 and declared bankruptcy in 1933. Both the Borderland and Low Moor records are housed at the Alderman Library, University of Virginia. The Wheelwright Coal Collection at the Margaret I. King Library, University of Kentucky, provided material (along with oral histories) on the town of Wheelwright, which existed under three different coal companies: Elkhorn Coal Corporation, Island Creek Coal Company, and Inland Steel Corporation. The Justus Collins Papers, a small collection at West Virginia University, supplied information on the Winding Gulf Company town at Davy, West Virginia.

Collections of company records were uneven, of course, some being more detailed and extending over longer periods of time than others. All were weak for the very early period of coal-town development, a not insurmountable problem since later descriptions of the towns left many historical footprints. No single collection was adequate to explore all the contours of coal towns. Rather, all had their strengths and weaknesses. Therefore, some towns are pulled forward to explore a particular aspect of company-town history while others recede only to be drawn forward later to elucidate another corner of the past.

Oral-history collections provided the hard-to-get, but invaluable, firsthand accounts of the miners themselves. The Appalachian Oral History Project in the 1970s interviewed hundreds of people from the region, many former miners or family members of former miners. These interviews have been transcribed, and their locations are given in George Parkinson's *Guide to Coal Mining Collections in the United States* (Morgantown: West Virginia University Library, 1978). This valuable guide also locates many other collections of company records. A small but rich oral-history collection is the Samford Oral History Collection at Samford University, Birmingham, Alabama, which provided all of the information on the company town of Docena, a town of the Tennessee Coal and Iron Company. Still another small but useful and growing oral-history collection is the one done by the National Park Service, New River Gorge, Oak Hill, West Virginia, which gives snapshots of life in dozens of coal towns that dotted the map in this rugged gorge along the New River. I also benefited from several interviews of my own and from unsolicited letters sent to me by former residents of Virginia coal towns who learned of the study.

Three major government studies of the coal industry must be mentioned: the U.S. Coal Commission produced a five-volume study of the industry in 1922; in 1947, the U.S. Coal Mines Administration produced *A Medical Survey of the Bituminous-Coal Industry*, sometimes called "The Boone Report" after the individual who headed the study, Rear Admiral Joel T. Boone; and in 1980 a presidential commission, under John D. Rockefeller IV, produced *The American Coal Miner: A Report on Community and Living Conditions in the Coalfields*. Throughout the book, I have followed convention and referred to these investigations as, respectively, the U.S. Coal Commission, Boone, and Rockefeller reports. These three studies provide a wealth of information on miners and their working and living conditions.

From the beginning, the goal of my study has been to explore the nature of the coal-town order in all of its complexity and variety, beginning with the background culture of the white majority and moving into the social community of individual towns. Another set of towns may have altered the focus or led to slightly different conclusions, but there is no reason to believe that the towns of this study, randomly chosen on the basis of the availability of records, has produced a distorted view of the coal town. Nor can one be sure that another set of towns would have evoked vastly different results. The conclusion seems inescapable: no single town represents all coal towns. The quest for the "typical" town has already generated a formidable stereotype. There is no need to replace it with yet another one. Towns went through phases of development; they were always changing and being subjected to the influence of major historical events, market forces, and technological changes in the industry. More important to understand is the complexity of life in company towns and the social, cultural, and economic factors that shaped this complexity.

Finally, I get to thank all those who helped to bring this book about. In a break with custom, I will begin by acknowledging my greatest debt, to my wife Barbara, to whom this book is affectionately dedicated.

My concepts have been influenced by the work of Robert Darnton, the late Herbert G. Gutman, Thomas Bender, Jacquelyn Dowd Hall, Eugene Genovese, and Tamara K. Hareven. Peter Kolchin and Edward L. Ayers gave generous amounts of their time to read drafts at a critical stage; their comments improved the book. Don H. Doyle, Michael J. McDonald, and an anonymous member of the University of Tennessee Press Editorial Board read the manuscript in its later stages and provided much good advice, as did Ronald Lewis. I must also thank friends and colleagues who took an active interest in the project and whose support was valuable, especially Vernon Burton, David Lux, Harold Livesay, Thomas Dunlap, James I. Robertson, Jr., Ronald Eller, and Doug Flamming. Tana McDonald ably guided the manuscript through the various stages of publication. Stan Ivester provided the kind of thoughtful and detailed copyediting that all authors hope for but few receive. Not all will agree with the final result, but their commentary has been nonetheless valuable.

This book could not have been done without the precious gift of free time to research and write. A National Endowment for the Humanities Fellowship for College Teachers, 1982–83, enabled me to do the bulk of the research on the project. In 1986, a timely residential fellowhsip from the Virginia Foundation for the Humanities and Public Policy gave me a semester free from teaching and administrative duties, which I devoted to writing. Robert Vaughan, David Wyatt, and the staff at VFHPP made my stay in Charlottesville enjoyable as well as profitable. Administrative duties slowed my progress in 1987–88, when I agreed to serve as interim department head. But reduced teaching loads and research funds from the Department of History at the Virginia Polytechnic Institute and State University allowed me to complete the final stages of work. I must also thank Loyal Jones, John Stephenson, and Berea College – as well as the Mellon Foundation for a fellowship that paid part of the research expenses in the initial exploratory stage.

Library staff members have been most accommodating to my research needs, including those at the University of Virginia, especially Gregory

Johnson and Michael Plunkett; Hagley Museum and Library; Eastern Regional Coal Archives; Samford University, especially Elizabeth Wells; Alice Lloyd College; Emory and Henry University; West Virginia University; and the University of Kentucky. I would also like to thank the staff of the New River Gorge National River Historical Collection, especially William Cox, who spent an afternoon showing me the old ruins of Kaymoor. Permission to reproduce photographs from the Borderland Coal Company Collection was generously granted by the Manuscripts Division of the University of Virginia Library. Credit should go to Westmoreland Coal Company Archive, Hagley Library, for permission to use the photographs, maps, handbills, and housing blueprints from the rich collection on the Stonega Coke and Coal Company at Hagley Museum and Library. I am grateful to Christopher T. Baer, assistant curator, for his help in locating photographs and illustrations and for guiding me through the collection. Ted J. Clutter, of the Virginia Center for Coal and Energy Research, Virginia Polytechnic Institute and State University, granted permission to use his fine map on the rail system of the Virginia coalfields; Walter R. Hibbard, Jr., director emeritus, granted permission to quote from his pioneering manuscript, "An Abridged History of the Southwest Virginia Coal Industry." I must thank Keith Dix for several illustrations. Stuart McGehee, curator, Eastern Regional Coal Archives, took an enthusiastic interest in the study and alerted me to useful materials in his growing collection.

Charlie Blevins and I talked and played music together in his Red Robin Inn across the street from the decaying ruins of Borderland, where he and his father once worked. Carry Marcum allowed me into her Blacksburg home and provided another rare firsthand glimpse, this one of life in the coal towns of southwest Virginia. To Blevins, Marcum, and all those who took the time to write to me and share their rich experiences, I am indeed grateful.

Introduction

The physical setting and power relationships between capital and labor have dominated the portrayal of coal towns. Migrants to coal towns did have a culture, but historians have found it of limited value as a source of strength and continuity. Instead, writers have centered upon the power and autonomy of the operators, seeing their hands everywhere, in the company house, company store, company church, even the company graveyard. Listen to a few of the statements of historians about company towns.

The "standardized living and working conditions" of the company town "quickly and ruthlessly destroyed old cultures." It was a system of "industrial slavery" which produced class solidarity that even overcame the boundaries of race.[1] In company towns, the operators "established a totally controlled community life" where they practiced "audacious robbery," overcharging the mining families and maintaining a monopoly over their business. "Outrageous deductions were [made] for a burial fund, doctors, and other services."[2] Company towns "created a system of closed, artificial communities" which "functioned to limit the growth of social freedom and self determination." It was an environment "not of the mountaineer's own choosing." It "left its residents powerless to control their own destinies."[3] In the words of E. P. Thompson, such claims rob the coal miners of "the dignity of agents" and bestow upon them "the passivity of vectors of impersonal forces."[4]

Confounding this image, however, are the miners of the New Left labor history or what has been called "the archetypal proletariat" in European labor history.[5] Labor historians begin with an exploited and oppressed working class as a natural part of the process of coal extraction. From this fundamental premise, it follows that the miners became completely alienated and joined the labor movement. In a recent study of black coal miners in America, Ronald Lewis states: "I have accepted the orthodox Marxist theory of class conflict as the best general explanation of those race, class, and community conflicts which occurred in the southern coalfields."[6] The theory works only in the southern fields; in the northern fields another theory is applied. According to Lewis, Marxist theory "postulates that the employer desires to maximize profits and so will attempt wherever possible to weaken the power of the workers to increase their wages by creating division within the working class."[7]

In an otherwise astute analysis of black coal miners in America, Lewis moves back and forth between theory and reality in laying out his argumentative framework until reification finally consumes the theory and overruns the reality. For example, he speaks, presumably in reality, of a system of segregation which "is developed" to subjugate blacks and prevent class solidarity.[8] Theoretically, "by forestalling solidarity in the working class, capitalists can exploit labor generally, the degree of exploitation being measured as the difference between the wages workers received and the value of the goods they produce."[9] Back to reality: "It is clear that exploitation is exactly what Alabama operators had in mind, and I have used their own words, deeds, and calculations, rather than theory, to demonstrate that this was the case."[10] Then mixing theory and reality, and avoiding the conspiracy implicit in his analysis: "Even if they did not follow a conscious policy of exploitation, their role and function within the social system produced the same ends."[11]

Having rendered their subjects powerless victims of the coal operators and slaves of a totalitarian commune, labor historians then proceed to empower miners with a heroic existentialism born of years of suffering in the gulag of coal. The stress is upon conflict. Violence and labor strikes "were collective and militant acts of aggression, interconnected and conditioned by decades . . . of social change, economic exploitation and oppression, political corruption, and tyranny." They were "products of decades of evolving attitudes toward and about work, life, existence, unionism, employers, law and order, social and economic justice, the state, the community, and the meaning of America."[12] With the focus on capital-labor relationships, the company town as a community rarely surfaces, except in the moments of a labor crisis.

In an entirely different approach, government investigations of the coalfields have focused on the coal town as an urban ecosystem. It is important to recognize the strengths and weaknesses of government reports because they have been a major source of information for historians and other writers on conditions in the southern Appalachian coalfields. The reports of the U.S. Coal Commission and the Boone and Rockefeller commissions need to be used with caution.[13] I do not mean to suggest that these reports were deliberately biased or that they knowingly misrepresented conditions in the southern Appalachian fields. On the contrary, the Coal Commission and the Boone reports amassed a treasury of data on company towns. The Rockefeller Report dealt mostly with very recent developments and borrowed upon prevailing stereotypes to contrast present conditions with the company-town era.

In addition to having a narrow focus upon the town as ecosystem, the designers of the government studies and the collectors of information have perspectives and attitudes that are distorted. Chapter 7 contains a more elaborate critique of these reports, but chiefly the reformers judged the towns on the basis of urban, middle-class standards of housing, sanitation, and leisure. Above all, the reports were interested in bricks and mortar, not the social history of mining settlements.

The most widely available treatment of Appalachian mining towns is the chapter of Ronald Eller's celebrated book, *Miners, Millhands, and Mountaineers*, entitled, "Coal, Culture, and Community: Life in the Company Towns." It begins with a quotation of Winthrop D. Lane, a New York newspaper reporter, describing company towns in the Guyan River Valley of Logan County, West Virginia, from the window of his moving railroad car. After Lane's description of houses as unpainted shacks on stilts in "camp after camp," Eller then begins:

> Winthrop Lane's graphic account of social conditions in the striketorn fields of southern West Virginia in 1921 was a profound indictment of the new industrial order in Appalachia. The transformation of the region had come quickly. Less than thirty years earlier, the mountains had stood in solitude. Great forests of oak, ash, and poplar covered the hillsides with a rich blanket of deep hues, and clear, sparkling streams rushed along the valley floors. No railroad had yet penetrated the hollows. The mountain people lived in small settlements scattered here and there in the valleys and coves. Life on the whole was simple, quiet, and devoted chiefly to agricultural pursuits.[14]

Clearly, industrialization is Eller's serpent in the Appalachian Garden of Eden. Eller views mine culture as a creation the operators imposed from the outside, not as an endogenous culture.

But the mining settlement did constitute a community. Little attention has been paid to life, work, and culture as distinct from the autocratic impositions of imperious operators or the exigencies of a capricious market. Sports, drinking, religion, visiting, and other leisure activities formed a vital part of coal-town life. Miners and their families also formed their own voluntary associations to satisfy their social, labor, and welfare needs. Through these organizations, mining families forged bonds of worker solidarity and communal independence. At work and play, mining families lived under the close scrutiny of the bosses, and their freedom was circumscribed by their dependence upon the operators for housing, social, and welfare needs. In this regard they resembled tenants or sharecroppers in the rural South. But the physical attributes of mining communities—such as the clustering of dwellings around schools, churches, and stores—plus the commonality of experience in the industrial workplace and the absence of laws of involuntary servitude combined to give mining families more freedom and opportunity than were enjoyed by agricultural labor. The lord-and-serf model of social relations has left unexamined the story of the formation of an endogenous culture and its functions within the company town.

If the social history of coal towns is to be understood, first it is important to know something about the preindustrial history and culture of Appalachia. Beginning a study of industrial towns with a clear picture of preindustrial Appalachia may seem unnecessary to some readers. But, ironically, it is precisely because the history of preindustrial Appalachia is so misunderstood that the interpretation of company towns has been distorted. Miners were not "people without history," to borrow anthropologist Eric Wolf's evocative phrase.[15] Mountain families migrated from a preindustrial society with a distinct history, folk culture, and world view. Through these lenses they came to grips with their situation and shaped their responses in accord with the realities of industrial life.

Presenting preindustrial Appalachian history and culture as a backdrop to the evolution of mine culture (chapter 1) magnified the difficulties of this study enormously. Detailed studies of preindustiral Appalachia simply do not exist. "The curious mix of academics, activists and professional writers continually drawn to Appalachia during the twentieth century has instead, and quite understandably, devoted attention to the plight of the bituminous coal miners."[16] Studies of industrialization, like Eller's, have represented preindustrial Appalachia as a static, egalitarian, and classless society. Eller begins his work as follows:

> Few areas of the United States in the nineteenth century more closely exemplified Thomas Jefferson's vision of a democratic society than did the agricultural communities of the southern Appalachians. Long after the death of Jefferson and long after the nation as a whole had turned down the Hamiltonian path toward industrialism, the southern Appalachian Mountains remained a land of small farms and scattered open-country villages. Although traditional patterns of agricultural life persisted in other parts of the nation—in the rural South, the Midwest, and the more remote sections of the Northeast—nowhere did the self-sufficient family farm so dominate the culture and social system as it did in the Appalachian South.[17]

The vision of an egalitarian, carefree, and independent yeomanry also captured the imagination of twentieth-century critics of industrialization. According to Mary Beth Pudup, whose study of southeastern Kentucky found concentrations of land, slaves, and political power within a few family lineages, the notion of a self-sufficient yeomanry "greatly dramatized" the "tragic dimensions of Appalachian industrialization." Pudup continues: "Juxtaposing the two historical eras—the modern coal dependent versus the premodern subsistence society – has become a standard interpretation of Appalachian historical geography."[18]

In related theoretical explorations, especially the internal-colonialism model, Appalachian studies have directed their blame for Appalachia's chronic social and economic problems in the twentieth century toward those outside the region, especially "coal barons," speculators, northern investors, and missionaries who have been cast as agents of colonization.[19] In this "sympathetic reading of Appalachian history," Appalachia has been exploited economically, socially, and culturally by outsiders.[20]

It is possible to separate myth from reality and to create a broad framework for interpreting the history of company towns that is also logically consistent. What follows is an attempt to do precisely that, beginning with preindustrial Appalachia.

To disentangle fact from fiction, I believe it is necessary to divide white mountain society into three groups. The first group is made up of large farmers with substantial acreages, some of whom used a few slaves, who constituted a small number of families. Many of them gained an advantage as early recipients of large land grants. As towns grew and became centers of government and trade, especially county seats, large-holding families dominated the commercial and political life of these trade centers and through them built links to outside interests. Large-holders, local artisans, and shopkeepers became the foundation of a second group, an incipient middle class in mountain towns and commercial centers. By 1880, on the eve of the Industrial Revolution, these towns-people composed a middle-class elite of business entrepreneurs, lawyers, doctors, merchants, and large landholders – the wielders of local political power and influence. This middle class supported secession before the Civil War because of its own economic ties to slaveholding agriculture and outside commercial and trading interests. Afterwards, its members became advocates of the New South creed, a blend of economic booster-ism, class snobbery – directed against less affluent, poorly connected, and unsophisticated backcountry people – and racism.[21] It was this mountain elite who welcomed commercial development because it stood the most to gain from the "invasion" of industrial capitalism.

Since the native middle class paved the way, sometimes acting as re-tainers to northern capitalists, often enriching themselves simultane-ously, capitalism can hardly be said to have invaded the region. The handwringing about "invasion" and exploitation from the outside is a distortion, unless one wants to exclude the local political and economic elite somehow as interlopers and unaccountable for the exploitation that capitalism admittedly brought to many areas of Appalachia.[22]

In Kentucky, investors "swooped down on the Kentucky hills" and acquired mineral rights to the land from "unsuspecting mountaineers" at a rate of "fifty cents to five dollars an acre." Kentucky laws permitted buyers for the coal companies to avoid land purchase and thereby avoid taxes during the period before the railroads were built. Subsequent rulings did nothing to correct the abuses, but instead enlarged the mineral rights. The coal companies gained not only entitlement to all the coal, oil, or natural gas beneath the surface but rights to harvest timber, build roads, and even divert streams. No thought was given to the protection of water and the environment. State officials in West Virginia produced thousands of pages of literature touting the state as the "Switzerland of America," boosted economic developement of the region, and promised to be a doormat for all with capital to invest. If capitalism was an invasion, the native middle class was a fifth column.[23]

In addition to the original settlers and an emergent middle class, a third group of mountaineers was made up of the subsistence farmers and all the landless below them trying to establish their own subsistence farms. By far the largest group, subsistence farmers depended upon factors like availability of land, fertility of the soil, age, time of birth, generation, and general economic and political conditions for their fortunes. They might be sons farming as tenants while awaiting the distribution of the family estate. As the population grew in Appalachia after 1830, subsequent generations watched their inheritances shrink. The Civil War brought destruction and interruption of farming. It took years to make the slow recovery after the war due to sagging commodity prices, western competition, and the impossibility of applying modern farm machinery to steep mountain terrain. It was this hardscrabble group that provided much of the labor for the textile mills, furniture plants, planing mills, leather industry, logging camps, railroad crews, and coal mines of the Industrial Revolution.

The real keys to rural Appalachia – both preindustrial and postindustrial – are family, fecundity, and mobility, not stasis, alienation, and immobility. Mountain families struggled to preserve their way of life, not by resisting change but by accomodating themselves to it. High birthrates, population growth, and land scarcity in large areas of Appalachia produced a mobile population well before the penetration of industrial capitalism. Pastoral Appalachia, where subsistence farming provided a comfortable living in cozy cabins generation after generation, is a warm and perhaps charming image, but unfortunately it does not fit nineteenth-century reality. Nor would it be entirely true to say that farm families were forced off their land.

Mountain families were free to choose. They did not have to migrate to centers of rural industry. The chronic misery of rural life was a powerful push factor, yet families had the means to adjust. Many families used all the means at their disposal to stay put. In fact, there is at least one known case discussed in chapter I, of the rejection of a better life elsewhere by a mountain resident who chose instead to remain in his own area of limited opportunity. Surely many other families made the choice to stay; there are numerous examples of similar behavior in the twentieth century.

Mining familes who came to the coal towns from mountain farms brought their memories with them. Insofar as they came from backgrounds where landed wealth was concentrated in the hands of descendants of early settlers, where family lineage was the basis of wealth, mobility, economic opportunity, and political power, and where those shut out of access to resources had little means of adjusting to demographic and economic problems, they were strangers neither to exploitation, oppression, political impotence, nor economic hardship. Nor did they share the cynical outlook toward modernization that later observers, using hindsight, have brought to bear in interpreting the past.

By now it should be clear why it is necessary to shake free from some of the stereotypes surrounding preindustrial life in order to understand company mining towns. If mountain life had been so idyllic, farm families would not have left. When they left the farms for the mines, they were not leaving modern homes with electric lights and indoor plumbing but small weatherboard houses perhaps in need of painting, roofing, or ceilings. Nor were they leaving stable communities. Some were tenant farmers whose outlook for freeholding was dimming. Nearly everywhere tillable land was scarce. Rural life held out limited opportunity; rural industry seemed more promising. As I will show in chapter I, mobility had been a necessity for decades. Migration to work in the mines was just one more move in a long history of migratory patterns designed to preserve cultural ideals.

Such historical perspectives are crucial to comprehending the assimilation to industrial life. Against a preindustrial backdrop of a limiting present and a dimming future, it need not be shocking to learn, for example, that many former mining-town residents were not alienated by the company-town experience. Some recalled with fondness their days in the company-town setting, in spite of the noise, poor sanitation, dust, danger, and company authority. The stereotype of an independent yeomanry idealized for its tranquil, secure, and wholesome way of life (to borrow a page from Tamara Hareven) as a backdrop to the company town with its crowded, dusty, noisy, and controlled environment can easily lead observers to ignore the oppression in agrarian society, making more of it in industrial society than those who experienced both worlds did.

Subsistence farmers were accustomed to long hours, heavy physical labor, candlelight after dark, heating and cooking with woodstoves and fireplaces, and cold, drafty weatherboard houses. None of the houses had indoor plumbing. Trash was disposed of in the nearest ditch or river. Contamination of food and drinking water caused typhoid fever, dysentary, and enteritis. Medical and dental care was scarce to nonexistent. Modern celebrants of a mythical mountain past might be surprised to learn that mountain families had little time and energy for telling tales or making baskets. They probably strung more beans than dulcimers. Mostly, life was a cycle of endless labor. Roads, railroads, towns, stores, electric lighting, indoor plumbing, weekly garbage pickup, better medical and dental care, and other forms of "modernization," especially jobs, would have been welcomed by farm families to relieve the isolation, laboriousness, and misery of mountain life and work. To suggest otherwise is nonsense.[24]

Rural industry was a distant magnet. It attracted perhaps more with its wage rates, towns, and social life than it repelled with its crowded houses, noise, dust, and danger.

The conditions of labor in coal towns were also far from idyllic. Coal mining and coke pulling were heavy physical labor that would easily exhaust the stamina of modern aerobics classes. In addition to being demanding, the work was dangerous.

Yet these conditions did not set coal mining apart from other industrial occupations. It is certainly not the intention of this study to gloss over either the abusive character of industrial labor or the harshness of coal-town life. Rather, I want to view life and labor within the economic and social contingencies of my subjects, the way they viewed them. For that reason, I have quoted freely from the oral histories of former mining families, which confirm that, for about the first two generations of labor, working conditions in American industry were strenuous, unhealthy, and deadly for all workers.

Culture and society came together in the coal town. Like the work of Herbert Gutman, much of this study rests upon a particular definition of culture and the need to maintain an analytical distinction between culture and society.[25] Mining families did not come to the company towns culturally empty-handed. Their culture of origin provided a context for the interaction between rural folk culture and the needs and demands of an industrial setting.[26] Anthropologist Sidney Mintz separates culture as a "resource" from society as an "arena" in which culture operates to "confirm, reinforce, maintain, change, or deny particular arrangements of status, power, and identity."[27] Sociologist Zygmunt Bauman has insisted upon the separation of culture and society in explaining behavior:

> Human behavior, whether individual or collective, is invariably the resultant of two factors: the cognitive system as well as goals and patterns of behavior as defined by culture systems, on the one hand, and the system of real contingencies as defined by the social structure on the other. A complete interpretation and apprehension of social processes can be achieved only when both systems, as well as their interaction, are taken into consideration.[28]

From hillside farm to mining town, laboring families acted under the limitations of both the host society and their own cultural ideals. Even — especially — in the migration, one can witness patterns of behavior in harmony with the cultural system and real contingencies as presented by the folk cum industrial society. Preserving the analytic distinction between culture and society "reveals that even in periods of radical economic and social change powerful cultural continuities and adaptations continued to shape the historical behavior of diverse working-class populations."[29] Important though it was, culture was not some reductionist force that would explain the total history of company towns.

Like the history of rural Appalachia, the history of coal towns was also dynamic. Towns went through stages of development that charted a history of paternalism (examined in chapter 3). As the individual town developed during frontier, paternalistic, and declining years, the prism of its population refracted differences in race, sex, marital status, and generation. Generalizations about the "average" company town, even if they could be drawn, are less important than analyzing the forces that were constantly altering the towns.

Unless they were convicts, most miners were not forced to reside in company towns against their will. In other words, miners were far from "wage slaves." Not even the first recruits, whose desperation might have made them more dependent upon the operators, were in bondage to the operators. The first generation of mine labor was noted for its tendancy to farm in the spring, summer, and fall and mine coal in the winter. In combining industrial with agricultural labor, farmers were carrying on a tradition of taking advantage of new economic opportunities as a way to preserve traditional ideals. Many farmer-miners eventually gave up trying to do both and moved to the company towns. But part-time mining remained a practice of some miners at least until the Great Depression. By then, another generation of mine labor was starting to live outside company towns and commute to work by automobile. After World War II a third generation of mine labor, more mobile still, abandoned the company town altogether. In the 1950s, most of the company towns closed. Mobility, to some degree, was always a source of the miner's freedom and independence.

Hence my story proceeds against a different preindustrial backdrop, not a golden age of an untrammeled yeomanry but a period of crisis on the land, agricultural decline, advancing tenantry, and a darkening future for the next generation. It is this perspective that I believe mining families brought to their social situation in the company towns. Once they had reached the towns, the migrants created a work culture in a dialectical process of assimilation where culture and society interacted and where this interaction caused the perduration, transformation, or renunciation of their culture of origin.

Mining families were always changing; they had to. The process of adaptation to change began in rural society when the Industrial Revolution was still a long way off.

1   The Stable Ideal

The restless mobility of the American nation has been a familiar theme, running through the pages of the past until it forms a saga of "an unsettled people."[1] From the Conestoga wagon to the Winnebago, gold diggers of San Francisco to microchip hunters of the Silicon Valley, whether Okies and Arkies, exodusters and sharecroppers, young or old, rich or poor, Americans it seems have been on the move. But presumably not all of them. Until the Industrial Revolution, "a race of fossilized frontiersmen" inhabited the backcountry South.[2] Numerous community studies have found a stable and static preindustrial society in the southern Appalachian Mountains of the United States.[3] Presumably, mobility played no formative role in preindustrial Appalachia.

According to this view, it was not until the penetration of industrial capitalism, roughly in the 1880s, that Appalachia was transformed from a bucolic, static society into modern, mobile, and uprooted communities plagued by family dislocation and community breakdown. Political and economic power became concentrated in the hands of outside capitalists; communities once self-sufficient and stable were impoverished; and mountaineers lost their independence, even became powerless. The region was reduced to the status of a colony of corporate America.[4]

The first purpose of this chapter is to emphasize the historic importance of mobility in Appalachian society, especially between 1880 and 1915. Beginning with the first European settlement in the eighteenth century, continuing through the upheavals associated with demographic and economic change in the nineteenth century, and marked by repeated cyclical in- and out-migration during the twentieth century, Appalachia has been a mobile society. From mass migration to itinerant labor, geographic mobility has been a central feature of the Appalachian South.

My second purpose is to analyze the cultural significance of Appalachian mobility. Rather than destroying family and community, mobility became a quest for what may be called the stable ideal, defined as a kinship-based society in a communal setting.[5] Much of Appalachia was able to achieve only a fragile stability through mobility.

By 1900, in large areas of the mountains where there was no large-scale rural industry, poverty was chronic. The penetration of industrial capitalism undeniably brought with it exploitation of labor, disruption of local subsistence economies, and environmental destruction. But poverty clearly predated the coming of industry, and it is misleading to suggest that the region's economic problems began with industrial capitalism. Acquisition and leasing of vast tracts of mountain land hastened the economic collapse, but overpopulation and land starvation had already dealt severe blows to local economies. Moreover, the poverty that existed before industrial capitalism continued to worsen in areas where rural industry made no impact. In both Appalachias, where rural industry developed and where it failed to develop, the population was not static.

A brief overview of Appalachian history will emphasize the cyclic phases of mobility during the first two centuries. A more substantial examination of the period between 1830 and 1915 will identify some of the major forces of change and mobility that preceded and then accompanied the Industrial Revolution in the nineteenth century.[6]

From the days of frontier settlement until modern times, many John-Boys have struggled to find the legendary stability portrayed in the popular television series "The Waltons." And they have had to move to do it. Movement has been of two kinds: mass population movements over long distances as part of global migrations, and individual moves including brief journeys away from the mountain home, seasonal migrations of longer duration, and ultimately forays into rural industries. Mass migration and itinerancy have been forms of mobility whose character is best described as preservative rather than acquisitive. In other words, mountain culture has not caused mobility, but cultural ideals have given context and definition to the movement.

Three historical developments – settlement, population growth, and industrialization – kept the mountain areas of the American South in an almost continuous state of motion and change from the eighteenth through the twentieth century.

Settlement, of course, has been one of the great contributors to regional change. Beginning in the 1720s and continuing until the American Revolution, scores of migrants, mostly Scotch-Irish and Germans, fled economic oppression in their homelands and settled on the American frontier. In the space of a century, the Scotch-Irish, who formed the majority of Appalachian settlers, were thrice removed, having been forced out of lowland Scotland between 1610 and 1690, and then out of northern or Ulster Ireland in waves after 1717 – in both cases due to British economic discrimination.[7] Southeastern Pennsylvania received large numbers of immigrants until the 1720s when vacant land became scare and new-comers began to search for less crowded areas to settle.

As Scotch-Irish and German migrants spilled out of southeastern Pennsylvania and into the valleys and mountains of Virginia and eventually into western North Carolina and eastern Kentucky and Tennessee, some made multiple moves on the frontier. Finally the great migration spent itself. Mass movement in the backcountry subsided briefly about the time of the American Revolution. Then the westward surge of the nation's population poured through mountain passes during the three decades prior to the Civil War. The area once again was enlivened by the movement of thousands, composed of prospectors, adventurers, planters from worn-out lands, or just ordinary men and women looking for free land. Some of these restless wanderers and drifters settled in the mountains too, although the waves of the nineteenth century tended more often to pass through, heading on further west to flatter, more open lands and other dreams and fantasies.[8]

In the broad sweep of history during the eighteenth and early nineteenth centuries, mass migrations were the sources of substantial population shifts in Appalachia. Movement continued in the nineteenth century, but it had different causes and characteristics.

A closer examination of Appalachia between 1830 and 1915 indicates the role of demographic pressures on the land as a tremendous internal dynamic for change in the nineteenth and twentieth centuries. Rapid population growth in an area of limited arable land helped fuel the onrushing engines of social change whose roar historians of southern Appalachia are now beginning to hear. It was not the only force for change. Nor did population growth affect all areas at the same time or with equal intensity. Local conditions mitigated its impact. Yet it was undeniably a powerful dynamic for change everywhere in preindustrial Appalachia and arguably equal to the Industrial Revolution as a source of instability.

The population juggernaut threatened everything in its path. Large families and the custom of dividing land equally among all male heirs drove many to the edge of the Malthusian precipice. Precise dating of what might be called a "population crisis" is problematic. Travelers' accounts, census returns, government reports, oral testimony, and demographic studies, however, all point in one direction: after 1830, population increases began to exert pressure upon available economic resources and continued to do so for well over a century.

High birthrates caused the population crisis. Between 1800 and 1900 the total fertility rate in the United States dropped from 7.04 to 3.56 as families found the means and the will to practice family limitation.[9] If

Appalachia had the means (and that remains to be learned). it did not have the will. A sample of families from the Upper Cumberland counties of Tennessee in 1900 found the median number of children born in completed families to be 6, and many women had given birth to 10 or more children. Average household size was 5.3 members. "For women in the region, the expectation must have been that, once married, they would continue to have a child every two years until menopause."[10] In the community of Cades Cove, situated in the Great Smoky Mountains of eastern Tennessee, "six to eight children per family was average" in the 1880s; "fifteen was considered large, but not unusual."[11]

In the Tug Valley, the counties of Logan in southern West Virginia and Pike in eastern Tennessee have been the subjects of a recent study of the famous Hatfield-McCoy feud.[12] The Hatfields settled in the valley in the 1830s. Anderson Hatfield was born in 1839 into a family of 11 children, 6 of them sons. His father Ephraim's land was scattered, some of it near the mouth of a creek and the remainder high up a hollow near the headwaters. Anderson's generation felt the "economic crunch" of the short supply of tillable land and high birthrates. Only Anderson and his brother Ellison "equaled in their lifetimes the land assets of their grandfather or their father. All faced the prospect that the land available for their own children would not meet bare survival needs." Ellison inherited two tracts of "unproductive" and "rough mountainous land [which was] wholly unfit for cultivation." He had 9 children, whose one-ninth share each would have been nearly worthless. Anderson had 13 children, who faced "a frustratingly barren future." Formerly these had been prosperous families in the Tug Valley.[13] In 1850, Logan County households averaged 6.4 members, and 30 percent of all families in the county were landless. In 1880, when household size averaged 5.7 members, over one-half of Logan's families were landless.[14]

Elsewhere in West Virginia, population in the mountain counties increased an average of 26 percent per decade for a hundred years after 1820.[15] Not until 1950 did fertility rates in the Appalachian region drop below the national rate.[16]

As early as the 1840s, the crisis garnered the attention of travelers in western North Carolina. In the mountain counties of Buncombe, Madison, Transylvania, Henderson, and part of Haywood, travelers noted signs of wealth and industry in the small towns and trade centers, and contrasted town wealth with the poverty and isolation among the rural folk.[17] Large families and shrinking patrimonies signaled the blight of poverty spreading over the countryside. In a region noted for its economic egalitarianism – compared to the inequalities associated with nearby plantation agriculture – growing class divisions between town and country seemed particularly striking to the visitors. Between 1790 and 1840, census figures reported a natural population increase of at least 20 percent per decade in this area.[18] In Kentucky, the population grew "with monotonous regularity" in county after county throughout the nineteenth century, especially in the highlands region of the south and west.[19]

Unfortunately, population growth throughout the Appalachian region was greatest in upland areas of small-scale subsistence farming, where the resources to sustain it were more limited than in the fertile valleys which could have supported a population increase.[20] After the Civil War, Appalachian farms averaged 187 acres, and the mountain region continued to suffer under "one of the highest birth rates of any area of the country."[21]

Mountain farmers adjusted to economic hardship in a variety of ways, if not through the practice of family limitation, then by finding ways to supplement the family diet. Hunting and fishing provided a substantial supplement to the family larder. Roots, berries, and nuts from the forest gave variety to the diet and provided a small source of cash income. Livestock fed on the mast in the woodlands, which functioned as a commons for all to use and relieved farmers of the burden to erect costly fences or grow large amounts of forage. Vegetable gardens and orchards produced fruits and vegetables, preserved through canning or in root cellars. A variety of farm products, especially butter, eggs, apples, fruits, and vegetables, could be sold or bartered. Prewar Appalachia faced serious challenges, but it was possible to make ends meets.

Mobility was an essential means of adustment to economic insecurity. The character of this movement, however, differed from the mass movements associated with the age of settlement. Rural itinerancy was the form of mobility associated with overpopulation and economic marginality.[22] Itinerancy was nonresidential mobility. It involved periodic alterations in economic activity in which odd jobs were taken to supplement the mainstay of farming. These "migrants in the homeland"[23] moved from place to place without actually changing their domiciles, perhaps within a fifty-mile radius of the family farm.[24] Mountain farmers who lived on the margins of economic security pursued a patchwork of activities in piecing together the family economic quilt.

It is not surprising that this form of movement has remained obscured from the view of historians. Itinerancy is far less discernible than mass population movements because itinerants leave no recorded traces in any kind of official record. Itinerancy is most difficult to verify and impossible to quantify with any presently known methodology. The manuscript census, which has proven so useful to the social historian in the study of persistence from one census to the next, is far too crude a record to reflect nonresidential mobility. In fact, an enumeration of a local settlement in one census might identify the same individuals on previous censuses going back several decades, suggesting a stable community undergoing little change. Yet all of the men of the settlement might have been on the move during the ten-year census interval in a scramble for supplementary work day in and day out, month after month, year after year. But so long as they were in the same county on the day of census enumeration, inhabitants would need only to reside in a county for two days in a ten-year period to pass most tests of persistence. The people of Appalachia have been far more mobile than the census reveals.

If oral histories are any indication, additive labor – i.e., multiple jobs, tasks, or economic activities carried on to make a living – has been one of the most characteristic, and perhaps formative, experiences of mountain people down through their history. As most subsistence farmers readily admitted, they had to be jacks of all trades and masters at none if the economic quilt was to cover their ever-changing needs. The evidence for this kind of mobility appears in individual case histories drawn from oral histories, family records, and scattered secondary sources.

A list of the activities farmers pursued to make ends meet, culled from oral and family histories, includes: digging natural roots for barter; midwifery and herbal medicine; casket building; timber cutting and sawmilling; working at local grist mills and toll stations; blacksmithing; hiring out at harvest times to other farmers; making wagon wheels, roof shingles, baskets, or chairs; gardening; distilling illegal whiskey; driving livestock; and, in the postwar period: hiring out to logging or railroad crews; working in furniture, leather, or rayon industries; and mining for coal or tending looms in a textile mill.[25] Not all of these activities required leaving home. Some of them could be accomplished without leaving the farm, or by leaving for brief periods only. Other part-time work could involve being away the entire winter. Over the years, additive labor provided a piecemeal living.

Farmers also built links to the market economy in places like Cades Cove to satisfy cash and social needs. In large areas of the South where staple-crop agriculture prevailed, the market economy threatened the household economy and the maintenance of traditional life. Indeed, in the cotton South, for example, the cash-crop/food-crop mix was critical to economic independence.[26] The fertility of Cades Cove soil and the freedom from overpopulation until the 1890s, however, allowed cove inhabitants to build viable relationships with regional markets in the cities of Knoxville and Maryville, and these ties to the outside world kept the community progressive-minded. Farmers in Cades Cove viewed market relationships as liberating rather than threatening.[27]

Linkages to regional markets in some areas of the mountains like eastern Tennessee and greater isolation in others areas like the Tug Valley of West Virginia provide one source of the dual image of Appalachia as both backward and progressive.[28] Regional differences in soil fertility, steepness of mountain slopes, breadth of valleys, access to markets, population growth, and general climatic conditions made many Appalachias, not just one. The great variation in local environment makes it imperative to consider regional idiosyncrasies as some of the most influential forces shaping mountain life.

For heads of households, additive labor meant itinerant labor, and the movement involved changes in routine, pace of work, and location. Making ends meet necessitated a makeshift life including odd jobs, seasonal migrations, or, in the case of tenants and sharecroppers, movement from farm to farm.

Additive labor became a necessity in the Appalachian household of the nineteenth century and grew into a tradition that has stretched into the twentieth century. A series of interviews conducted with subsistence farmers in western North Carolina in the late 1970s illustrates how additive labor became a family tradition. If men were jacks of trade, women became the jennets, and children were also expected to contribute at early ages. The family became an integrated labor machine, each person functioning and contributing to the common good of the whole. Lee Workman's father owned a "modest Catawba County farm." In addition to farming, he supplemented the family income by shoeing the neighbor's horses, repairing their wagons and plows, making their grain cradles, and catching possums in the winter to fatten and eat. Workman's neighbors tanned hides, cut and sold railroad crossties, temporarily signed onto railroad construction crews, and logged in the winter.[29]

Women and children contributed in a variety of ways. As early as five or six years of age, boys and girls began to help out.[30] Fathers counted on daughters and wives to perform numerous chores with little help or respite from the range of domestic duties they were otherwise expected to accomplish. In addition to washing, sewing, cleaning, and cooking, women made soap, tended bee hives, milked cows, cultivated the gardens and canned the produce, kept the chickens, churned the butter and gathered the eggs, all the while typically bearing children every two years. Additionally, the labor services of women and children freed up the men's time, which could more readily be plied in activities to meet cash needs.[31] Mobility and versatility of mountain labor served to preserve a traditional way of life.

Farm tenancy in the southern Appalachians has not been studied extensively. Recent community studies, however, have noted significant levels of tenancy and sharecropping in mountain areas. What is even more surprising, tenancy appears to have developed well before the Civil War. In Georgia, white tenants were present in numbers great enough to provide an alternative supply of labor. High population densities and poor tenant farmers "characterized" the Georgia uplands. In the east Tennessee mountain community of Cades Cove, over one-half of the farmers were tenants in 1860. Many of the remaining farmers had lost their market independence and held vital links to the market economy by the time of the Civil War.[32]

Farm tenancy as a sign of land scarcity and poverty seems unquestionable. In 1880 Randolph McCoy lived with his family in Pike County, Kentucky, near the northeastern border of West Virginia, the area of the famous Hatfield-McCoy feud. "Ranel" and his wife Sally had produced sixteen children, an unusually large number even by the "standards" of the Tug Valley. Eight of them were boys, and Ranel had only three hundred acres to divide among them. Two boys hired out as farm hands, and others sharecropped on nearby farms. In a society where land ownership was the source of status and social mobility, the stigmata attached to hiring out or sharecropping "was a greater disgrace than premarital sex or illegitimate birth."[33] Sharecroppers and tenants were also highly mobile, although the range of their mobility apparently did not extend beyond neighborhood or county boundaries.[34]

Yet farm tenancy was also adapted to conservative ends. By 1900 in Cades Cove, which had a limited supply of arable land, tenancy had become a means of distributing a scarce resource while simultaneously controlling the behavior of community members. Over one-third of the heads of household were tenant farmers, mostly sons in their twenties awaiting the distribution of the family estate. The use of tenancy as a means of guaranteeing landownership to future generations may have been practiced elsewhere in the mountains. Opportunities on western lands and in factories relieved the pressure after 1910.[35]

Demographic and economic conditions in Wise County, Virginia, provide a microscopic look at population growth and growing desperation. In the extreme southwestern corner of the state, on the Kentucky and Tennessee borders, Wise was formed in 1856 out of Dickinson County, and it retained a largely agricultural economy until the 1890s, when it became the most important coal county in the state. In 1860 only 3 percent of its entire land mass of 413 square miles was arable; the rest remained in wilderness.[36] Translated into acreage, only 7,900 acres of land in the county could be tilled. Yet Wise had a population of 4,508 residents.[37] If equally divided, the county might have had 1.7 acres of arable land per capita. If we assume the average household size of 5.3 members in the nearby Upper Cumberland region of Tennessee, Wise County would have had 851 households in 1860, each with less than 10 acres under conditions of perfect equality in land distribution. By 1880 the population had grown by 72 percent to 7,772 persons, and each household would have been reduced to 5.4 acres under similar hypothetical circumstances. In fact, small-scale farming did dominate Wise agriculture. By 1910 over one-half the farms in the county were under 50 acres. Studies have shown that under normal conditions the fertility of a field is exhausted in three years' time, and therefore a farmer desiring to cultivate 12 acres a year needed at least 50 acres of arable land, a norm many Wise County farmers failed to meet.[38]

Wise's population grew vigorously in the twentieth century. Although some of the growth reflected in census figures included an in-migration to the coal-mining towns and lumber camps, natural increase still sustained a surging population.[39] In the 1920s, when the first readily available figures appeared on rates of birth and death, Wise had a birthrate of 48 compared to the state rate of 29 per thousand. Death rates were below the state average (9.84 for Wise compared to a state average of 11.28 per thousand). The natural increase in Wise County in the 1920s is stunning when compared to countries today plagued by population growth. Wise's rate of 38 per thousand was far greater than the rates of India, Egypt, Ethiopia, or Mexico — areas now experiencing severe population problems.[40]

Much work remains to be done using local tax lists, land books, and census records to gauge the impact on individual counties and communities and to relate the population crisis to other historical changes. In the absence of any studies of historical demography, one cannot be certain that natural increase (births minus deaths) alone propelled the population explosion of the nineteenth century. Nevertheless, nothing else offers a more satisfactory explanation. No mass movements of people into Appalachia are noted anywhere between the closing decades of mass settlement in the 1850s and the growth of rural industries in the 1880s. Instead, all signs indicate that Appalachia's history during this period was a unique departure from national trends. In this century, America made what demographers call the "demographic transition" to reduced levels of births and deaths. The effects of modernization, including improved medical care as well as the knowledge and will to practice birth control, caused the transition. Appalachian development, on the other hand, has been characterized as an "arrested demographic transition."[41] The region became "isolated from the effects of modernization" which lowered fertility levels elsewhere in the nation, and in Appalachia, especially in the rural areas, the transition stalled.[42]

Between 1900 and 1930, the population of mountain counties grew by 55 percent (nonmountain counties grew 33 percent). Russell County in southwestern Virginia had a population of 6,714 in 1830 and sufficient land to support the population. In 1930, the population numbered about 26,000 and there were fewer than three acres of arable land per capita.[43] Mining "was virtually dead as an alternative employment, and poverty was 'chronic,'" according to a New Deal report.[44]

However, the inhabitants of Appalachia who were really desperate were not those who lived where mines, mills, and other rural industries opened nearby but those who lived in isolated areas where industry did not exist to relieve population pressures. Areas like the entire Blue Ridge Mountain region of Virginia or the Norris Dam Basin of the Tennessee Valley, for example, experienced the same problems of agricultural decline and overpopulation, but these areas had few sources of alternative employment.[45]

Some refused to leave and "often remained at conscious financial loss."[46] In 1854, Issac Hart of Athens, Tennessee, wrote to his cousin, Colonel J. W. Hampton Tipton in Cades Cove, to tell him that he would do better to move west:

> We made 100 bu. of fine wheat. We do not have to labor under the same difficulties as you do. We have thrashers. . . . You have to flail after the old dugout, go to the thicket, cut a pole and lay on all day. At night fan out 5 or 6 bu. with a sheet. Then you go 15 or 20 miles to get flour to eat.

Hart felt it was hopeless to try and get Tipton to come. "Your attachment is so strong for them mountains that it will be hard for you to part with that grand scenery."[47] Twentieth-century Appalachia has not lacked its stay-putters either.

Even more telling evidence that rural poverty plagued counties where industrial capitalism failed to penetrate is the case of Martin County in eastern Kentucky. Martin County held 1.4 billion tons of coal reserves, but it remained undeveloped and retrogressive until the Norfolk and Western Railroad built a twenty-four-mile branch line into the heart of the coal reserves in the 1970s. Prior to that time, the population had been declining for thirty years, the principal source of income being government welfare. When the coalfields opened, unemployment in the county dropped from 40 to 4 percent, per capita income rose from $1,000 to $7,000, and the population grew to 14,000, over 5,000 of whom were employed in coal mining. Salaries ballooned to $40,000 a year for an oiler on an electric shovel while the typical miner exceeded $30,000 per year.[48]

Additive labor, mobile men, and family labor lessened the impact of demographic burdens and economic depression until the arrival of factories and mines. Migration to nearby industries became the next step for many in the quest for social stability.

Between 1880 and 1915, industrial capitalism made its impact upon the Appalachian region. Appalachia was "discovered" as a "strange land and a peculiar people." Travelers came looking for an exotic culture. They found what they were looking for through "selective perception" and went away to write for middle-class audiences in the North. Simultaneously, surveyors, engineers, land agents, railroad men, investors, and other economic interests were making another discovery—that Appalachia held one of the world's largest untapped reserves of timber and coal.[49] Unfortunately, the discovery of the mountaineers as backward and benighted served to justify considerable exploitation of mountain land and labor. In some areas, the acquisition of and control over the land hastened the collapse of an already staggering economy.

In the postwar years, the general decline in agriculture and a continued growth of mountain populations made further adjustments necessary. The coming of rural industries expanded the opportunities to adjust without having to leave the region. The confinement of the postwar migration mostly to the South, along with the familial and communal character of the migration to rural industries, indicate how cultural values continued to contour the reactions to economic problems in the region. Many in the first generation of industrial laborers attempted to farm while pursuing some combination of mining, logging, and millworking—giving to additive labor a prodigious calling beyond the bounds of human energy and stamina for most. Although there is evidence of coal mining as a part-time occupation for some as late as the 1920s,[50] more and more mountain farmers found themselves drawn permanently and inexorably into the industrial setting. In many cases the move from farm to rail yard, mine, and mill (the railroads, coal mines, lumberyards, and textile mills being the major sources of employment) was a family or community effort. Friends and relatives who had made the change earlier assisted latecomers.

The cases of L. F. Minor, Ernest Carico, and Ernest Mead are examples of that generation of mountain farmers who watched their inheritance in land shrink to levels where alternatives to farming were necessary. L. F. Minor was born in 1892 on a farm in Hancock County, Tennessee, one of the counties with a high fertility ratio. The Minor family had once owned 3,500 acres of farmland in the county. In 1974, after having spent fifty-six years in the coal mines, most of it as a miner with the Stonega Coke and Coal Company, Minor was asked why he had left such a handsome estate for a dreary coal town. His reply:

Well, I'll tell you. My great grandfather he divided up all this land with his children – he had seven. And some of them had 600 acres of land – some of the boys died – and some of the girls had 300 acres and so on like that. Well, they growed up and then they had children, and then, they inherited so much and when we left down there it'd got down to we had 100 acres – my father died – so we decided that . . . we'd . . . try something else, and so we just moved up here in Virginia. At that . . . particular time, of course, Hancock County never did have any industry much.[51]

Ernest Carico was born in 1911 in the Sandy Ridge area of Wise County where one hundred people lived in a three-square-mile radius. The soil was poor and sandy, and all who lived there were poor. His father owned fifty acres, which he farmed part-time. In the winter he worked in a coal mine. When he died, the small family estate was divided evenly among his six surviving children, leaving each with eight acres of land. Unable to make a living on such a small share of poor soil, Ernest went to work in the coal mines full-time soon after he was married in 1932.[52]

Ernest Mead, born in 1915 in the same region, saw his inheritance shrink to six acres as one of eight children. He followed a path nearly identical to Carico's, except he tried to farm after work. He would leave home at four in the morning for a five-mile walk to the entrance or "drift mouth" of the mine. After a day in the mine, he arrived back home at about dark, chopped wood, fed the livestock, and worked his garden by the light of his miner's cap. After taking a bath, he would collapse into bed at about ten in the evening.[53] Working two or more jobs was not unusual for these men. As we have seen, many had done so before the mines opened.

Thousands of native white mountaineers migrated to lumberyards and planing mills; furniture, leather, and rayon plants; mining towns and textile-mill villages during the late nineteenth and early twentieth centuries. Beginning slowly in the 1880s and building till World War I, mountain inhabitants gave up trying to make a living on the land. No count of the total numbers involved, not even a good estimate, is possible, but it may have been the greatest mass movement since the age of settlement. According to a U.S. Department of Agriculture Report, a general trend in Appalachia between 1900 and 1930 was the movement from poor farms to industry.[54]

The move from farm to industry was gradual, probing, and halting. Rural industry proved to be a "refuge from the Malthusian threat" just as the case had been in less-favored agricultural areas of Europe in earlier centuries.[55] According to an official of the Stonega Coke and Coal Company, which at its peak employed nearly three-fourths of Virginia's coal miners, Stonega from its beginning depended mostly "on the natives of this county and the contiguous territory, as new men imported were reluctant to make this their new home."[56] Farmers would mine in the winter and farm in the spring and summer.[57] The tentative character of this movement exacerbated already troublesome labor shortages at the mines.

The Low Moor Iron Company leased a mine and built a company town at Kaymoor, West Virginia, in the New River Gorge area. In the spring of 1906, the general manager reported a shortage of seventy-five men at the Number One and Two mines because "a number of miners who have farms in West Virginia and Kentucky go, in the spring of the year, after the winter's work, back to their farms and return again in the fall."[58] Often these men boarded in the mine camps but returned to their homes at night, adding to the transient and unstable character of early camp life. Factory and mine were new sources of additive labor which the first generation of migrants combined with agricultural activities as part of their occasional forays into the industrial world. For a while they moved "gingerly between the two."[59]

The metaphor of uprooting is misleading to describe the process of farm-to-industry migration. Rather, the decision to leave was made in the context of the cradle of the family, and with the reassurances of prior migrants, already established in industrial settings, that industrial villages were communities containing like-minded families with common cultural and economic ideals, aspirations, and experiences. Undoubtedly in many cases the promises turned out to be rosier than the reality, yet the decisions to go were made with the not insubstantial belief that the road from farm to mine did not lead into some great abyss.

The migration depended upon family and friends to smooth the pathway from the agricultural to the industrial commune. Workers' stories reveal a chainlike pattern of migration not unlike that discovered by historians of the mass immigration experience.[60] Family crises pushed some to decision. Melvin Profitt grew up in Knott County and worked in the coal camps of Perry and Letcher counties in Kentucky. His grandfather had owned a farm until he mortgaged it to pay a $300 doctor bill. When the grandfather died, the doctor foreclosed on the mortgage and put Melvin's father and the family off the farm. His dad worked as a sharecropper for fifty cents a day, plus five pounds of meat and a bushel or corn per week. When the landlord increased his own part of the share, the father quit and went to the mines.[61] According to the Reverend Stuart H. Frazier, a black preacher who went to work for the Chesapeake and Ohio Railroad in 1929:

> Well, it was sort of like a chain reaction. You see, Virginia's farming country. Well, when the mines, the coal mines opened up, well here was the kind of money that those people had never hear of. And many of them came out here and worked in

the mines. And they commuted home the same way, although many of them moved their families into the mining communities. And it was sort of clannish-like. For instance, I come out I'd get a job for . . . my brother, or my uncle . . . or good friends. . . . And there for a long time, most of the men – Blacks who worked at the round house – came out of Louisa County, Virginia. They were either related or good friends. . . . Lots of whites also came out of Virginia.[62]

Hilton Garrett came to Wheelwright in 1923 from Alabama on a train from Birmingham. He came alone on the encouragement of a friend who had preceded him and who wrote him that men were needed. After he "made a pay day," he sent for his wife.[63]

Makeshift work, an effective pathway around the challenges to the indigenous culture and the insufficiencies of the local economy, often led to rural industry. In 1911, Robert Messer was born into a family of eight children in Clay County in eastern Kentucky. His father was a small farmer who, like most small farmers of eastern Kentucky, had to combine a variety of economic activities to make a living: "My daddy he made cross ties, he peddled, he peeled tan bark, and he worked around."[64] Messer grew up sandwiching school between periods of work. Just like his father's, it was a catch-as-catch-can life spent constantly on the move working here and there, doing anything for a dollar, which he gave to his father and mother. He hired out to hoe corn for fifty cents to a dollar a day and "peddled:"

> We peddled eggs. . . . we picked blackberries in the summer and peddled them. . . . And we'd take them to Straight Creek . . . and we'd peddle chickens; we'd peddle geese, anything. We raised an acre of cane. . . . And we'd sell the molasses. . . . If we had $25 in the spring to make out on, we thought we was rich. . . . I worked all the time.

At age twenty-three Messer married and continued his hustling for work at a dollar a day cutting trees and selling pulpwood until he found a job in the coal mines of Clay County, where he worked for twenty-five years. [65]

The coal mines simply offered a better life. In the 1890s Charlie Blevin's grandfather migrated with his seven sons from Paintsville in Johnson County, Kentucky, to Borderland, West Virginia. Charlie's father was about five years old. It took three days to make the move with a wagon, team, and milk cow tied to the wagon. When they got hungry, they milked the cow and drank the milk. According to Charlie, "By the turn of the century Johnson County was still a backward place. The mines over there hadn't ever got built up like these mines right in here [Borderland]. The C&O hadn't made it up there then. It was all just farming and timber, and it was even pretty hard to get your timber out there at the time." But it was not hard work that caused the migration. Instead, the Blevins brothers left Paintsville because "they figured they could better themselves coming in here and getting on this railroad . . . or working these mines." Grandfather, father, and Charlie Blevins all worked in the Borderland mines.[66]

The character of Appalachian mobility reveals much about the nature of mountain society and the role of cultural values in molding the responses to economic and demographic change.[67] Population growth, land scarcity, and agricultural decline exerted tremendous pressures on rural society. To deal with changes, families developed strategies that reflected their desires to preserve a kinship-based social order. These strategies included additive labor, farm tenancy, linkages to the market economy, and greater exploitation of family labor. Mobility was an essential part of the efforts to preserve traditional society, but within certain limits. Few chose to move to western lands, even when better opportunities beckoned. In the postwar years, the range of alternatives expanded significantly to include opportunities not only on western lands but in urban and industrial centers of the North. Instead of migrating to these areas, most chose the low-wage furniture, textile, or lumber industries or the more dangerous and volatile coal industry as a better means to combine cultural and economic goals.

Yet the relationship between mobility and Appalachian culture remains only partially explored. Obviously, the stable ideal provided a cultural context that influenced patterns of mobility. But the broader social significance of mobility for Appalachian culture, to turn the matter around, remains unclear.

In an area of limited market contact, little economic diversification, and a hierarchical political system – such as the Tug Valley of West Virginia – violence, heavy drinking, brawling, illegal distilling, and other crimes did exist.[68] In another area connected to outside markets which was more economically diverse and guided by republican government, such as Cades Cove in Tennessee, only localized pockets like Chestnut Flats exhibited traits of the culture of honor.[69] Loggers, herdsmen, hunters, and itinerant workers generally spent long periods spearated from their families. Elliott Gorn has noted that, in earlier periods, "The frontier town or crossroads tavern brought males together in surrogate brotherhoods, where rough men paid little deference to the civilizing role of women and the moral uplift of the domestic family."[70] What role did a society of mobile men play in perpetuating premodern forms of social behavior? Land transfer to males and the expectations of women to keep "the place" going in the absence of men gave to Appalachian society a decided maleness. This male-dominant society needs more careful elaboration in future research as an example of the juxtaposition of culture and economy.

To what extent did the intersection of a premodern culture and structural linkages to the market-cum-industrial economy begin to reshape backcountry society? How was political culture shaped by mobility? Under what conditions did republicanism take root? On the structural level, how did mobility affect levels of voter participation and the functioning of local government? After the 1920s and the decline of rural industry, the inhabitants of Appalachia were forced to leave the region entirely to find work. Was this mobility more alienating than the previous migration to rural industries? Was it a selective out-migration in terms of age, gender, and outlook? The answers to these and other questions remain as prerequisites to a full understanding of culture and mobility in Appalachian society.

From the vantage point of land stripped of timber, hillsides ravaged by rain and erosion, mines worked out, and ghost towns with rotting tipples and houses, it is easy to romanticize the bucolic and pastoral life of rural Appalachia. But farm life was far from idyllic. The lives of the Messers, Caricos, Minors, Blevinses, and Meads strip away the sentimentality about life in the country and expose the chronic misery of rural life before the migration. Eventually, the migrants would see the trade-offs and costs of their choices just as surely as the historians have. At the time, however, what lay ahead were economic opportunities in the coal towns and the beckoning promise of a better life.[71]

2   Interlude: The Rise of King Coal

Coal fueled the Industrial Revolution in the United States. Production increased from 100,000 tons in 1800, to 1 million tons in 1832, to 10 million tons in 1851, and 20 million tons in 1860. After the Civil War, railroad locomotives began to burn coal. Pig-iron and steel mills also pressed demand to the unheard-of-figure of 110 million tons by 1885, the year in which coal replaced wood as the nation's leading source of energy. Extraordinary as it was, in less than two decades even this figure would more than double again. By 1900, the United States' production of 243 million tons topped the output of Great Britain by 43 million tons, making America the world's leading coal producer.

The opening of the southern Appalachian coalfields helped bring about this rise to industrial greatness. It was also a precursor of company mining towns. A brief survey of the major events and other factors leading to the establishment of the Stonega Coke and Coal Company, the chief builder of coal towns in the Big Stone Gap field of Wise County, Virginia, will serve as a microcosm of the course of this development.

Until the late nineteenth century, nearly all of the coal produced in the United States came from the mines of Pennsylvania, Ohio, Indiana, and Illinois. The nation's iron and steel factories had grown up there close to the waterways and rail lines. As demand for coal increased, industrialists turned their search for new sources of the black gold elsewhere. During the 1880s, a genre of local-color writers began to provide descriptions of not only "a strange land and a peculiar people" but, along with their stories of exotic residents, sightings of some of the untapped mineral wealth reported to be scattered throughout the southern mountains. More significant in the "discovery" of the wealth in natural resources than the casual reports of the literati, however, were the maps and surveys of cartographers engineers, surveyors, and land agents. Gradually their efforts took full measure of both the timber and the roughly 50 million acres of coal reserves, the largest supply of bituminous coal in the nation. With the aid of local lawyers, merchants, and businessmen, outside capitalists purchased at prices as low as twenty-five cents an acre, or leased under fraudulent promises, millions of acres of mineral- and timber-rich land. By the turn of the century, agents from

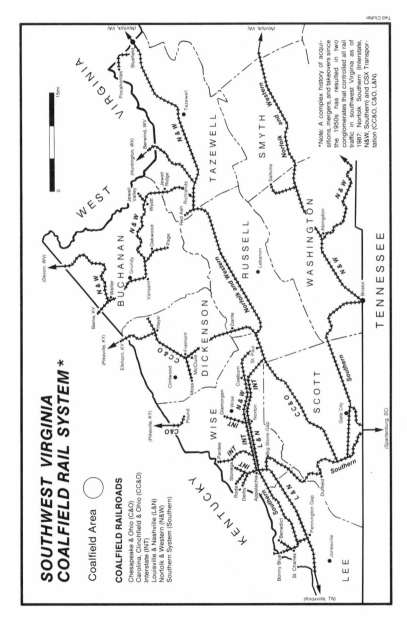

Map of southwest Virginia coalfield rail system, 1921. Courtesy of Ted Clutter, Virginia Center for Coal and Energy Research, Virginia Polytechnic Institute and State University.

some of the nation's financial centers, especially New York and Philadelphia, had acquired rights to large areas of mineral-rich lands.[1]

Major Jedediah Hotchkiss, a leading cartographer in the Confederacy under Robert E. Lee, is an example of the pivotal role played by private developers in identifying and promoting the mineral wealth of Appalachia. Born and educated in New York, Hotchkiss came in the 1840s to Staunton, Virginia, where he served as a tutor for a wealthy family. When the Civil War began, he joined the Confederacy, and during 1861 served as Lee's topographical engineer in southwestern Virginia. During his service he took note of the massive outcroppings of coal in the Flat Top Mountain area. Later he managed to hire himself out to survey and evaluate the holdings. A seam of coal thirteen feet thick, twice the height of any known seams at the time, was discovered extending westward from Tazewell, Virginia, into the West Virginia counties of Mercer, McDowell, and Wyoming. Hotchkiss then worked diligently to lure a group of Philadelphia capitalists to purchase some of the land and to launch the construction of a railroad to the valuable holdings. An economic depression in the 1870s slowed his efforts at securing a railroad. Meanwhile, he traveled throughout the northern United States and England seeking investors and even founded a journal to publicize the holdings. Consequently, in 1881, Hotchkiss's efforts paid off when Frederick J. Kimball, vice-president of the new Norfolk and Western Railway, grew interested in the Flat Top coal lands and the Norfolk and Western began the construction of a railroad into the heart of the region. A branch line reached Tazewell County in 1883, and a new mining town, Pocahontas, sprang from the venture. Mining coal began in the Pocahontas coalfields, which were among the largest in the United States.[2]

Due to the efforts of Hotchkiss and other private speculators, a land boom spread over the coal regions of southwestern Virginia and southern West Virginia. All of the land and coal was worthless, however, if it could not be gotten out of its mountain redoubts. There was no use to open mines if the coal could not be transported to distant markets. Railroad building accompanied the investments in land. Between 1870 and 1900, four major railroads extended lines into the central Appalachian coalfields: the Chesapeake and Ohio (C&O) into southern West Virginia, the Norfolk and Western (N&W) into southwest Virginia, the Louisville and Nashville (L&N) into eastern Kentucky and Tennessee, and the Southern into western North Carolina. Spur lines radiated from these major arteries, gradually unlocking the wealth of a millennium and launching a coal boom.[3]

Between 1900 and 1930, coal became king in southern Appalachia where coalfields were established in: southern West Virginia (Fayette,

Raleigh, Kanawha, McDowell, Mercer, and Mingo counties), eastern Kentucky (Johnson, Floyd, Magoffin, Pike, Knott, Letcher, Harlan, Perry, Leslie, Clay, and Bell counties), southwestern Virginia (Buchanan, Dickinson, Wise, Lee, Scott, Russell, and Tazewell counties), eastern Tennessee (Campbell, Claiborne, Anderson, Morgan, Hamilton, and Marion counties), and northern Alabama (Bibb and Shelby counties). Coal production in the Appalachian fields tripled in the 1890s and then experienced a stunning five-fold increase up to 1930, when it reached 80 percent of the nation's total production. In the relatively brief period of three decades, Appalachia became the coal bin of the nation.[4]

Appalachian operators succeeded in capturing a lion's share of the coal business for several reasons. For half a century, anthracite from the North had been America's staple coal. The volatile matter of anthracite amounts to only about 4 percent (compared to high-volatile bituminous coal which can exceed 33 percent), making it very difficult to ignite but cleaner and longer burning. However, anthracite seams run deeper, often beneath the underground water table, and therefore anthracite coal is more expensive and dangerous to mine.

In 1902 United Mine Workers of America President John L. Lewis's call for a strike in the anthracite fields proved fortuitous for the newly opened bituminous fields. The low-volatile coals of West Virginia, especially the "smokeless fields" of New River, Winding Gulf, and Pocahontas (these coals contained 16 to 24 percent volatile matter), offered the nearest substitute and gained a foothold. As early as 1910, the supremacy of anthracite coal was broken, and bituminous coke and coal replaced it as the nation's industrial fuel. Moreover, southern Appalachian coalfields were nonunion, and this may have given their operators an additional competitive advantage. Exploiting both the cost advantage of nonunionized companies over their unionized northern competitors and the hiatus in northern production due to the strike, the southern West Virginia operators increased their share of coal shipped to Great Lakes markets from 1 to 23 percent between 1900 and 1930.[5] These patterns of development and their impact upon Appalachian localities can be seen clearly by focusing on a single section, southwestern Virginia, and more specifically Wise County.

Wise County was formed in 1856 and named after General Henry Wise, the governor at the time. Gladeville (renamed Wise in the 1920s), with a population of 250, was designated the county seat. Agriculture was the principal means of making a living. In 1860, the U.S. Census counted more hogs than the 4,508 people living in the county. The 1870 census found 39 square miles of agricultural land in Wise with 678 farms, or about 1 farm for every 37 acres of land, if evenly divided. Far more consequential were the 451 square miles of coal lands, a total reserve approaching 6 billion tons. Confederate General John Daniel Imboden was instrumental in acquiring land and promoting the mineral wealth of the region. Imboden represented a pattern of ex-military officers who served in the region during the Civil War, became familiar with its mineral wealth as a result of their service, and emerged to boost development of the resources. In 1872, he exuded to a gathering of legislators and distinguished citizens of Richmond: "Within this imperial domain of Virginia, lie almost unknown to the outer world, and not fully appreciated by their owners," mineral deposits surpassing those of England, which might "attract hither millions of money, and enterprising thousands of people" to restore Virginia to "a foremost rank amongst the States of the Union."[6]

Imboden envisioned a "New South" of industry and progressive growth much like the vision of the more well-known boosters and newspaper editors of the period, especially Henry Watterson of the Louisville *Courier-Journal*, Henry Grady of the Atlanta *Constitution*, Captain Francis W. Dawson of the Charleston *News and Courier*, and journalist J. D. B. De Bow of *De Bow's Review*. Imboden invested in lands along the C&O Railroad in West Virginia and worked throughout the 1870s and into the 1880s, buying up land and mineral rights in Wise County. In 1880 he purchased 47,000 acres of mineral land in the county and his son gained one-sixth interest in an additional 100,000 acres. He worked feverishly to promote the building of railroad lines to these properties.[7]

Meanwhile, in 1880 wealthy mine owners in the anthracite coalfields of Pennsylvania took an interest in the Big Stone Gap coalfield of Virginia and Kentucky. The gap gets its name from a deep gorge cut in Stone Mountain by the Powell River. Lying in a narrow basin 12 to 15 miles wide and extending northeast to southwest for 36 miles, the field's area was approximately 540 square miles. In the eastern portion of Wise County the field reached heights of four thousand feet above sea level. One of the Philadelphia businessmen, John Leisenring, purchased 67,000 acres in Wise and titled it under the name "The Virginia Coal and Iron Company." Two years later, working through Imboden, Virginia Coal and Iron (VC&I) purchased another 25,000 acres. The field could not be immediately opened to mining, however, because railroads had yet to be developed. In 1890 VC&I laid a line from Bristol to Big Stone Gap called the South Atlantic and Ohio Railroad. The next year the Clinch Valley branch of the N&W was completed to Norton (named for Eckstein Norton, president of the L&N) after crossing Tazewell and Russell counties through St. Paul and Coeburn (named for W. W. Coe, president of N&W). The Cumberland Valley Branch of the L&N from Harlan County, Kentucky, reached Norton in the same year. The construction of these railroads opened the region up to coal and coke development. The first car-load of coal left the county in 1892, the first carload of coke in 1895.[8]

Production increased rapidly. Within ten years coal output rose to 2,563,000 "short" (two-thousand-pound) tons, and by 1903 there were over 3,400 coke ovens in the Big Stone Gap field, which altogether produced 80 percent of the coke in Virginia. The boom was reflected in a dramatic growth of Wise County's Population from 9,345 in 1890 to 19,653, 34,162, and 46,500 in the three decennial censuses thereafter. The 1900 census counted fifty manufacturing operations, 1,196 farms, and twelve mining companies. By 1920, two-thirds of the land in Wise County was owned and controlled by four large companies: Stonega Coal and Coke; VC&I; Virginia Iron, Coal, and Coke; and Clinchfield Coal.[9] With the purchases of land and mineral rights and the laying of railroad lines, the coal oper-ators could turn their attention to subsequent stages of hiring labor, punching holes in the earth, and creating mining towns. Throughout the mountains the ring of iron and steel could be heard signaling the end of the preindustrial age for large numbers of mountaineers and the begin-ning of the Industrial Revolution.

3   Building Towns

The building of coal towns began in the 1880s, peaked in the 1920s, and virtually ended with the coming of the Great Depression. Thereafter, market conditions, especially the competition of oil, gas, and hydroelectric power, reduced coal demand in the United States. Mechanization in the industry made it possible to produce more coal with far less labor. The number of miners plummeted. Automobiles meant that miners no longer had to live within walking distance of the mines. These changes are analyzed in the Conclusion. The present chapter examines coal towns at their zenith of development, when different forces shaped the industry and mining populations changed dramatically.

Coal towns were the product of a variety of forces, despite historians' tendency to see them as little more than the creations of industrial capitalists. The power of the operators is most evident in the form of paternalism. Since some towns had better housing and other facilities than others, operators in those towns are sometimes said to be "more paternalistic" than those where the facilities were inferior. But company towns were not merely extensions of the will of the operators. Moreover, the towns were not static but moved through phases of development, and these need to be analyzed. The history of coal towns was indeed a history of paternalism, more or less, but paternalism was not some reductionist force operating independently of other forces. Age, sex, marital status, and generation were structural features that had a profound impact upon town life. The course paternalism took was also affected by cross-currents of market conditions for labor and capital – such as high demand for coal and a shortage of labor until after the war – as well as terrain, the availability of local services, and especially World War I which redirected the course of coal-town development.

Company towns characterized the southern Appalachian coalfields. In 1925, when the U.S. Coal Commission completed its study of the industry just past the peak of the coal boom, it found nearly 80 percent of West Virginia's miners living in company towns. About two-thirds of those in the remaining fields of the region (in Alabama, 65.9 percent; in

Maryland, Virginia, Kentucky, and Tennessee, an average of 64.4 percent) lived under similar circumstances. In the North, Pennsylvania had the largest number of miners living in company towns (50.7 percent); followed by Ohio (24.3 percent); Kansas, Missouri, and Iowa (an average of 18.5 percent); and Illinois and Indiana (average of 8.5 percent).[1]

The naming of the company towns was an operator's prerogative. The operator who built the camp usually supplied the name, often before the residents arrived. There were no restrictions on the name save that of postal authorities whose agreement was routinely given to whatever name the operator chose. If the operator wanted to name the town after his wife or his mistress, he was free to do so. A number of towns bear the names of English villages, reflecting the cultural preferences of many operators. The rather widespread use of the word "glen" followed by another personal or family name, such as Glen Jean or Glen White, may reflect Scottish ancestry or perhaps the influence of Sir Walter Scott.

An analysis of place names in the "smokeless" coal fields of West Virginia reveals a variety of naming practices, but the most common was to name the settlement after a company official. About 50 percent of all the smokeless fields were named after a pioneer operator, founder, owner, engineer, general manager, or some other company official (for example: Kimball after the N&W president; Gary after the U.S. Steel president; or Berwind after Edward J. Berwind, owner of the New River and Pocahontas Consolidated Coal and Coke Company). Some took women's names, such as Helen, named after the C&O president's daughter; Ennis, maiden name of the wife of the original operator; or McAlpin, the operator's mother's maiden name. Mabscott was a combination of the names of the town's first coal operator and his fiancée. Carlisle, Scarbro, and Skelton were named after English cities; Lanark, a Scottish home. Pocahontas and Matoaka were Indian names. Some were mere locations: Northfork and Slab Fork. Stone Coal was a name to distinguish coal from charcoal. In 1907, after a coal explosion, operators changed the name of Stuart and reopened under the name Lochgelly, an official's relative. Derby was the name chosen for a town of the Stonega Coke and Coal Company when Philadelphia officials stopped off in the coalfields to plan a new site on their way to the Kentucky Derby.[2]

Railroad construction camps often moved in advance of coal towns. Unlike the anthracite mines, which opened in the vicinity of well-established incorporated towns, southern Appalachian coal lay in remote, rugged, and unsettled areas far from independent towns. Tents and tar-paper shacks lined the route of the Clinchfield and Ohio Railroad, completed in 1912 from Spartanburg, South Carolina, to Elkhorn, Kentucky. Single men dominated the camps, though a few women and children traveled with them. Crews were usually of mixed ethnic and racial origins, including native-born whites, blacks, convicts, and substantial numbers of Italian immigrants. The men were paid $1.50 for each day of work. The railroad deducted $1.00 a month for lodging whether the laborer spent one or thirty days in camp. Deductions for medical care, transportation, and food often meant that the men ended the month owing the company.[3] Under such conditions of housing and labor, "anything could happen – and often did."[4]

Usually, the coal camp, like the railroad camp, began with temporary housing – tents or boardinghouses – until more permanent dwellings could be built. Gradually, within a year or so, the camp grew to include a company store, the most essential structure in the town, except perhaps the saloon in the early towns. As a multipurpose building, the company store included administrative offices of the company and a commissary (the term miners customarily used for the grocery store). In time, changes in a town's demographic makeup might bring more family dwellings, grade schools, leisure facilities, and churches. In 1925, an estimated five hundred company towns dotted the map of southern Appalachia. In southwestern Virginia, the Stonega Coke and Coal Company (SC&C) was the major founder of company towns.

SC&C incorporated under New Jersey laws on 19 April 1902 in order to assume operation of the mines and coke ovens of the Virginia Coal and Iron Company (VCI). VCI had been built between 1890 and 1896. Although ownership was in common and VCI held a large block of stock, Stonega operated as a lessee, not as a subsidiary of VCI. Initially, the lease covered 5,800 acres, but grew to over 20,000 acres by 1909. By then SC&C had moved into a new field office at Big Stone Gap. SC&C continued to grow, absorbing two adjoining companies and doubling the size of the company in 1910 with the purchase of the Keokee Consolidated Coke Company and Imboden Coal and Coke Company. In the same year, the New Jersey corporation was dissolved and SC&C incorporated in Delaware – probably to take advantage of more advantageous tax laws. A new lease was executed with VCI covering 25,800 acres. In 1923, SC&C moved into West Virginia with a lease of the Sun colliery, which it abandoned in 1932. During World War II, according to company claims, SC&C mines employed 70 percent of all coal miners working in Virginia. SC&C's first major postwar construction project came in 1945-47 with the opening of the Glenbrook colliery in Harlan County, Kentucky, the largest colliery in the state at the time. The old town of Keokee, which had been abandoned in the 1930s, was rebuilt, adding a hundred modern houses with detached garages. It was sold in 1963. On 30 April 1964 SC&C absorbed the old Westmoreland Coal Company, and the company name was changed to Westmoreland to keep the older name.[5]

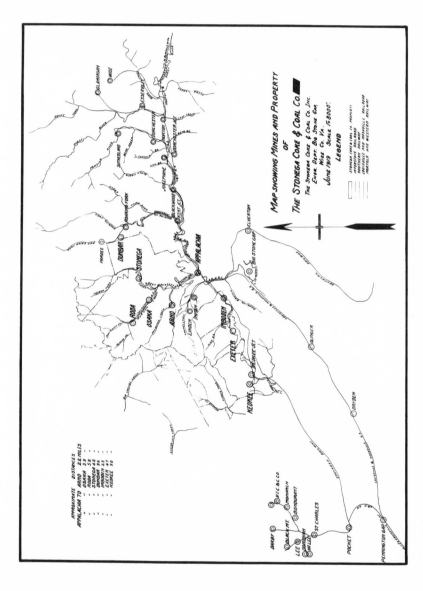

Map of towns of Stonega Company. Courtesy of Westmoreland Coal Company Archive, Hagley Library.

SC&C founded or operated ten company towns. Stonega was built in 1896, followed by Osaka (1902), Roda (1903), Arno (1908), Imboden and Keokee (purchased as operating units in 1910), Exeter (1917), Dunbar (1919), and Derby (1923). When operating at full capacity, according to a company official in 1935, SC&C employed four thousand men.[6]

A variety of factors determined the quality of housing in company towns. At Stonega's collieries, the Wentz family of Pennsylvania, which had controlled VCI, also occupied the top rungs of corporate management. John S. Wentz served on the board of directors from 1902 to 1918 and as president from 1902 to 1904. His son, Daniel B. Wentz, served on the board from 1902 to 1926 and as president from 1904 to 1926. Other members of the Wentz family held lesser positions. The Wentzes established a paternalistic environment in their towns. In small mining operations of Kentucky and West Virginia, especially in areas employing large numbers of immigrants, living and working conditions were harsh.[7] But at SC&C, company engineers and private contractors laid out the towns with worker "contentment" in mind almost from the beginning. Stonega was the largest and most fully developed town.[8]

In 1895 work began on the Stonega colliery. In 1897 a Bristol, Virginia, newspaper described the site: "Two years ago, along the banks of Callahan Creek, which empties into the Roaring Fork of Powell's River in the mountain fastness of Big Stone Gap, was a gloomy wilderness. . . . Today it is teeming with life and activity." About twelve hundred people lived in the town, and 350 coke ovens turned out tons of industrial fuel. A store, post office, school, church, and telegraph and telephone lines served the community. Newspapers described housing for the miners as "comfortable and convenient" and "much above the average of mining towns." Most of the housing was single-family dwellings, although an occasional house held two families. Boardinghouses, maintained by black or immigrant women (usually Hungarians or Italians, as were most foreign laborers), housed the single and unaccompanied miners. At its peak, Stonega had 702 single-family dwellings. In 1898, Bristol ran an excursion train to Stonega so that visitors could admire "the marvels" of this industrial village carved out of a wilderness.[9]

Stonega engineers let the terrain, ethnic and racial prejudice, and considerations of status guide their master plan. Street layout in Stonega was "primitive, governed largely by the hilly terrain, the serpentine railroad track that provided the lifeline to the outside world, and Callahan Creek." The miners' houses fronted the railroad and a dirt track. Company buildings – the commissary, park, and recreational facilities – and the first church were clustered together. Company officials lived in the more spacious and convienently located two-story dwellings near the cluster.

The miners' four-room, single-story dwellings were "sprinkled on hill-sides" and were the first structures to be seen upon entering the town. Other shacks for laborers occupied available space as the remaining terrain allowed. The company assigned blacks to the least desirable housing, and immigrants, whom they sought to lure (see the following chapter), to more favorable quarters.[10]

The local terrain presented engineers with difficult problems. Building the town on the slope of a narrow hollow or gorge presented miners and builders alike with problems of drainage, house foundations, and the heating of stilt-type houses, and it complicated the otherwise routine matter of getting furniture, coal, and groceries to the houses. The layout of the towns at Kaymoor and Borderland, West Virginia, and Dunbar and Exeter, Virginia, are examples of how terrain and the location of the coal affected town development.

Kaymoor was a company town of the Low Moor Iron Company, the first producer of pig iron in Virginia according to the company, which was headquartered near Clifton Forge in Allegheny County, Virginia. Abiel Abbot Low, a native of Salem, Massachusetts, made his fortune in the New York import trade before investing in railroads and industries of the "New South" during Reconstruction (1865–77). In 1873, as a member of the board of directors of the C&O Railway, Low joined with Collis P. Huntington and other capitalists to finance and build a rail line, part of which followed the gorge carved out by the New River in southern West Virginia. As the railroad was being built, Low acquired four thousand acres of Virginia iron ore lands in Allegheny County and eleven thousand acres of coal lands in Fayette County, West Virginia, the eventual location of Kaymoor. George T. Wickes of Low Moor was the on-site manager and was responsible for opening the iron mines at the site near Clifton Forge.

Between 1878 and 1899, Low Moor located ore veins, limestone quarries, and mines at Fenwick, Dolly Ann, Jordan, Rich Patch, Low Moor, and Longdale, most within 20 miles of Low Moor at Clifton Forge. Coal for coking was purchased from the West Virginia mines along the New River division of the C&O, the only transport available for the New River operators. By 1900 Low Moor had two furnaces, two limestone quarries, eleven iron-ore mines, two coal mines, twelve company stores, and a marketing agency for its coal and iron. The Kaymoor mine was not opened until 1899, by which time the coal industry was growing rapidly in Fayette County.

On 23 August 1900, C&O car number 19978 rolled off the Kaymoor One siding to the cheers and relief of miners, construction workers, and supervisors bound eastward for the 125-mile journey to the coke ovens of the Low Moor Iron Company. Low Moor now had its own coal mine, named after James Kay, the first superintendent. It was one of the seventy-five mines the C&O served between Thurmond and Hawk's Nest. Low Moor and the pig-iron industry fell upon hard times, and Low Moor began to liquidate some of its holdings in 1925, including Kaymoor which was sold to the New River and Pocahontas Consolidated Coal and Coke Company for over $1 million. Kaymoor One continued to produce coal until it closed in 1962.[11]

Kaymoor was divided into several communities. There were two mines: Kaymoor Two's mine tipple, headhouse, and power station were located about one-fourth of a mile down the New River from the truss bridge that joined Fayette and South Fayette. That mine closed in 1926. Kaymoor One, the most important of all the southern Appalachian mines in coal output, population, and longevity, was located two miles up the New River from Kaymoor Two. Due to the terrain and location of the coal, both Kaymoors had two community centers near the mine sites, the "Bottom" and "Top" of each site. The bottom sites were in the gorge near the C&O line and the New River. The top sites, that opened because not enough space existed in the gorge to house all of the miners, were perched on the rim of the cliff above the gorge. Both had houses, stores, schools, churches, and a population of mining families.

In the early 1920s, Kaymoor had 131 single dwellings and 560 people, 140 of whom were employees. In 1901, 50 houses were built, followed by 45 in 1902, 17 in 1905, and 19 in 1918. All except the newer 1918 houses were thirty-four feet square, of board and batten on a foundation of posts, and heated by coal in fireplaces or stoves. In 1923, 78 houses each had electricity for two dollars per month and 25 had cold running water; the remainder used springs, pumps, or hydrants. Houses had coal sheds and privies and rented for five to eight dollars per month unfurnished and furnished respectively. The 19 houses built in 1918 were precut bungalows shipped to Kaymoor by rail and carried on the "haulage" to the mountaintop where they were assembled. The haulage was an open cable car that raised and lowered freight or passengers – it had a capacity of 15 people – up and down a seventy-foot cliff as it lurched along precariously. Houses were customarily enclosed by fences so that families could keep a cow, chickens, or pigs. Lots were usually laid out for gardens, too. Single men lived and boarded with other familes or at Leana Woodson's boardinghouse for fifty-five cents per day (in 1919). The boardinghouse could accomodate 15 men and was usually full. The haulage was the only means of traveling between Kaymoor Top and Bottom. This geographical layout divided Kaymoor's miners into four separate communities and hampered community identity.[12]

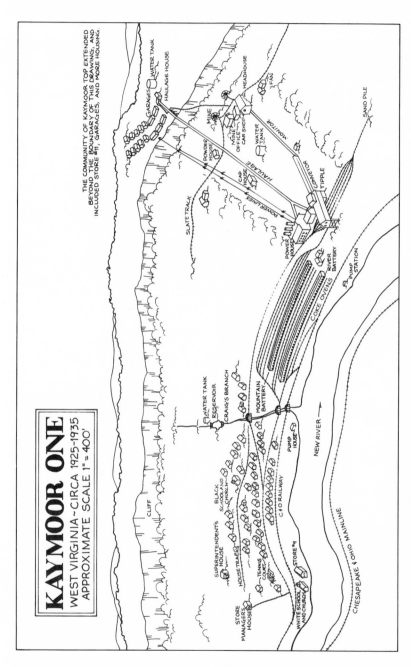

Layout of Kaymoor One. Courtesy of Eastern National Park and Monument Association.

Borderland was a company town of the Borderland Coal Company, and it derived its name from its dual location in Mingo County, West Virginia, and Pike County, Kentucky, an area divided by the Tug Fork of the Big Sandy River. The Borderland mines were situated in Kentucky along with a stable, school, shop, drum house, an upper tipple (the most visible above-ground structure, where coal is sorted and dropped into railroad cars), and most of the miner's houses. Coal was mined in Pike County, moved on rail cars to a platform where it was dumped and carried by aerial tramway across the Tug Fork into West Virginia. According to a company inventory in 1922, Borderland had 73 frame and 21 brick dwellings at its Number One plant and 67 frame and 23 brick dwellings at Number Two nearby. Brick dwellings for miners were not customary and had been built reluctantly during the severe labor shortage created by World War I. In 1916 each house cost the company $1,400 to build. Borderland's frame houses cost $1,100 each to build. In both cases, the quality would have been superior to local housing. Visible across the Tug River in Mingo County, situated alongside the Norfolk and Western Railroad, was the superintendent's house, houses numbered one through four, the company store, engine house, lower tipple, coaling station, and the power plant.

In its halcyon days, Borderland held three thousand acres of coal lands with an estimated 20 million tons of coal. Profits of the company were $1,250 in 1904, the first year of operation, and peaked at $110,000 in 1910. In the same period, the amount of coal mined increased from 246 to 3,781 railroad carloads. Coal sales generated the most profit (86 percent), followed by company-store sales (10 percent) and powder (3 percent). Before World War I, Borderland paid a regular dividend of between 15 and 30 percent; on 1 January 1918, it paid 60 percent – its highest dividend ever – rechartered itself in Virginia, and patented the trademark and name of the Borderland Coal Company. A new tipple was build in 1918 at a cost of $116,000. But company fortunes declined sharply after the war, partially due to an decrease in coal price and demand.[13]

However, as one of the major towns of this study, Borderland exhibits ideosyncrasies which set it apart as a company. At Borderland Coal, problems with labor and unionization were severe. In fact, the company's ultimate demise was caused in part by labor unrest. In addition, Borderland was unique as a company dominated by a single individual, Edward L. Stone, who was founder of the company and chief stockholder, president between 1907 and 1919, and chairman of the board from 1919 until 1934 when the company went bankrupt and ceased to mine coal. Of course, there were other individuals of significance in the company, namely James P. Woods, Roanoke attorney, U.S. representative

Borderland under construction. Courtesy of Manuscripts Division, Special Collections Department, University of Virginia Library.

Borderland Number Two plant. Courtesy of Manuscripts Division, Special Collections Department, University of Virginia Library.

from Virginia's Sixth District, and vice-president from 1905 to 1922 and president, 1922 to 1932. L. E. Armentrout was the most important day-to-day figure, the on-site manager from 1905 to 1915, and vice-president and manager, 1915 to 1927. Ernest B. Fishburn figured prominently as secretary-treasurer throughout the company's existence. It was always clear, however, who the boss was, and it was Edward Stone.

Stone was born in 1864 in Liberty (now Bedford), Virginia, and reared in modest circumstances, never receiving more than an elementary-school education. Orphaned at the age of ten, his career as a self-made man began as a classic tale of the American dream. While at the school playground one day, the editor of the Bedford *Sentinel* came looking for Stone's cousin to carry papers. Unable to find him, Stone volunteered and thus began his career in the newspaper business. Working himself up from delivery boy through a series of newspaper jobs, he quit school at an early age to support himself. On one occasion, at age sixteen, when the editor was in court, Stone was entrusted to get the entire paper out by himself, which he accomplished by noon and was out playing ball in the street when the boss returned. Stone was a scrappy youth who sometimes interrupted his work to take on a passing youngster. Luck paid another visit in 1885. Stone worked then for a printing firm in Roanoke, Virginia. When the manager died, the position was offered to Stone at the young age of twenty-one. Eventually he gained control of the business and became president of the Stone Printing and Manufacturing Company. In 1890, he married Minnie Fishburn, daughter of J. A. Fishburn, a prominent Roanoke businessman. Borderland Coal was just another of his many and varied business interests, which also included a foundry, a bridge and iron company, and a bank.

Stone Printing, however, was his "first love." His principal hobby was book collecting, and he had a library appraised at $50,000 at his death. In an average year, his income was about $58,000 during the first two decades of the century. He was generous with his wealth, giving to assorted charities such as the Roanoke Relief Fund, the War Relief Clearing House, the Boy Scouts, and the Coal Miners' Relief Fund—even though the striking miners were from his own Borderland facility. In the latter case, his position was that children should not have to suffer from their parents' mistakes. It is an example of the kind of anti-union sentiment he maintained throughout his life. He vehemently resisted unionization of his Borderland mines yet allowed unionization in his Stone Printing plant. He gave to institutions such as Roanoke College, which he helped endow, as well as Roanoke Hospital and Tuskegee Institute. After a protracted illness, this New South businessman died in 1938 at the age of seventy-four.[14]

Life in the town of Borderland was influenced not only by its location but by economic considerations and the attitude of the company's major stockholder. Situated in a narrow hollow on the Tug River, houses were squeezed between the river and the railroad. Coal dust from the nearby tipple and rail cars must have easily reached the living areas, giving miners' houses and clothing a daily bath of dust. Profit considerations motivated all coal operators, but Borderland was a small company lacking economies of scale. Paternalism cost more than Stone was willing to pay, except in a few brick houses. Perhaps because of his physical distance from them, Stone never expressed concern for mine laborers and their living and working conditions. The town never had the leisure facilities of larger companies like SC&C.

The building of the towns of Dunbar and Exeter indicates the influence of local conditions while simultaneously revealing the process of town-building. At Dunbar early in 1918, SC&C officials decided to locate a colliery on Pot Creek, immediately above the town of Roaring Fork, near two seams (Taggart and Marker). A tram road was built four hundred feet above the railroad line, and the coal was to be lowered by a trough conveyor. A group of men set to work building temporary shacks. Once completed, the shacks were filled with carpenters and laborers. The carpenters began building permanent houses, and the laborers began to clear the forest for a tipple, grade for tramways and inclines, punch openings for coal mining, put in foundations, and do all the other work necessary for opening a new colliery. A chief mining engineer was sent in to supervise the mine openings and tram roads.[15]

The original plan called for 250 single-family dwellings. House locations were surveyed, plotted, and the town was sketched on paper. Then company officials realized that they did not have sufficient space to locate standard four-room single-family dwellings. Thus the decision was made to adopt a ten-room, double-occupancy house, each to house two families. By 1 Janauary 1919, 28 of these dwellings had been completed and 16 were under construction. These were frame dwellings with poplar siding set upon brick piers for foundations. Inside the houses were plastered walls; all were electrically wired, with open fireplaces for heating in living and dining rooms. Two shallow wells were drilled at a depth of 50 feet and hand pumps installed for a temporary water supply. A permanent well of 275 feet was drilled and encased for 80 feet to serve the entire town. During the same year at Exeter, a steam shovel was brought in to change the course of Pigeon Creek, and 132 single-family dwellings were built upon a former swamp.[16]

Coal towns arose under various circumstances. Borderland, for example, was the creation of a small company guided by one man, a New

Edward L. Stone, ca. 1914. Courtesy of Manuscripts Division, Special Collections Department, University of Virginia Library.

Borderland, 1916. Courtesy of Manuscripts Division, Special Collections Department, University of Virginia Library.

South son, and had regional company headquarters in Roanoke, Virginia. SC&C, however, was a large corporation whose company towns were the dreams of absentee capitalists in Philadelphia who ruled through a corporate staff headquartered in Big Stone Gap, Virginia. Kaymoor was a "captive" town whose mine was opened primarily to provide coal for pig-iron foundries at the company headquarters in Clifton Forge. In each case, company management determined the layout of the site and the nature of housing, whether multifamily or single-family dwellings. The environment posed special problems of spatially separating dwellings, schools, stores, and churches from the noise and dust of the mining facilities. Company paternalism varied from company to company, a blend of economics and the attitudes of management.

Coal towns did evolve. Not only is the "typical" company town an elusive quarry because of local conditions and idiosyncrasies of management, the actual towns were always in some stage of development, never frozen in time. Such evolution wrought great changes in the character of the towns.

Three general stages of development marked the company town: first, a pioneer or frontier phase lasting from the late 1880s, when the first towns began to be built, until World War I; second, a paternalistic phase from World War I until the Great Depression; and third, an aging and decaying phase, roughly from the mid-1930s until the closing of the towns in the mid-1950s. This chapter will deal with the first two stages of development, leaving the final stage for the Conclusion. As with most models of change, many towns do not fit neatly into this model of development, especially in chronological terms. The town of Stonega, for example, passed quickly out of the frontier into a paternalistic phase while Wheelwright, Kentucky (described below), lingered in a more extended frontier-like phase. Stages overlapped; nothing as precise as definite dates for the completion of one phase and the onset of another is possible. However, more significant than having chronological precision, the phases refer to conditions within the towns themselves and their evolutionary development from founding to closing.

To characterize the general stages briefly, the frontier period was a rugged, pioneer time when towns were first being laid out, sometimes in forbidding terrain deep in the mountains, when operators paid little heed to the quality of life or the conditions of labor. Just as in the railroad construction camps, so in the coal camps: housing was usually temporary, consisting of tents or tar-paper shacks. Nearly all the labor force was male. During the paternalistic phase – which marked the end of the frontier period – operators paid more heed to the needs of the miners themselves, looked more toward family labor, and added schools, churches, beauty parlors, recreation centers, libraries, and other facilities to make life more varied and enjoyable. Data from several time periods on the actual number of coal-town residents, their marital status, or comparable information such as sex ratios, would allow more precise calculations of the change from frontier to paternalistic periods. Unfortunately, such information is not readily available.

Nevertheless, the ratio of single to married men during a town's existence appears to have had a major impact upon the character of town life. An increase in family labor mitigated the problems of heavy drinking, gambling, and violence and necessitated the building of the facilities mentioned above, giving the towns a more communal ambience. Even though not exclusive to these years, the move toward the use of family labor marked the World War I period, as the following chapter will explain. Following on the heels of the paternalistic phase was a period of aging and decline characterized by neglect of housing and disregard for the town as a community. Such forces as mechanization of the mines, along with the automobile and unionization, accompanied this transformation. The reasons for changes in the towns were both historical and idiosyncratic.

Pocahontas, Virginia, was one of the earliest coal towns. Construction began in the fall of 1881, even before the N&W had completed its rail line to the town. By 1883, when the railroad arrived, Pocahontas had developed into a boom town with fifty houses, a company store, a butcher shop, a dressmaker, a millinery, a ten-pin bowling alley, an ice house, a school, a chapel, two saloons, a newspaper, a brass band, one hundred coke ovens, and forty thousand tons of coal lying on the ground waiting to be hauled away. At the meat market, miners could buy whole chickens for twenty-five cents, beef for six cents a pound, butter for twenty cents a pound, and eggs for ten cents a dozen. Underground loaders netted $2.00 to $2.40 per day; common labor earned $1.27 to $1.40 per day; coke drawers got fifty-five cents per day. Sanitation was primitive: privies emptied into the Laurel Fork of the Bluestone River. Liquor flowed freely, even before the saloons were established. Miners could purchase a drink at "blind tigers," coin-operated machines where, for the deposit of a quarter, a miner could get "a drink of uncertain quality delivered by a hand of uncertain origin." When the state granted liquor licenses, twenty-one saloons and three breweries established themselves at Pocahontas: Virginia, Anheuser-Busch, and Pabst. Churches of every denomination vied with the saloons for the miner's soul and his paycheck too.[17]

Less is known about life in the early years of the mining settlement than in any other period. It was a time when the conditions of labor were at their worst. Work was often strenuous with the aid of very little machinery. Miners worked – many for the first time underground – in the dark, sometimes in pools of water, at difficult tasks for long hours in constant danger and uncertainty. Falls of rock and coal from the roof and explosions of methane gas and coal dust placed the miners at tremendous risk. Conditions of mining constantly changed, sometimes daily.[18] Fragmentary evidence suggests it was also an era of primitive living conditions. Men were often separated from their home communities and families; they lived in cramped and crowded quarters, spent long days in the mines, and returned to the barrackslike boarding houses where heavy drinking and gambling relieved the boredom and fistfights settled the inevitable disputes.

As a company, TCI began in 1860 as Tennessee Coal, Iron and Railroad Company in Tennessee. After 1907, it was taken over and operated as a subsidiary of United States Steel under the name of the Tennessee Coal and Iron Company (TCI). It was one of the largest corporations in the South. It owned 340,000 acres in Alabama, 112,000 in Tennessee, and 1,420 in Georgia; it had twelve thousand to thirteen thousand workers on its payroll. TCI mined one-half of all the coal and produced one-half of all the iron, three-fourths of all the coke, and all of the steel in the state of Alabama. It had mines and coke ovens in Alabama at Pratt, Blocton, Blue Creek, Blosebury, Gample, Ellen, Jasper, Birmingham, and Bessemer and in Tennessee at Tracy City, Whitewell, and Victoria.[19] Docena, on the outskirts of Birmingham, became a company town of TCI. From 1890 and 1905 it was a prison camp; in 1907, after the switch had been made from convict to free labor and the prisoners distributed among camps at other mines, TCI recruited a labor force made up largely of black tenants and sharecroppers from the surrounding region along with smaller numbers of whites. They lived in tents and began the construction of more permanent facilities.[20]

Similarly, in 1916 the Elk Horn Coal Corporation opened a drift-mouth mine and established a tent camp at Wheelwright in eastern Kentucky. The miners worked ten-hour days for seventeen cents an hour. Floorless frame dwellings lined with building paper hauled in by oxen from the nearest railroad, eighteen miles away, replaced the tents. A series of wells with hand pumps supplied water. Sanitation was primitive with outside privies, and Wheelwright still looked like a frontier town to Wood Cooley when he arrived in 1928: "It looked like back in the Western days, you know, when you had a bench on the front porch. Everybody'd set out there and whittle all day. All the houses were painted yellow and they had black lattice around them."[21]

Boarding and boardinghouses characterized pioneer camps. They housed the populations of single or solitary foreign mine workers – who were more prevalent before World War I – and sometimes served as temporary housing for small families awaiting vacancies in permanent dwellings.[22] T. B. Pugh, a former miner familiar with the pioneer camps of West Virginia, remembered every camp having a boardinghouse for the "unattached miners." The Pugh family itself lived in a boardinghouse for two weeks awaiting the arrival of furniture which came on the freight train in a bundle that was made recognizable by the familiar bark of their dog inside.[23] Lloyd Vick Minor, a former miner from southwestern Virginia, recalled his father going to work at the coke ovens at Osaka where he had to apply and wait for a vacancy in a company house. Like other oven workers, while waiting he lived in a boardinghouse. Osaka workers also lived with young, childless couples who rented spare bedrooms to the waiting men. Once it became clear to oven workers, temporarily separated from their families, that they were going to remain as permanent employees, they applied for and moved into the first available house. Their families then joined them at the site.[24]

A substantial, if incalculable, proportion of frontier populations was composed of foreigners. The Borderland colliery had an immigrant majority in its population during the coal-camp era, according to its founder Edward Stone. Houses with four to five men each were usually rented to a single individual, presumably a responsible foreigner, who in turn rented to others.[25] In 1913, about fifteen years after the first mine opened at the site, the Stonega colliery sucessfully lured a number of Greeks away from a competitive mine in nearby Dante and began the construction of three three-room houses in which it hoped to accommodate thirty Greek miners. Recruitment of foreigners for the mines and the building of boardinghouses continued up to the outbreak of World War I, when foreign labor began its exodus from the coal fields.[26]

During the coal-camp era, the boardinghouse residents gained a reputation, deserved it seems, as a rough-and-tumble crowd that engaged in drinking, gambling, and violent brawling. T. B. Pugh recalled:

> The thing I remember about the boarding house there [Sewell, West Virginia], since it was just above our house, they'd get drunk, and there'd be more throat-cuttings there than anyplace you ever heard of. Just about every week, somebody would be stabbed, or shot, or have his throat cut. Throat-cutting was common and stylish.[27]

The historian of Kaymoor believed that the heritage of "pioneer individualism" among native white mountaineers contributed to violence, especially in the years before the town became firmly established as a community. Miners had handguns, and the company hired untrained guards who were deputized by the local sheriff to maintain law and order. It was an explosive situation. In 1904, John Boggs shot Fred Kale over

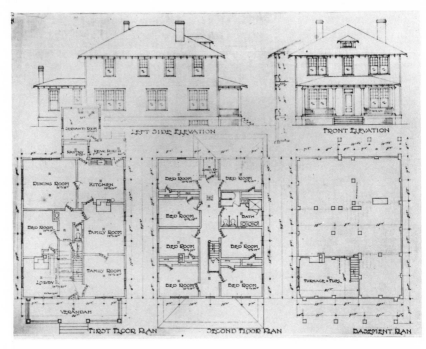

Exeter boardinghouse plan, 1918. Courtesy of Westmoreland Coal Company
Archive, Hagley Library.

a woman. The two began the argument in a bar in Nuttalburg, then returned to Kaymoor Top and settled their dispute in a shootout. Payday
nights were often bad times for drinking, gambling, arguments, and
fights. Violence followed young single males. Occasionally domestic violence also occurred, as in the case of a Kaymoor Two woman who borrowed
ten cents in scrip to purchase shotgun shells which she used to kill her
husband after he repeatedly threatened her for unknown reasons.[28]

Violence continued in some towns past World War I, although for the
most part the war marked the end of the rugged pioneer phase. Martha
Clark, a black miner's wife, reported a killing nearly every Saturday
night when she and her husband moved to the town of McRoberts, Kentucky, in 1928.[29] Not unlike the western frontier, the coal camp drew a
congregation of young, single or unattached males who had been uprooted from definite expectations of social behavior and placed in a strange
and unfamiliar environment where anxieties and tensions of life and
work sought relief in exaggerated and sporadic outbursts of unbridled
behavior. It was an all-male world where coal operators exploited the
workers and the environment. The workers released their frustrations

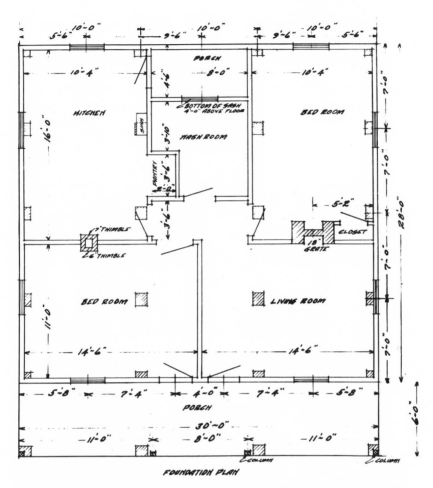

Room arrangements, Stonega Company, 1917. Courtesy of Westmoreland Coal Company Archive, Hagley Library.

and aggressions upon themselves and other miners. Since ethnic and racial prejudice prevailed, the confrontations easily involved mixed groups.

The ever-increasing demand for coal, the intense labor shortages until World War I, and the discontent of labor – expressed most emphatically by the movement of miners from mine to mine but also by sporadic strikes – exerted pressure on coal operators to improve conditions in coal towns and pressured them to improve the the camplike environment of the frontier phase. In some cases, the move toward a town setting came early in a coal town's development, as operators sensed the necessity for a more paternalistic relationship between themselves and their miners. Other operators were moved to this position by World War I and the more intense labor shortage it wrought. In still other cases, towns were begun during and shortly after World War I and escaped the harsh and crude conditions that had faced earlier generations of miners.

SC&C was one of the companies that appear to have recognized the importance of a contented labor force early in their history. The Stonega colliery moved rapidly to establish town facilities within two years of the opening of the mine. It operated a hospital for its mining families from 1902 until 1957 at Stonega. It also engaged in petty acts of paternalism. On 23 December 1916, for example, SC&C gave all of its employees a Christmas present. Married men got $5.00 in cash, single men $2.50, and salaried workers received 5 percent of yearly earnings. In spite of the inequity, the company claimed:

> These presents were highly appreciated by all employees and together with the Christmas treats which were given to the children – these treats included a pound of candy, an orange, an apple, a box of popcorn, a toy, and a pair of gloves, mittens, or toboggan – made the 1916 Christmas the happiest the employees of the Stonega Coke and Coal Company had ever had.[30]

Local officials of the company were obviously anxious to demonstrate to the Philadelphia office that they were in step with emerging company plans to create a contented laboring population.

It was in 1916 when SC&C first gave full elaboration of its belief in paternalism, or what it called "contentment sociology." The medical department's portion of the company's annual report stated: "Further, we have learned that 'Efficient Service of Manpower' is the real goal of the Industrial physician, and that preventive surgery, personal hygiene, and contentment-sociology, are mile-posts on the road to this goal." The report prided itself in having no epidemics of disease during the year, and only two cases of typhoid fever. Welfare nurses, hired by the company, served the interests of a happy family life "for better work of the men." A safety program encouraged the prevention of accidents and the prompt treatment of those that did occur. The report concluded:

> Contentment is necessary for the stability of labor and prevention of unions and lockouts. Playgrounds, amusement halls, night schools, and domestic science classes have been carefully worked out for the benefit and contentment of the employee and his family. Again, the Church, for the first time, is strongly represented at all the Collieries, it being such that each denomination has sent to the Company one or more of their strongest pastors.[31]

Contentment sociology came in the form of applied medicine at another colliery too. At Docena, much attention in the early years was paid to living and working conditions of the miners. Labor turnover rates were high due to "unsatisfactory provisions of housing, bath houses, and safety measures." Consequently, in 1913 TCI organized its health department. Dispensaries and small emergency hospitals were established in various communities of the company, and more attention was paid to preventive medicine – especially in dealing with diseases of malaria, typhoid fever, and enteritis. Labor unrest in the form of strikes had troubled the TCI company in 1902 and 1904, leading to the announcement that TCI would operate on a nonunion basis thereafter. Soon afterwards, the Lloyd Nolan Hospital was centrally located near Docena to serve all the mines of the company and continued to operate until 1957.[32]

Since the Bureau of Mines and state boards of health exerted their own pressure for health and sanitary improvements in mining towns, it is difficult to say where paternalism ended and forced compliance to outside directives began. Regardless, applied medicine was in the best interests of the operators, both from the standpoint of labor stability and on the grounds of production levels. Of course, it also benefited the miners.

Epidemics of contagious diseases could have devastating effects upon mine labor and productivity. In 1920, SC&C noted in its annual report that the post of company doctor had existed for years, but now "we know that industrial medicine is important because the health of the employee is the biggest production problem." SC&C's medical department kept yearly records of diseases among the mine population. The company attributed the absence of epidemics among children in 1915 to "rigid measures of quarantine" enforced by the medical staff and plant police force. They found that the company's population had escaped the usual cases of typhoid, although several cases of dysentery "of a virulent type" had been reported at the Keokee colliery. The eyes and throats of all schoolchildren were examined for the first time, and fourteen cases of trachoma were identified. The report finished with a rallying cry: "Sanitary privies, public baths, and Social Betterment Nurses, the Text for 1916." The following year's report talked of launching a "crusade on the Negro urinal diseases" – partly an expression of racism and partly a reflection of the reality that black miners suffered improportionately to their numbers from venereal disease – and proposed to study the best way of collecting and disposing of rubbish and garbage, called for a more rigid supervision of cow stables and hog pens, and mentioned public bathhouses once again where miners could wash off the coal dust before going home. In 1918 all collieries were infected with smallpox "brought in by Negroes from the South." An epidemic raged at Arno and Osaka before compulsory vaccination brought it under control. Cases of measles, scarlet fever, whooping cough, and diphtheria "as always" were noted, but the best record ever was achieved for typhoid fever.[33]

At Kaymoor, a smallpox epidemic raged through Fayette County in 1904. The cost of inoculations reached $60,000, which coal operators balked at sharing. A flu epidemic, national in scope, spread over the gorge area in 1918, causing drastic curtailments of activity to prevent its spread. Schools were closed, the theater was shut down, only one customer at a time was allowed in the barber shops, and all public meetings were discouraged as company doctors at Kaymoor One "worked day and night to prevent the inexorable spread of the deadliest influenza epidemic in American history." The epidemic so "devastated Kaymoor" that production plummeted. Kaymoor Top had an excellent supply of water with eight drilled wells and two springs supplying fresh, clean water to the residents on the rim. Kaymoor Bottom drew its water either from the New River or a reservoir fed by a branch, and this water was more easily contaminated. Company doctors monitored the water supply closely to prevent disease but were not always successful in preventing contamination.[34]

Health and sanitation remained problems for coal operators as long as there were company towns. Not unlike the problems of crowded urban populations, the concentration of hundreds of people in narrow gorges and valleys strained even determined efforts to provide a good supply of clean water and an adequate system of sewage and garbage disposal, and it easily overwhelmed a lackadaisical attention to health and sanitation. An early photograph of Stonega shows privies located over Callahan Creek. But SC&C moved quickly to upgrade sewage and water facilities in its towns. The company built a complete sewer system at Andover in 1915; the following year at Roda, pipes were laid between a water tank – filled from artesian wells – to house fronts, and fire hydrants were made accessible to all residences.[35]

Gradually, through improvements in sanitation (Wheelwright residents got flush toilets in 1942), inoculations, bathhouses (which collieries added generally in the 1920s), and health education programs, operators were able to control epidemics of communicable diseases such as typhoid fever, smallpox, and diptheria and others like tuberculosis and hookworm. Inexplicably, the number of cases of pellegra, a dietary-deficiency disease, went from eleven cases (1 percent of all communicable diseases) in 1924 at SC&C to forty-five cases in 1940 (still only 1 percent).[36]

Generally, however, as the diseases of the frontier era waned in the paternalistic period, they were replaced by other less-fearful health problems. At SC&C, for example, there were 1,497 cases of influenza in 1924 (34 percent of communicable diseases) and 2,177 cases in 1940 (72 percent). During the same period, there were 41 cases of diptheria, 58 of hookworm, 40 of smallpox, 86 of tuberculosis, and 19 of typhoid fever in 1924, but in 1940 only 1 case of diptheria and none of smallpox, tuberculosis, hookworm, or typhoid.[37]

Venereal diseases proved more tenacious. Cases of gonorrhea and syphilis were reported year after year at SC&C and Wheelwright. Educational campaigns were never able to do more than limit the number of cases. Based upon blood tests, Wheelwright estimated 10 percent of the mine population had syphilis in 1941, the same estimate as for diarrhea. The medical director complained that a one dollar injection fee was as low as he could make it and "a lot of natives won't take even free treatments." He did not say why, but one might speculate that venereal disease was not viewed by the "natives" in the same easygoing and open manner as diarrhea. The total number of reported cases had declined by 1950 when Wheelwright reported six cases of syphilis and nineteen of gonorrhea, down from thirty-five and seventeen in 1942.[38]

Contentment sociology also motivated operators to act in areas beyond medicine. George Wolfe, manager of the Winding Gulf colliery, wrote to his boss Justus Collins to suggest that a better strategy for securing labor might be to build places of amusement rather than to continue building houses, especially since 26 houses were empty. "Do something to make people better satisfied," he advised, such as building a movie house and a poolroom. He also noted that people had raised five hundred dollars for a church and, according to the contract, the company was obliged to match that sum. Wolfe argued that providing whites with a church would also enhance labor contentment because "we are the only operation in Winding Gulf without a single church for whites." He complained to Collins that there was no form of amusement and that people "quarrel, bicker, and fight constantly." He also proposed a schoolhouse "for our colored children." Two years later, Wolfe complained about the labor situation again. By then, 222 houses had been completed and, according to Wolfe, "we have less manpower than ever." The war had exacerbated the labor shortage. Single men had left the colliery, and married people would no longer take in boarders or "herd together." Once again he made his pitch for doing something to retain labor, this time calling for the upgrading of living conditions. SC&C took note of "holding Colored labor at Keokee" in 1915. It was a camp remote from other mining camps and towns. The company decided to build an amusement hall thirty feet square. One side was partitioned off as a dance hall while the other served as a poolroom and lunch hall. It was built at minimal cost, and SC&C believed "they" would appreciate a building for social gatherings, so that this "will probably prove to be a good investment."[39]

Other contentment-sociology practices, clearly designed to stabilize labor, included an agreement at SC&C to give miners free house rent after twenty years of continuous service. The practive began in 1916 but was discontinued around 1935 as the need for paternalism no longer prevailed in the labor market of the 1930s. Between 1922 and 1940, SC&C also carried out a campaign for cordial relations between miners and foremen through improving-foremanship conferences. These short courses were designed "to impress upon the foremen the necessity of fostering and improving" the relationship between workmen and bosses. Foremen were "taught" to give the individual miner more attention so that he would "feel that his superiors have a real interest in his welfare." These conferences were targeted specifically at organized labor: "Every precaution is being taken to see that existing conditions, insofar as they relate to our labor, are not interfered with from outside sources."[40]

Paternalism took a variety of forms. At Borderland, a new commissary was built to "make it easier for us to get and keep miners and other operators." At most collieries, houses seem to have been reasonably well maintained for similar ends. Docena repainted its houses every five years as a rule, and the records of SC&C document yearly repairs, repaintings, and remodelings of company houses, especially during the 1910s and 1920s. Kaymoor had a housing department responsible for repair and maintenance of its houses, including painting and the replacement of roofing and rotted fence posts. Before 1914 the houses were not painted, but after 1919 they were all painted white with green trim. In 1922, L. E. Armentrout, general manager at Borderland, appealed to President Stone for approval to paint all company houses, reminding him that they had not painted in 1921 due to the strike. A satisfied labor force lay behind his appeal:

> It has been our aim as you possibly know for a good many years to take better care of our employees than most of the companies. I feel that we have better houses than 90% of the operations. We keep them in better repairs, and always try to keep them painted up, so that they make a good appearance from the outside.[41]

In spite of the motivations of the operators, when given a choice, the miners and their families preferred the practice of contentment sociology over the alternative of neglect of disregard for the welfare of coaltown residents, as the case of Wheelwright, Kentucky, shows. In this company town, some mining families lived under three different operators, one of whom added many of the conveniences commonly associated with paternalism. Wheelwright did not follow the model chronological breakpoints from coal camp to coal town. Nevertheless, it manifested a similar evolution, from a frontier era with few facilities for recreation, to a paternalistic period when the operators modernized the town and, finally, to an era of neglect. Accordingly, it provides an example of miners' reactions to changing company practices, especially in the case of miners who lived under all three managements.

Wheelwright was a company town founded by Elk Horn Coal Corporation, under whose management it operated from 1916 to 1930, when the colliery was purchased by Inland Steel. It continued under the management of Inland Steel until 1965 when it was sold to Island Creek Coal Company. In 1966, Island sold the houses and public buildings to Mountain Investments, Incorporated, for $1.3 million. In 1979, Mountain sold its property to the Kentucky Housing Corporation for $1.2 million, and the following year Kentucky donated all the utilities to the incorporated city of Wheelwright and began to renovate and sell the houses to individual citizens. During the time Wheelwright was under Elk Horn, it retained some of the vestiges of the frontier stage of development. Streets were unpaved, houses kept their outside toilets, and each yard had its own pile of ash and coal. Garbage and refuse were collected and hauled to "Garbage Hollow." Elk Horn built only one four-room frame school house for white children; black children had to meet in the one-room black church. Nevertheless, some of the features of paternalism were in evidence. An old wooden structure that served as a theater for silent movies; a community center with a soda fountain, poolroom, and barber shop; and two stores completed the facilities under Elk Horn management.[42]

Wheelwright modernized after 1930. Inland Steel built a water system and filtration plant. A garbage and trash incinerator, along with a sewage system and flush toilets, ended the coal and ash heaps, outdoor toilets, and summer bouts of diarrhea. Inland also placed one hydrant per eight houses for fire protection. It transformed the old boarding-house into a swimming pool and built a bowling alley. Over four hundred houses were reconditioned and enlarged, and miners were given an option to add a room at the company's expense. Three-room houses rented for $11.50, four-rooms for $14.50, and homes "in the high rent district" were available for $20.00 to $25.00 per month. Telephones were made available, and gas lines were run to all houses, ending the messy and laborious coal-burning fireplaces. Inland loaned the county $15,000 for the construction of a high school and offered fuel, electricity, and water at no cost. It provided two scholarships, to be given on a competitive basis to children of employees and nonemployees alike (divided about fifty-fifty). *Life* magazine produced an article on Wheelwright as a "model" coal town. Inland also modernized the mines with a fan ventilation system, new power substations, a steel and concrete tipple, an aerial tramway for refuse disposal, and a new headhouse (where coal cars exit) and cleaning plant. It purchased all-steel cars for the mines and built a new inside repair shop and outside machine shop. A miners' bathhouse was also completed with showers, individual lockers, and separate quarters for black and white miners. When the technology eventually developed, Inland added cable television.[43]

Unlike other companies, which added facilities in the interest of labor stability, Inland's modernization, coming at a different time in history, seems to have been motivated by economics. Inland owned a bituminous mine in Pennsylvania in 1929 which produced coal with a high sulphur and ash content. It wanted coal of low sulphur and ash to mix with its Pennsylvania coal, and it had been buying it in the Elk Horn field before purchasing the Wheelwright colliery and leasing an additional eleven thousand acres of land from Elk Horn. Modernization of the facility was simply "good business."[44]

Island Creek took no interest in the town of Wheelwright. It sold the houses and recreational facilities quickly to Mountain Investment. Technically, the town was no longer a company town. Under this arrangement, rent escalated from two to ten dollars per room. When miners who lived in Wheelwright during these changes in ownership recall the town, their fondest memories – as might be expected – are of the Inland years. Wood Cooley said of Island Creek: "They ain't got a care about the town." Everett Hall recalled Elk Horn as being good to the people and good to work for, but the town was not modern; he associated modernization with Inland. About Island, he had little good to say because they only wanted to get the coal out, "that's all they worry about." He characterized the differences in terms of the sun's rising and setting: the dark periods were under Elk Horn and Island, and the daylight was the period of Inland's operation.[45]

Although it is possible to identify stages in the development of company towns and distinct features of each stage, a common feature in all periods of development was segregation. Company towns were thoroughly segregated. Racism and nativism were familiar residents in the coal town, regardless of location in the southern Appalachian fields. "Hunktown," "Niggertown," and similar terms were common in the parlance of native white miners. Racism was far more virulent than nativism. Separate housing areas and epithets hurled at foreigners were common in coal towns, harsh reminders of the secondary status assigned to immigrants by native-born whites. Loathsome as these were and difficult though it must have been for hardworking men, women, and children far from their homelands to get used to, nativism never resulted in as thorough-going a separation as racism. Immigrants were able to use the same areas of the company store, recreation centers, and schools as whites — which was not the case for blacks. The state of West Virginia diverged from the South by not having the Jim Crow system of laws and statutes legally separating the races. Nor were blacks disfranchised, as they were in in other southern states such as Alabama and Virginia. Consequently, they were legally free to participate in the democratic process.[46]

Clearly, black miners were segregated, but no convincing case can be made that separate but equal facilities prevailed in West Virginia. At the Winding Gulf colliery, George Wolfe, the manager, wrote to Justus Collins in 1917 about a promise to build a black church, saying "We have fought this thing off for a long time" although he felt this "never has been right." Blacks had been forced to use instead the lower part of a building on the west fork of Winding Gulf, although "all of the colored people live on the east fork." In spite of his concern, he suggested they might stall further. In 1923, a number of black miners threatened to leave Collins's Winding Gulf facility because whites' houses, more conveniently situated near the company store, were painted and theirs were not. Also, blacks complained of having only one schoolroom and teacher for over forty pupils. At the company town of Tams, West Virginia, whites' housing also appears to have been more centrally located and certainly less crowded than blacks'. In 1920 it was estimated that, in the "colored section" of seventy-five houses, there was an average of seven people; in the foreign section, about ten people occupied each house; and in the white American section, the average was five. All the houses had three to four rooms. At Kaymoor's twin towns at the top and bottom of the New River Gorge:

> Racial segregation was more obvious at Kaymoor Top than at the Bottom. The two main clusters of houses at Kaymoor Top were reserved for whites, while black families lived in homes scattered up the "holler." At Kaymoor Bottom the limited space prevented clearly defined segregation barriers, but white families lived in the choice locations near the tracks while black families were placed in homes high along Craig Branch in the back rows.[47]

The Borderland Coal Company illustrates how racism and nativism guided the decisions of an operator in planning such town facilities as housing. In the words of the president, Edward Stone:

> Several years ago — and, in fact from the earliest beginning, and during the trying times of the Company — the majority of the men in the field were foreigners. The houses we built were the usual standard miners houses. . . . If these foreigners were left to their own inclinations, conditions in the houses would not be anything like the standard of an American workman.

Housing area, unidentified town, Stonega Company. Courtesy of Westmoreland Coal Company Archive, Hagley Library.

As Borderland made its transition from the frontier to the paternalistic stage, roughly around 1916, Stone noted (in the same letter):

> With the passing of the foreign men the coal miners' conditions improved considerably....
>
> Probably two years ago authority was given for the building of 50 modern brick miners' houses, each one costing from three to five times what the original temporary temporary houses cost.
>
> The old houses are generally occupied now by colored employees, and these houses afford colored employees better living conditions than they were used to at home, as was the case with the foreign miners, when a similar comparison is made.

Although Stone's statements about the quality of company housing for the earliest inhabitants – compared to what they had left – contained a measure of truth, it is obvious that hierarchical attitudes guided housing arrangements, with native whites, foreigners, and blacks receiving housing in a descending order of quality.[48]

There is also evidence of entire collieries in West Virginia being restricted by race. A black miner's wife related that at one time blacks could not live in the company town of Concho. In fact, "they didn't even allow them to go through." Annie Kelly said that no black people lived in Elmo; "they didn't allow them even to stop." When the interviewer asked if that was because there were many blacks at Nuttall, Annie responded that she did not know, but that "there was coloreds at Fayette and a couple of families at Michigan, but none at Elmo." Nor did Elmo have any immigrants. On the other hand, Keystone, West Virginia, had a reputation as a predominantly black town. Without knowing more about these towns and the reasons behind preserving them as racially unmixed, little else can be said, except that such conditions call into question racial equity in the state. About segregation in the towns of West Virginia, there is little to doubt. Nuttall, Tams, Elverton, Kaymoor, Quinnimont (a railroad company town), and the Winding Gulf colliery at Davy, to name those of certainty, all had segregated housing, schools, churches, lodges, dance halls, and other facilities.[49]

Certainly the racial situation in West Virginia was tense at times. During the 1916 gubernatorial primary, for example, a black miner and a white miner got into a fight at Winding Gulf. The black man was jailed, and a mob of blacks tried to spring the prisoner, killing a white deputy in the process. George Wolfe exclaimed that the "mob spirit has been crystalized in this state by this political primary. . . . All the Negroes in Raleigh County are armed." Wolfe's comments may have been exaggerated; nevertheless, the effort to free the prisoner was a startling outpouring of black sentiment. Though organized at a black lodge in Hotcoal, the movement included blacks from McAlpin, Big Stick, Lynwin, Pemberton, Sullivan, and Tams. After several days, Wolfe noted that the chances for "a race war" at Winding Gulf were over, but whites were still aroused. He felt that if whites in Raleigh County wanted peace they would have to be tough and make blacks afraid to gather a mob. More than thirty blacks were arrested and jailed, and one black preacher weighing over 350 pounds "died of fright." These events, of course, do not indicate anything about separate facilities. Yet it is difficult to imagine that racial animosity of this intensity did not produce inequality. Of course the very existence of separate facilities, as the Supreme Court finally recognized in 1954, was inherently unequal.[50]

Outside of West Virginia, ethnic housing enclaves and racial segregation characterized all coal towns. Wheelwright was thoroughly segregated by race, and ethnic minorities were forced to live apart from native-born whites. Three separate boardinghouses sheltered foreigners, blacks, and native whites. "Hall Hollow" was the name of the black settlement. When Hilton Garrett, a black miner from Alabama, came to Wheelwright in 1923, Jim Crow was well entrenched and remained so until the 1960s. When asked why he could not go to the soda fountain and be served, Garrett explained it was due to Jim Crowism. The interviewer responded: "I never heard of that. How'd that get started?" Garrett replied in a way that suggested he believed the interviewer had to be putting him on: "It was going on when I was born." Garrett was a barber who also ran the black boardinghouse. Marvin Gullet, a native white mountaineer, also recalled when black laborers came to build the railroad and settled into their own "nigger camp." He remembered that blacks and whites worked together in the mines, although the company tried to keep each group together. However, there was very little mixing in daily life, and no black person could ever enter a white church or home.[51] Foreigners were also intensely disliked by local farmers, who tried at first to drive them out until they realized money could be made by selling them farm produce. Farmers often referred to foreigners openly as "Whops," "Dagoes," and by other names. Poles and Jews became the targets of considerable hostility. Blacks had their own school in Wheelwright with only three or four teachers. It was built after the white school, located up on a hill, apart from the white school down in the town. When a swimming pool was built in 1942, no provision was made for blacks to use it.[52]

SC&C's towns were similarly divided. When the company began to sell its company houses in the 1950s, the inventories referred to houses at Osaka in "Slabtown," a black section, and "Hunktown" at Roda, an ethnic enclave. House numbers indicated a clustering of dwellings in both enclaves. Schools, churches, lodge halls, amusement centers – every facility mentioned in these towns – had separate facilities for the races. In 1916 the increasing number of blacks made it necessary for the company to provide more housing. Therefore they remodeled an old supply house, a building thirty-five by eighty feet, and divided it into sixteen rooms, finishing the inside with cheap building paper. In this facility they placed sixteen families in what must have been very crowded quarters. When the commissary burned in the town of Stonega and a new one had to be built in 1915, it included a "refreshment parlor," a twenty-five-square-foot room separated "by glass front display cabinets" into two compartments, "one for white patrons, the other for colored." Around the same time, whites demanded a barbershop, and the fencing of a "colored cemetery" at Stonega was discussed in company correspondence. First-aid teams, which collieries trained and used in mine rescue missions, were also segregated. In 1915, SC&C had nineteen white first-aid teams and three "colored." It became customary, for the first time in 1915 and yearly thereafter, to hold "meets" in which rescue teams competed in mock disasters. Photographs of the Fourth Annual Colored first Aid Contest at Andover in 1924 reveal the winning black team in bib overalls with no trophies. White rescue teams, on the other hamd, were usually pictured in suits and holding trophies.[53]

Docena was also segregated in spite of its overwhelming black majority. Estimates of the town's racial composition vary. Former residents estimated the composition of both the mine labor force and the town of Docena to be 85 percent black. Docena was built on a square called a "prado." The white school and church were located on one side; on the opposite side was the company store. A large grassy square lay between. The mines were located at a distance, out of sight of the town. Whites' houses were on streets around the square; blacks were housed further away, on the outer edge of these houses. According to a former black resident, "when you went to the store to get meat, there was a place for colored and another for whites." The social barrier was the most formidable: "They [whites] would take and go on with you, but that was just about it." Docena had a black baseball team, the "Black Barons," and their own separate cemetery, social club, churches, and bathhouse. Mail was delivered in the white section first by a mailman who called out the names of those getting mail before going to the black section and repeating the process. The wives and daughters of black miners washed, ironed, and worked as maids in the homes of white management. According to a mine foreman, relations were harmonious in the mines "until the integration business started." Blacks were paid the same and worked side by side with whites, although miners tended to "buddy together" to load coal – whites with whites, blacks with other blacks. When asked why more blacks were not foremen, a white foremen replied gratuitously that they could not pass the state board exam.[54]

Between 1880 and 1930, the growth and development of company towns incorporated industrial capitalism in southern Appalachia, "lift[ing] pre-industrial natives from a simple agrarian-based existence and set[ting] them down in industrial villages and towns." In 1934 the Big Stone Gap *Post* spoke highly of SC&C and the changes it had wrought in Wise County. Prior to the coming of SC&C, Wise had less than three percent of its land cleared and under cultivation, and a small population dependent for a living upon raising cattle and hogs, hunting, trapping, selling pelts, and digging ginseng. Compared to local standards, SC&C brought an elevated standard of living.[55] Electricity, indoor plumbing, a regular income, health care, recreational outlets, commitment to public education and housing "that was as good or better than the norms of the area" were the positive aspects of industrialization.[56] Unfortunately, mining families were also introduced to the negative features. Exploitation of labor, dangerous work, low wages – especially for coke workers and nonloaders – and the noisy, dusty, and crowded conditions of many company towns demonstrate that industrialization was not altogether beneficial.

Altruism seldom motivated the operators to provide social institutions, recreational facilities, good health care, or comfortable homes. Labor expediency in a labor-short market, together with the financial security of the operating company, set the boundaries for paternalism. Operators believed that paternalism was simply another cost of doing business. It had to be paid if a company wanted to remain competitive. Large producers, like Stonega Coke and Coal, could more easily absorb the costs of paternalism. Smaller producers, like Borderland, attempted to get by with little investment in paternalism.

By 1900 the demand for coal had reached levels where the operators rarely had all the miners they wanted. When native labor proved inadequate to labor needs, operators turned to immigrants and southern blacks for additional workers. The shortage became especially acute during the years of World War I. From 1900 to 1920, owners tended to rely more heavily upon paternalism to hold their miners in the towns. Meanwhile, the operators recruited blacks from the rural South and foreigners to dig the coal, run the coke ovens, and load the trains.

4   Recuiting Labor: Immigrants and Blacks

Problems in mountain agriculture, population growth, and mounting poverty pushed some rural whites to look for relief in the local mines. It is impossible to estimate the total number of potential migrants these conditions created in the mountains. Not everyone wanted to move to a coal town, either. It was a difficult choice in spite of the deterioration of rural life. Also, there were other alternatives, such as the textile, planing, and lumber mills; furniture and rayon plants; mica and iron-ore pits; or rock and limestone quarries. Nor is it possible to discern the total labor needs of the hundreds of coal towns that sprang up and developed. Nevertheless, between 1900 and 1920, the bituminous coal industry of southern Appalachia enjoyed its most spectacular years of boom and expansion. Never before and never since has the demand for coal miners been so great as in these decades. The competition for labor was fierce at times, and operators occasionally exceeded the bounds of ethics and propriety in their attempts to find miners and increase production. The rapid development of the industry between 1900 and World War I produced a scramble for labor; the war simply made the scramble more desperate. The war also wrought significant changes in the composition of the workforce as foreign-born miners vacated the mines in great numbers. These developments propelled the coal town toward paternalism and away from the rough and tumble of the pioneer years.

The recruitment of immigrants and native blacks marked these decades of boom. Coal managers vigorously recruited foreign and black labor in order to supply the growing demand for miners. Native-born whites remained the principal source of mine labor, but immigrants and blacks became significant additions to the labor force before the war and established a definite presence in coal-town life. The bituminous fields in the North also used immigrants and blacks. However, there were considerable differences in the labor mix between the northern and southern fields.

In 1920, according to the investigation of the U.S. Coal Commission, there were about 525,000 bituminous coal operatives in the United States.

Nearly 60 percent were native-born whites, one third foreign-born, and less than 10 percent blacks. Approximately one-third of these operatives, 183,000, labored in the southern Appalachian fields: West Virginia had 87,700; Kentucky, 44,200; Alabama, 26,200; Virginia, 12,400; and Tennessee, 12,200.[1] The southern fields differed fundamentally in the proportions of these three groups. No southern state had as many foreign-born workers as the northern fields, and all southern states used more black labor.

Among the southern fields there were also significant variations. West Virginia attracted the largest proportion of immigrants and Alabama the largest proportion of blacks. Between 1907 and 1911, West Virginia briefly had a foreign-born plurality in its mining population, which rose to 46 percent of the labor force during these years. By 1917, however, the foreign-born workers had left the southern coalfields in large numbers and made up only 25 percent of West Virginia's mine labor force.[2] West Virginia also attracted the largest number of blacks, 18,376 in the peak year of 1930, but they never reached one-fourth of the labor force. In Alabama, black workers were not as great in number, about 7,000 workers at their peak, but as a proportion of the labor force they made up over one-half of Alabama's miners for at least the thirty years between 1900 and 1930, peaking in the latter year at 53 percent. In the remaining states of the southern fields, Kentucky, Tennessee, and Virginia, neither black nor foreign labor ever reached one-fourth of the labor force, and both groups began to decline in importance as early as 1910.[3]

White migration was simply inadequate to meet the demand for labor, and coal companies complained of labor shortages throughout the period between 1900 and 1920. Labor agents scoured the South in search of black tenants and sharecroppers; others worked the major entrepôts of immigration: New York City, Baltimore, Philadelphia, and Bridgeport, Connecticut. Stonega professed to have two labor recruiters, "on the road continuously" in 1913.[4] Besides their own recruiters, coal operators retained labor agencies to recruit miners. The Industrial Corporation, Incorporated, a labor recruitment firm in New York whose slogan was "We Circle the World," offered to Edward L. Stone, founder and major stockholder of the Borderland Coal Corporation, a supply of miners from New York or Pittsburgh of up to 25 men per month. They promised to avoid the "hobo and excursionist" element of ordinary recruiting agencies. Borderland would be able to supply its own man to examine the workers. If a worker's fare was advanced, he would sign an agreement to reimburse the company out of the first wages. The price of any food, protection, or guards furnished would be agreed upon later.[5] These terms reflected customary labor recruitment practices of the age. Workers were

William Goodwill, Miner at Goodwill mine, West Virginia, 1937. Courtesy of Eastern Regional Coal Archives, Craft Memorial Library, Bluefield, West Virginia.

advanced the costs of transportation from wherever they were hired to their destination mine. These costs plus any additional costs incurred, such as feeding and guarding the recruits, would be borne by the workers themselves, to be deducted from their first paychecks. It was commonly referred to as "bringing men in on transportation," and the practice spread during this period. Labor firms developed specialties in the labor market. For Kaymoor, the Atwood Employment Agency recruited white workers, the George Rison Agency black workers, and Low Moor, the parent company, used its own recruiters for immigrants.[6]

As the demand for coal rose, many operators believed immigrants could fill the void of labor. Low Moor recruited foreign-born miners for its limestone quarries and iron-ore mines in Clifton Forge and Covington, Virginia, as well as its Kaymoor coal mine in West Virginia. On 20 May 1907, the general manager wrote to the Menotti Bank of Philadelphia to inquire about getting 20 Italians to work in the iron mines, promising "good houses, a bake oven, and everything in nice condition," and a salary of $1.50 per day. Menotti replied that they could supply them. Already Low Moor had 80 Italians working at one mine and 40 to 50 at another. The 20 Italians were finally recieved on 23 June on the following terms: Low Moor paid the escort's expenses from Philadelphia and back at the rate of $1.25 per man. Transportation for the workers was advanced and deducted from their first paychecks.[7]

Coal companies spent considerable sums of money to recruit miners. Stonega kept careful records of the amounts it spent. The sums varied from year to year, but generally the trend was upward. In 1906, Stonega spent $6,115 on transportation advances; in 1912, $10,958; in 1918, $77,782.[8] In spite of the company's efforts, it often failed to recover the transportation advances. In 1916, Stonega imported 2,545 men at a cost of $38,263. Since one-fourth of the men left before working off their transportation expenses, it cost the company a net $15 per man imported above what was refunded.[9]

The seller's market in labor during these years pitted the operators against one another in mustering the skill, ingenuity, and determination to acquire an adequate and stable supply of labor at the lowest cost possible. In April 1904, a Low Moor labor agent reported difficulty getting the 15 men the company had requested because he was allowed to offer the recruits only $1.25 per day when others were paying $1.35 to $1.50. By 1906, Low Moor had been forced to go to $1.35 and to advance board at the rate of $10.00 per month in order to remain competitive.[10] In July 1906 the general manager at Low Moor, George Wickes, spoke with Judge Christian of Lynchburg regarding the practice of sending labor agents out from Low Moor to entice workers away from other mines. Such was a clear violation of the state's enticement statutes. When the judge told Wickes he thought the law so weak that it would not be upheld in court if challenged, Wickes quickly advised his labor agents to "go ahead and take the chances." The judge also informed Wickes that the railroad contractors had assigned men to watch and catch violators of the law.[11] The railroads were undoubtedly experiencing similar problems in the labor market. The practice of trying to entice workers away from other companies did not end quickly. In 1916 the Stonega Company noted that numerous other companies had written personal circular letters to SC&C employees soliciting their work; better wage offers caused some to leave.[12] Clearly, abiding by the laws benefited the companies while violations worked to the advantage of the miners. Greed being what it is, however, the temptation to gain the advantage in a tight labor market pushed some beyond the law.

Working through friends and relatives of employed miners was another technique companies applied to remedy the labor shortage. E. D. Wickes, manager at Kaymoor, reported on 11 June 1906 that he had asked "one of my Macedonian friends and one of my Hungarians" to write to their friends and relatives in New York and encourage them to come to Kaymoor.[13] Stonega canvassed its foreigners for names of friends who might be willing to come if transportation were advanced.[14] In 1916 the mine superintendent at the Winding Gulf colliery of Justus Collins in West Virginia claimed he was slowly picking up good families – through the influence of friends and relatives – and with good prospects of keeping them.[15]

In spite of the difficulty of acquiring workers, coal operators developed preferences in some cases for specific ethnic groups over others. These biases might grow out of a previous experience, good or bad; sometimes the bases of their choices were not clear. Employment agencies, anxious to win contracts, accommodated these biases. The Atwood Employment Agency, with offices in Chicago, New York, Philadelphia, and Roanoke, required companies to respond to a series of questions before entering into an agreement with them. "What nationality is preferred?" and "What nationality will you accept if unable to secure preference?" were the first two questions on the form.[16] On 27 May 1907 the manager of one of Low Moor's mines stated a preference for "a gang of negroes or Polanders or Russians."[17] Atwood responded that Roanoke would be a better place to deal for blacks and their Philadelphia office for Poles and Russians.[18] In April 1906, E. D. Wickes, superintendent of Kaymoor, described the latest recruits to his boss:

> Tony arrived with twenty-one men last night. One got away in Jersey City, two in Washington, four at Charlottesville.
>
> Some of the men are very good looking, but it is the worst lot I have seen, taken as a whole: Irish, German-Jews and Italians. I got seven started in the mine the first thing this morning; the others will go in Monday. Five Italians promise to be all O.K., and as they will be apt to send for their friends after a time, we may get

out even in the long run, but I don't see how Tony slipped up so. The only way it seems to me to be sure of what I am getting is to go myself. Our New York transportations for this place have never proved a success. The first lot I got last week will turn out pretty well from present indications, but they are all green and I have to take good men to run them. This *last* lot, some of them have not even been accustomed to hard work. I have great hopes, however.[19]

In order of rank, Italians, Poles, Hungarians, and Slavs were the most significant ethnic minorities. For reasons that are not clear, Italians were most coveted as miners.[20]

On the other hand, coal operators wanted to avoid hiring others, such as labor activists. In spite of Low Moor's shortage of seventy-five men in 1906, the manager assured a company official in New York that, after a visit to the Kaymoor and Fenwick mines, he had secured the cooperation of the men "to help us get the agitators out."[21] During this time, a labor organization, presumably the United Mine Workers of America, sent men into southern West Virginia to try to organize miners along the Kanawha River. A month before writing this letter, Wickes had noted a number of men who had left Kaymoor because of their unwillingness to get mixed up in labor disturbances. They were "replaced by known non-union men and first class men."[22]

Most immigrants came to the mines from similar backgrounds and for the same reasons in their countries as native white Americans had: high birthrates, great natural increases of the population, shrinking family estates, and widespread poverty. The crisis was much more intense in Europe, however, especially in the East. By 1900, people were starving to death at the rate of fifty thousand a year in Galicia, and only the importation of grain averted mass starvation in Russian Poland.[23]

Steve Tomko, for example, was born in Hungary. His father and mother "worked continuously in the fields" and made their living working on the farms of others. Some of his father's brothers who had already immigrated to the United States sent back money which allowed the elder Tomko to leave in 1902 to work in the coal mines at Glamorgan, Virginia. He worked for two years before he was able to save enough to send for the rest of the family. They joined him at the Glamorgan colliery in 1904. Steve entered the mines there at age thirteen.[24] John Sokira provides another example of the familiar pathways emigrants took from rural Europe to southern Appalachia. Sokira's parents were sheepherders in Czechoslovakia, where he was born in 1887. The emigrated on 12 June 1900 to work in the Brookside mine. John also entered the mine at age thirteen; he worked as a coal miner for fifty years in Kentucky, Pennsylvania, and Illinois.[25] In 1910 the West Virginia state commissioner of immigration announced that, on a single payday, postal money orders amounted to $6,000 mailed from Glen Jean, $3,800 from Scarbro, and $2,800 from MacDonald, for a total of over $12,000 sent back to families in Europe.[26]

Coal operators recruited black labor in the same fashion as they sought immigrants. On 20 May 1907, Wickes wrote to the Lynchburg Labor Agency to ask if it would be able to supply on a regular monthly basis "negro laborers for our mines" – three underground and one outside. He stated a current need of ninety to one hundred at the underground and thirty to forty at the outside mines and offered a wage of $1.50 to $1.75 per day inside and $1.50 outside, the same wage he held out for immigrants.[27] A copy of the letter was mailed to a friend at the American National Bank in Lynchburg, and the friend later promised to contact "colored men here who assemble colored labor."[28] W. M. Dues, a black labor agent in Lynchburg, contacted Wickes the next day and offered to furnish black labor for a fee of $45 per month plus expenses. Wickes, however, requested to see Dues in person before making any commitments. Meanwhile, Wickes did give him the approval to begin assembling a group of ten to twenty laborers, "nothing but good men," for his Dolly Ann mine. He also indicated that they would be paid $1.60 to $1.65 a day and that Dues could expect $1.50 per man plus round-trip train fare from Lynchburg to Covington, all to be deducted later from the laborers' time.[29]

Black miners were primarily poor migrants from the rural South. One study of West Virginia's black miners in the 1930s found only 14 percent born within the state, out of six hundred interviewed. Of the migrants, 47.8 percent came from Virginia, 11.8 percent from North Carolina, 11.2 percent from Alabama, 4.5 percent from Tennessee, 3.3 percent from Georgia, 2.5 percent from South Carolina, and 4.9 percent from a mixture of five other southern and six northern states.[30] Other scattered reports mention Alabama as the source of much black labor. Steve Tomko, for example, indicated that a number of blacks at Glamorgan had been recruited and brought in from Alabama.[31] Regardless of their origins, most were in flight from the starvation wages of southern agriculture. Jess Travis of Patrick County, Virginia, revealed in an interview with the author that he had migrated to West Virginia in 1911 to work in the mines. When asked why he had left a young wife behind to go work in a distant mine, he answered that he made only fifty cents a day as a sharecropper in Patrick County but earned three times that amount in the mines.

Unlike immigrants and the white majority, blacks appear to have been hired to do the most difficult work, such as manning the coke ovens. In 1908 the Imboden mine of SC&C had eight hundred men who had come from Alabama, Tennessee, North Carolina, Kentucky, and West Virginia. Of this number, five hundred were black workers, all of whom were employed at the coke ovens. Each worked a three-oven set and received eighty cents per oven per day. Each oven would produce two and one-half tons of coke.[32] The work was hot and laborious, and hernias were the most frequently mentioned occupational problems associated with the "pulling" of the heavy coke with long-handled rakes. According to the wife of a former black miner from Gary, West Virginia, no white men worked at the ovens there.[33]

The extent to which coking was a black activity is unclear, however. One former miner at Imboden stated that poor farmers had initially done this "extremely hard work" until blacks were brought in to replace them. Even if they wre used predominantly as cokers, apparently blacks were not trapped into these jobs. The same informant also related that black cokers "graduated to the mine" and made "some of the best coal diggers."[34]

Nevertheless, black majorities at the coke ovens at Imboden and Kaymoor, and frequent references to certain mines having more black labor than other mines—such as the Osaka mine of the Stonega Company, where coke ovens were located—strongly suggests, if it does not prove, that blacks were sought as cokers. It was not uncommon for industry of this age to employ black labor for the more arduous and unpleasant tasks in the industrial process. The Aluminum Company of America (ALCOA) founded the company town of Alcoa, Tennessee, in 1919 and sent labor recruiters into Alabama, Georgia, and Mississippi in search of blacks to work in the potrooms and the carbon plant, where it was "extremely hot." In 1920, the ALCOA labor force was made up of 1,482 blacks, 1,708 whites, and 130 Mexicans.[35]

Blacks were also hired, according to one study, to provide a "judicious mixture" of whites, blacks, and foreigners which operators might use to forestall unionism by pitting one group against the other.[36] In some of the Appalachian fields, such as those in northern Alabama, where blacks were often imported as strikebreakers and kept on to work in the mines after the strike was settled, black labor might have served this function.[37] The present study has found no direct evidence, however, that blacks were deliberately recruited as part of a strategy to defeat trade unionism. Other than exercising a predictable amount of caution to avoid labor activists, regardless of color, and the idiosyncrasies of some owners to prefer some ethnic groups over others, most operators were too desperate for labor to be particular. During these boom decades, they were anxious to hire workers wherever they could find them. Later, perhaps, when beset by labor problems under different circumstances—i.e., where the supply of labor more nearly matched the demand, as it did after 1920 – the manipulation of labor would have been both more likely and more effective.

The mix of native whites, blacks, and immigrants varied from colliery to colliery; that much is certain. The "typical" mine of the bituminous fields does not appear to have been very common. It is true that southern Appalachian mines made greater use of black labor and less of immigrants. Yet the trend was toward a white majority. Even these characteristic features, however, might fail to describe the composition of the workforce at particular mines.

The Winding Gulf colliery of Justus Collins in southern West Virginia employed 467 miners in 1916: 313 white American, 111 black Americans, 22 Italians, 11 Russians, 6 Hungarians, and 4 Slavs.[38] Proportionately, 66 percent of the Winding Gulf miners were white, 24 percent black, and 10 percent immigrant. At the Kaymoor facility in 1912, there were 165 inside workers: 58 native whites, 50 native blacks, 40 Russians, 5 Poles, 5 Englishmen, 2 Austrians, 2 Hungarians, 2 Italians, and a Frenchman. Of the 30 outside workers, there were 16 whites, 6 blacks, 5 Poles, 2 Italians, and a Russian. In the coke yard were 8 whites, 11 blacks, 8 Italians, 7 Romanians and an Australian.[39] At Kaymoor, immigrants, blacks, and whites were present in nearly equal proportions. The Minden, West Virginia, mine once had a reputation for employing more foreigners than other mines did, for reasons that are unclear.[40] A section forman at the TCI town of Docena, Alabama, estimated his section of 396 men to be composed of 85 percent black workers and 15 percent white.[41] According to one Kentucky informant, no blacks or foreigners occupied the coal camp at Knott while other camps at Bluebird and Wisconsin were more likely to have black miners. Another informant reported camps with no foreigners or only one black family. Still another former miner referred to the heavy recruitment of immigrants and blacks for the southern West Virginia mines during the heyday of the labor shortage.[42] The only safe generalizations are that mine populations varied from town to town and from time to time.

Some of the reasons for the variations might be surmised from the history of labor recruitment recounted above. As I have pointed out, some operators developed distinct biases toward specific ethnic groups and asked recruiters to find workers of their preferred nationalities. This could make a difference in the composition of the labor force at the mines where this policy was being pursued. We have also seen how some operators recruited black labor for the more difficult and undesirable industrial tasks, such as working the coke ovens. At those facilities with a lot of coke ovens in blast, black labor may have been a larger proportion of the total labor force. The success of labor agents no doubt also influenced the labor mix at specific mines. At times operators had much difficulty finding recuiters who could supply black or immigrant labor on a regular basis. The recruitment process itself may have made a difference, especially the technique of having coal-town residents write letters to their friends and relatives to encourage them to come to work at specific mine sites. Perhaps this created streams of migrants which fed and enlarged the labor pool and created in the process "atypical" majorities at certain collieries. As noted in chapter 3, migration from farm to mine at times assumed chainlike characteristics as first-comers from a Virginia county subsequently encouraged friends and relatives to follow. Latecomers could draw upon the knowledge of earlier migrants and depend upon them for support and assistance in the process of uprooting and resettlement in the coal town.

Larger forces determined who came. Between 1890 and 1910, when immigration to the United States reached an all-time high, immigrants came largely from southeastern Europe, mostly peasant farmers on the brink of starvation, including Italians, Poles, Hungarians, and Slavs. Blacks from the South were fleeing peonage-prone sharecropping and the low-wage desperation of casual day-labor. Whites, especially small farmers from the mountains, found the coal mines a refuge from the plague of high birthrates, land scarcity, large families, and agricultural distress. The timing of these migrations and their ebb and flow could produce dramatic swings in the coal-town populations.

The most striking feature of mining settlements during these decades appears to be the fluidity of the labor force, which also makes generalizations about the labor mix of a particular colliery rather risky. One miner pointed out that in the early years of mining (he began in 1908) there was a big turnover of men because some would mine in the winter and farm in the spring and fall.[43] As shown in chapter 3, it was not unusual for Appalachian farmers to enter the mines at first on a part-time basis. In 1907 the Kaymoor superintendent reported the loss of "one of the Polanders" and expressed concern about holding the rest until "we get the transportation out of them."[44]

On 10 June 1916, Lee Armentrout, manager of the Borderland Coal Corporation—which had its mines in Pike County, Kentucky, and its tipple and rail lines in Mingo County, West Virginia—wrote to Edward L. Stone complaining of losing men at mine number one. He reported that labor conditions "were getting very serious" and that he was "placing an ad in several different newspapers today." After Stone received the letter, he asked Armentrout to look into the causes. In his reply, Armentrout reported to his Roanoke boss that some miners were going to Detroit and writing back to attract others. Others had gone to Dayton to work for the Barney-Smith Car Company, and they would probably also write back and attract friends. Armentrout also noted that Borderland employed "a good many natives" who "at this time of the year are off looking after their little hillside crops." Finally, he stated his belief that, as far as moving to other mines was concerned, "we usually pick up about as many as we lose." The turnover continued. In October, Armentrout wrote, "some of our Hungarians" have left after having been told by labor agents that they would find better conditions elsewhere. He concluded: "If they didn't move every few months they could not be miners as that seems to be their habit."[45]

Bringing men in on transportation was one thing; holding them was another. In April 1907, the Low Moor general manager estimated that only about 4 percent of those workers who were imported stayed, even at the relatively good wage of $2.50 per day.[46] The Stonega annual reports for the years 1905 to 1916 recorded the percentages of "transportation men" who left without giving service to the company. If one eliminates both the lowest figure (5.6 percent for 1906) and the highest (30.4 percent for 1909), the average is over one-fourth of the imported workers each year leaving Stonega before they had reimbursed the company for their transportation costs.[47] Stated another way, one-fourth of Stonega's labor force turned over each year. Some of them, according to Stonega officials, "have gone to our neighbors to avoid payment of transportation costs."[48] By this practice, workers were able to get their fare paid to a colliery, enjoy temporary food and board, and then leave to find more permanent employment elsewhere without ever reimbursing the company for their transportation.

The popular image of coal miners in captivity to their bosses cannot be sustained by this evidence of extensive mobility during the decades of the coal boom. When the U.S. Coal Commission studied miners in the bituminous fields, the fluctuation of the mining population was so great that it was difficult to locate families in 1923 whose earnings and expenditures could be checked against a single mine-company payroll for an entire year.[49] Over 90 percent of mining families in the northern fields had lived in the same district for five or more years in 1923, but only 26 percent of southern families had done so.[50] Miners had alternatives, and substantial numbers worked the labor shortage to their advantage. The Chesapeake and Ohio Railway counted seventy-five collieries in the New River district between Thurmond and Hawk's Next, West Virginia, a distance under twenty-five miles.[51] Miners of the Stonega Company in Wise County, Virginia, might move around among the collieries in Virginia, southern West Virginia, or eastern Kentucky and Tennessee. Alternatively, miners from nearby colleries moved freely about to and from Stonega's mines. Although a single industry dominated the region, no single company did, making for a lively competition for miners throughout the region.

Individual mobility and its motivations are difficult to discern. It has been said that the mobility of mine labor was a consequence of the powerlessness of miners.[52] How often might a miner move? Where would he go? Were the movers mostly single males without families, or did family men move just as frequently? The kinds of records needed to address these tantalizing questions are usually not available to scholars. Fortunately, some clues were found in the records of the Stonega Company in the form of job applications from 1929. Only twenty applications were found, and two of these had incomplete information. Nevertheless, they provide a revealing picture of the job history of these applicants.

On the average, applicants were 27.8 years of ages and had 8 years of previous mining experience when they applied. There were eleven married and eight single men among the applicants, and they were predominantly American-born whites (at least fourteen out of nineteen). Two of the applicants had been at the previous colliery for 17 years, but the average for the remaining sixteen (in two cases the records were incomplete) was 18.5 months on the job. Prior to that, the applicants had stayed in their jobs for an average of 24 months, some staying as little as six days, others as long as 10 years. Equally interesting are the reasons they gave for leaving previous collieries. For the most immediate change, eight listed a slack period at the colliery, three "wanted a change," two "left voluntarily," three offered "no reason," and in one case water had filled the mine. Prior to that, eight gave "no reason," four "left voluntarily," three "wanted a change," and one left because of low coal. In other words, economic conditions, such as the shutting down of the mines, appear to have been more important in the later period. No one gave slackness as a reason in the earlier move.

It is also significant to note, however, that in all previous jobs the applicants had moved as frequently for personal reasons as for anything else. According to these applications, then, miners moved every 18 to 24 months without being forced to do so, and married men moved as often as single men. Perhaps Joseph Tony of Big Stone Gap was not exaggerating when he told an interviewer that his father moved the family "ten times in one fall. He found a place that didn't suit him, he'd move out."[53]

In the midst of these uncertain and fluid times in the southern coal-fields, World War I came and produced even more instability in the work-force. It accelerated previous trends away from foreign labor and increased a reliance upon native-born whites and, to a far lesser extent, native blacks. Foreigners left the Appalachian coalfields in large numbers dur-ing the war years. The impact on individual mines could be great. The Winding Gulf colliery in West Virginia claimed to have had 35 percent of its labor force made up of foreigners in 1915 but only 10 percent a year later.[54] The Borderland Coal Corporation experienced an even more dra-matic decrease of 90 percent of its foreign-born workers,[55] many of whom "have left to a great extent for their own homes on account of the war."[56] By 1931, the Stonega Company had only 44 foreigners left, or less than 2 percent of a total work force of 2,739 miners. Blacks made up 20 per-cent, and the white majority had increased to 78 percent of the mine labor force.[57]

The war also altered the character of the labor pool and the coal towns. Many of those who left were single. They were replaced by married men with children. According to the draft laws in effect at the time, single men and married men with no children were both eligible for the draft. Married men with at least one child could get an exemption. On 25 Au-gust 1917, the manager of Winding Gulf stated he was very short of men and that this was likely to continue.[58] Earlier, in June, he had reported 245 men registered for the draft at the Winding Gulf colliery and 265 registered at another facility at Davy.[59] The Stonega annual report of 1917 noted that the draft had led to the loss of young, single men, es-pecially motormen, brakemen, and drivers, many of whom had volunteered so they could get the branch of service they preferred.[60] According to one Stonega vice-president, "Our labor is shifting down to married men. We have lost a great many single men, and we are not recruiting very many single men, so it is going to be more and more a matter of taking care of families."[61]

The need for single-family homes was suddenly greater than the supply. The bunkhouse and the boardinghouse were inadequate to attract fam-ily men, and all available family housing soon filled. The demand for coal, of course, remained high, and even increased, and so too did the need for coal miners. George Wolfe, the Winding Gulf manager, wrote in August 1917 that it took one house for each man: "people will not double up these days" like the foreigners once did. He believed he could get more men from the South—"Negroes from the Alabama coal fields"—if he had the houses. Since he did not, he suggested that mechanization might be the quickest solution to the shortage of men and houses.[62]

Stonega could not build houses fast enough, either.[63] Borderland put ten wooden houses under roof in 1917 and laid the foundation for five more. Some of these were brick houses which, according to one company official, were "the best class of houses I have seen at any operation and will I think assure us of a good class of employees."[64] Later the Borderland board of directors approved the construction of thirty more houses.[65]

Recruitment proceeded at a torrid pace. Stonega recruited in the principal towns of Bessemer, Alabama; Atlanta, Georgia; Knoxville, Tennessee; Louisville and Lexington, Kentucky; Cincinatti and Cleveland, Ohio; Detroit, Michigan; Buffalo, New York; Bridgeport, Connecticut; Newark, New Jersey; and Pittsburgh, Pennsylvania.[66] The company avoided the Carolinas and Georgia (except Atlanta) because it feared the strict transportation laws and their severe penalties. Also these states had few experienced miners. Meanwhile, Stonega did everything possible to keep labor agents away from its doorstep. The towns of Appalachia and Norton, which were dominated by Stonega, enacted laws to prohibit labor agents. When several were caught in the vicinity, attempts were made to prosecute them. "This, however, failed and it was necessary to resort to more effective measures."[67] The measures were not revealed.

Collieries went to great lengths during these years to get laborers. George Wolfe looked up the addresses of all past miners, wrote to them, and got many to return. He even hired "old cripples, especially an Hungarian," at sixty dollars a month to "hang around junction points" to try and get men to apply at the mines.[68] On 26 June 1917, Stonega decided to give free transportation to all men who would come to work for them.[69] After years of requiring men to pay their transportation costs to the mines, Stonega was now so anxious to get miners that they were willing to offer free transportation. In spite of these extraordinary efforts, the labor shortage continued until the slump of the postwar period. Then the economic bubble burst. Never again would labor be so dear in the coalfields of southern Appalachia.

5   Mining Coal

Life and work in mining settlements in some aspects resembled life and work on the farms, especially in the division between "a man's work" and "a woman's work" and the tradition of mothers and fathers training daughters and sons to enter this world of work. Other continuities were the task system of mining coal, especially the diversity of labor and its gradations from the lighter tasks of drivers to the heavy physical labor of loading coal, and the rural ambience of life and work inside and outside the mines – including the cultivation of gardens, the tending of livestock, and other activities.

The separateness of the labor of men and women increased in coal towns. Women did not work beside men in the mines as they had on the farm. Views about work and a woman's place, together with certain economic and social conditions, excluded women from underground work. This practice differed from British mines, where women worked underground until 1842. In that year, after an investigation produced sketches of women and boys chained to heavy tubs of coal which they pulled through the mines, Great Britain passed a law to forbid women working underground.[1]

In the United States, women did not enter underground mining until 1973, according to government records, although a few apparently worked underground during World War II.[2] Stonega reported 38 women in a workforce of 2,977 in 1939, 77 out of 3,209 in 1942, and 84 out of 2,415 in 1945.[3] There is no indication as to where they were employed; presumably they were used mostly as clerks and service workers. In 1990 there were about 4,000 women in underground mining. Until recent times, however, there were strong taboos against women in the mines; some miners even refused to go into a mine where women had been, claiming women in the mines were signs of bad luck. Some women accepted their historic exclusion from the mines. In 1980 an interviewer asked Annie Kelly, a coal miner's wife from the coal town of Elmo, West Virginia, "Did any women ever think of being coal miners like they are today?" The miner's wife responded emphatically: "Nooo. Never would have dreamed of anything like that. I don't think it's right now, either."[4]

Convention alone does not seem to be a satisfactory explanation for the absence of women in the mines. After all, hundreds of them went to work in other industrial settings. The Piedmont textile mills employed large numbers of women. In the North, silk and textile plants provided employment opportunities for wives and daughters in the anthracite fields, and women readily took advantage of them.[5] The crucial difference between the textile mills and the mines was the physical strength required to accomplish most mining tasks. Pulling coke from the hot ovens and loading it onto railroad cars, laying track, setting timber props between the floor and roof, and picking and loading the heavy coal mixed with slate rock required a brawny labor force. The lighter tasks of pumping water, opening passageways, driving teams or locomotives, slate-picking, or working around the tipple were few in number and were usually accomplished by young boys or old men.

Industrial work opportunities for women in factories near the bituminous fields were almost nonexistent. Lacking employment opportunities for women outside the household, miners' families found other ways to supplement the family wage. According to an investigation in the 1920s, taking in boarders and lodgers was the primary source of secondary income.[6]

Women also found limited amounts of work as sales clerks or in washing clothes and cleaning the homes of company officials and professionals. Between 1916 and 1948, Lula Lall Jones, for example, worked a series of odd jobs for the superintendent's and store manager's wives and in a doctor's office.[7] The highest percentage of "gainfully employed" women, which included all of these outside activities, was in West Virginia, where about one-fifth were so employed.[8] But, for the majority of women in the bituminous fields, income-generating labor outside of the household was uncommon. Black families had the greatest proportion of gainfully employed wives, and only about 2 percent of these worked away from their homes.[9]

In rare cases, even the proximity of alternative employment might not necessarily draw women outside the household. Christine Cochran, a black miner's wife, lived in the coal town of Docena, on the outskirts of Birmingham. With considerable ambiguity, she explained her choice not to work outside the household in terms of the kind of life that "made the housewife too lazy" because she just sat at home, spent the money, and took care of the family. She believed that white women felt the same way.[10]

Even if women did not work in the mines or industry in large numbers, they performed a prodigious amount of labor.[11] Many coal towns, especially in the earlier period and up to the 1930s, allowed miners to keep livestock – hogs, chickens, and cows – and to have gardens. Feeding and tending livestock and cultivating gardens occupied a considerable portion of the time of miners' wives and children. Lack of refrigeration and labor-saving devices and the prevalence of coal dust made house-keeping an arduous and time-consuming activity. Annie Kelly recalled that most coal miner's wives went to the company store the first thing each morning because fresh food could not be stored at home.[12] For the rest of the day, she said, there was the house to clean, and there were dishes to wash, children's hot lunches to prepare – because children did not eat lunch at school – and supper to fix for the family. One or two days of the week were set aside for the laundry, which had to be done in washtubs with a washboard, then hung out to dry. Since miners did not have bathhouses until the 1920s, bathing followed laborious rural prac-tices. Water had to be hauled and heated on the cook stove each evening. When the miner arrived home, it was poured into a tub, and he would get on his knees to wash himself.[13] According to Kelly, there was pre-cious little free time: "I always got up at 5 o'clock and went to bed when I wanted – usually 8 or 9."[14]

Daughters helped mothers in the domestic economy, and sons pre-pared for their destiny as coal miners. Only in rare moments did males and females glimpse another world, such as during a labor strike in 1943 when women in Concho, West Virginia, walked the picket lines because men were not allowed to do so. They established a tent camp where they lived twenty-four hours a day on food sent in by sympathetic food-store chains such as Kroger and Atlantic and Pacific. Meanwhile, the men stayed home and kept house. As one miner's wife put it, "We thoroughly enjoyed it."[15]

Maleness is one of the most striking features of the coal town, and nowhere is it more evident than in the world of work. Coal mining was a volatile industry and an insecure occupation. Danger and uncertainty had definite implications for the men and women who lived and worked in such close and constant touch with unemployment and death. Men could not presume anything so grand and secure as a career. In an uncer-tain and unstable industry where jobs, status, and earnings depended upon the miner's skill and capacity for hard physical labor, it made emi-nent sense for women and children to provide whatever supplementary labor and support they could to insure against catastrophic loss. Family income might be curtailed or reduced at a moment's notice by a roof fall or mine explosion. The slow and debilitating effects of lung damage from rock or coal dust might reduce the breadwinner's capacity for work.

At the collieries, digging coal was of primary importance, and any-thing women did was secondary to that fundamental activity. The coal mine, visibly represented by the tipple and surrounding buildings, was the focus of attention, the raison d'être of mining settlements. The hum of activity was music to the ears of mining families. A quiet tipple meant shutdown, no work, financial strain, tension and perhaps problems within the family. As long as coal rolled from the drift mouth of the mine, the coal town and its way of life could continue.

In 1951 the Stonega Company produced a profile of the typical miner at its colleries, shown in table 1. The typical miner wore a size eight shoe, two sizes smaller than the national average; was five feet, nine inches tall; weighed 154 pounds; had a fifteen-inch collar; and wore a size seven hat.[16]

If this late profile of the physical size of the average miner prevailed throughout mining history, it raises some interesting questions about the labor market. For example, it suggests that the cramped conditions of mining coal created a process of natural selection where smaller-than-average men came to prevail. What effects this might have had either upon ethnic and racial minorities or during times of economic decline — such as the Great Depression, when work was scarce — can only remain matters of speculation.

The world of male work was the dominant factor in mining settlements, the subject of most conversations, and the preeminent concern of everyone. The conditions of men and women living together in dwellings and all laboring side by side at the same work produced a commonality of experience equally great in its capacity to weld together a community of hardship in the hollows of Appalachia. The very nature of mine work, its organization, and its dangers had a significant impact on this communal understanding that miners and families brought to the coal towns.

Table 1
Company Profile of Typical Stonega Miner, 1951

	LOW	HIGH
Age	36	41.5
Years in mining	14	20.6
Years with Stonega	4	16.6
Proportion of mining years with Stonega	2/16	10/16
Years of education	5.4	6.6
Total of family members	4.6	5.7

SOURCE: *The Stonegazette*, May 1951, box 535, WCCR.

Under the ground, mining coal involved laboring under conditions in sharp contrast to agriculture. The transition from farm to mine involved a change from a well-lighted, well-ventilated, open workspace to a dark, cramped, and uncertain environment. Farming was an occupation either without a boss or with one who only loosely supervised. At the mines a man had to answer to a foreman. Working on a farm required mostly individual labor under relaxed constraints of time and production. The mine was a competitive place where time and production determined earnings, status, and social mobility. Generally, mining involved the assimilation of preindustrial workers and their habits and values into an industrial discipline. Mine labor was also of mixed racial and ethnic origins, a heterogeneous labor force not readily assimilable. Labor historians have argued over the consequences of this process of integrating preindustrial workers into an industrial discipline.[17] To what extent was the conjunction of work and culture in mining towns a disruptive and alienating experience? What customs and traditions served the ends of integration?

Getting coal out of the ground was far more difficult and complex than it might appear to the casual observer. No examination of mining settlements would be complete without showing some appreciation for the techniques of mining coal and the nature of the work during what is commonly called "the handloading era," that period beginning with the opening of the mines in the late nineteenth century and lasting until the rise of mechanical coal loaders, which many companies adopted in the 1930s. Mining in the handloading era retained attributes that made it more akin to a craft than a factory discipline. The discipline was looser, and the skill and knowledge of mining coal came from the collective experience of the miner.

In the handloading period, the nature and organization of mine work provided an industrial work experience that encouraged ties of kinship and friendship. The "room and pillar" technique was the standard method of mining. It was a system universally used in the eighteenth-century collieries of England and, to a lesser extent, in the nineteenth century.[18] The "room" is nothing more than a tunnel which the miner burrows through the coal seam, advancing at the rate of ten, fifteen, twenty, or more feet per day. The front of the tunnel, where he and maybe a helper or apprentice work, is called the "face." On both sides of the tunnel are solid walls of coal, really pillars left to support the roof. Close to the face of the tunnel, these solid walls are broken by "break-throughs" or "cross-cuts," narrower tunnels cut by the miner for ventilation and to communicate with one another. Individual rooms are as high as the seam of coal, anywhere from two to eight feet, and the width of twenty-four feet was fairly uniform. With some variation, mining proceeds with miners driving the tunnels forward through the seam of coal at their own pace in rooms about sixty feet apart (from center to center), pausing occasionally to make cross-cuts to the other tunnels. Miners were paid by the number of tons of coal they sent out of the mines during the day.

It was also common, if not uniform, to make two openings in the initial penetration of coal seam, ten to twelve feet wide and about thirty feet apart. These openings or "butt headings" were driven parallel to one another, and sometimes they advanced gradually as rooms were tunneled at right angles to them. Alternatively, the headings might be driven to the limit of the coal seam before room tunneling began in the opposite direction back toward the original opening. One of these headings served as an air course and the other as the main haulage tunnel for coal cars. Rail tracks were laid down the main haulage road and from the individual rooms to the main tracks. Switch turnouts were established at the junction of the main and room tracks.[19]

Though widely used as a system of mining, the room-and-pillar method of mining coal varied widely. At Kaymoor, a double-entry system with still a third tunnel to carry the air supply was used.[20] Borderland Coal used a single-entry system at its mines in Pike County, Kentucky. Rooms were developed from the entry only, with no barrier pillars along any of the cross or main entries.[21] The few pillars that were left were not mined until the headings had reached the limits of the coal seam. Then began the process of "pillar robbing," whereby miners engaged in the more dangerous phase of taking out the pillars themselves, literally laying the roof on the floor. The Borderland practice of driving the rooms as the headings advanced, and leaving the pillars to stand for a few years before drawing them in a retreating line, was practiced from the opening of their mines until about 1927, when it was abandoned as inefficient, unsafe, and unprofitable.[22] By then the Borderland mines had only a few years left before the company went bankrupt.

The Stonega Company had also practiced pillar robbing, which it called the "advanced room system of mining." In 1916, however, Stonega abandoned the method. Thereafter, headings were driven to the limit of the seam, rooms were then driven from the top of the heading, and the pillars were drawn immediately upon the completion of the rooms. This allowed for a higher recovery of coal, minimized the cost of track and timbering, and was much safer.[23]

Underground, coal loaders were the company's bread-and-butter workers. They were the production men paid on a tonnage basis, unlike the "day men" or "company men" who supported them and were paid by the hour or day. Due to the complexity of their work and the transmission of knowledge about hewing coal through an apprenticeship system, loaders were viewed as the craftsmen of the industry. When the term "miner" is used, it typically refers to the loader, at least until the 1930s when conveyors and other machinery began to alter their status. Customarily dressed in bib overalls and brogans, they worked with the tools of their craft – pick, shovel, pry bar, breast auger, saw and ax, tamping bar, and lamp – symbols of their special knowledge and skills that each miner purchased and maintained. With no formal system of training, loaders passed along their craft to others.[24]

A day in the life of a miner might begin in the early morning hours around three or four with the rise of the miner's wife to prepare breakfast and the lunch pail. In 1926 the family of Merle Travis lived in the company mining town of Ebenezer, Kentucky, where his father worked for the Beech Creek Coal Company. In Ebenezer, the sound of the tipple whistle awoke miners and their spouses, like Merle's parents, who were known as "Uncle Rob" and "Aunt Etter." Years later, in 1947, Travis recreated the whistle in "Over by Number Nine," recorded for Capitol Records, in a collection entitled *Folk Songs of the Hills*.[25] Upon arising, the miner dressed, ate breakfast, and took the sometimes long walk from his house to the mine.[26] Automobiles were not common among mining populations until after World War II; the miner had to live within walking distance of the mine until roads and automobiles made commuting possible. If it was a drift mine, as most Appalachian mines were, he simply walked into the mine to his room.

The job of mining was divided into four basis tasks: undercutting, boring, blasting, and loading. Undercutting required the miner to lie on his side or back and, with a pick, chisel out a wedge-shaped section at the base of the face. This part of the job might take two to three hours to complete, and in the early days before good drainage was provided, miners sometimes had to lie in water while making this cut.[27]

Once he made a cut of three or four feet, the miner bored holes into the face above the wedge with a five-foot-long auger, called a "breast auger," which he cranked, using the weight of his body to force the bit into the coal. Then he loaded the bored hole with black powder. Techniques were no doubt idiosyncratic, but according to one miner, an eight-by-ten-inch sheet of paper was formed into a cone and filled with enough powder to break the coal into chunks. The placement of the hole and the amount of black powder were important steps in the mining process if the miner was to have a good tonnage day. Use too little explosive and the coal chunks would be too large, requiring additional time and effort in pick work to break them into loadable size; use too much and the result would be an excess of slack, a fine coal waste that was less valuable than lump coal and for which the miner received no pay. A large explo-

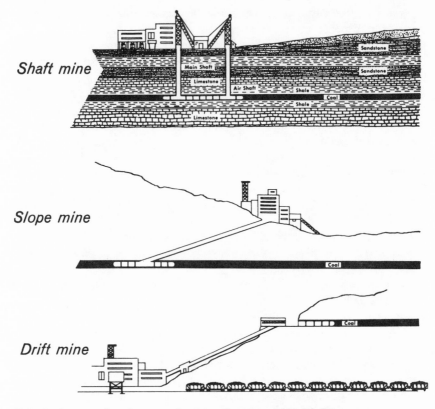

Principal types of underground mines. Courtesy of Keith Dix.

sion could also weaken the roof, increasing the danger of roof falls. Only through experience did miners learn the best placement and the proper amount of explosive.

In order to fuse the charge, the miner inserted an iron rod into the hole, extending into the black powder. After packing dirt in the hole around the rod, the miner slowly withdrew the rod, leaving a small hole as a channel for the insertion of the fuse. The fuse was a thin roll of wax paper with a little black powder in the one end that was inserted in the hole and fed to the bottom. A foot or two of the fuse was hung outside of the hole to be lighted with the miner's lamp. The miner then took cover behind one of the pillars, yelling "fire in the hole" to alert any casual visitor of the impending explosion. The "shot" coal was then loaded by hand and shovel onto a rail car in the miner's room and pushed to the

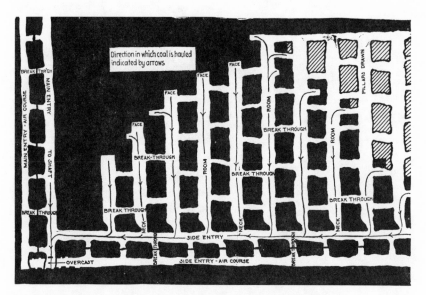

Panel of working section of a mine. Courtesy of Keith Dix.

entry to be hauled away. Coal was loaded by hand and with a number four shovel, each shovelful holding approximately twenty-two pounds.[28]

In one of the best-known songs of coal-mining history, a miner loaded "Sixteen Tons" of coal. The song was written by Merle Travis on 8 August 1946 and was included in his *Folk Songs of the Hills*. Ernest Jennings ("Tennessee Ernie") Ford made a recording of the Travis song in 1955 which rocketed to the top of the popular charts in just three weeks. Russell Ames, a collector of folk songs, called it a "traditional miner's song." A labor journal claimed the hit had been sung for years throughout the mining areas. Subsequent investigations failed to substantiate these claims. Nor was it entirely true that miners actually loaded sixteen tons of coal per day. About eight or nine tons was the average for the 1920s. According to Jay Watkins, a Beech Creek miner who had actually worked with Travis's father, Uncle Rob, in the 1920s, the legendary sixteen tons was an initiation rite. It was customary for the older miners to "slack off" so the newcomer could load sixteen tons on his very first day and thereby prove his manhood.[29]

Many other jobs besides hewing coal were available to men and boys at the mines. Indeed, the complexity of mine labor enhanced the longevity of mine work beyond the years of exhausting labor as loaders. Coal loaders were supported by a number of company men, paid by the hour or day. On 6 December 1922, Stone noted there were sixty-five miners

Opening a mine. Presgrave-Huddle Collection, Manuscripts Division, Special Collections Department, University of Virginia Library.

Making the undercut, Pocahontas, 1938. Courtesy of Eastern Regional Coal Archives, Craft Memorial Library, Bluefield, West Virginia.

and seventy company men at the Number One mine; at Number Two, thirty-seven miners and fifty-eight company men.[30] His goal was to get more miners and reduce the number of company men, to at least a ratio of one to one. Because of the shortage of miners during World War I, company men had increased at Borderland to one and three-fourths per miner in some areas and as high as two and one-fourth in other areas of the mines.[31] On 23 May 1913, the Stonega general superintendent, Taggert, wrote to Reeder, the vice-president of the company, of his plans to extend the motor haulage in Stonega Number Three by 1,900 feet, in order to increase the number of loaders or miners from twenty-six to forty.[32] As cost-conscious businessmen, coal operators strove to limit the number of company men per miner to a marginal level.

Company men tended to be organized on a task basis at the mines. On 31 January 1913 the Stonega superintendent, C. G. Duffy, reported the crews of day men at the Stonega mines listed in table 2. Each group of company men supported an equal or greater number of loaders. In addition, mines might employ a roving crew, consisting of a boss and three men, to be available for use in any of the mines where they were needed. Such crews might be employed for specific tasks, such as taking up steel track in areas of the mine where the rails were no longer necessary or laying additional track.[33] Most of the terms used to identify day men readily describe their function, except perhaps pumpers, who bailed water from the mines, or pushers, who shoved loaded mine cars from the face to the entries of the rooms or shoved empty cars to the face. The

Table 2
Crews at Stonega Mines, 31 January 1913

Number Two Mine	Number Three Mine	Number Four Mine
4 motormen	4 motormen	2 motormen
2 track men	2 track men	2 track men
3 slate men	4 slate men	3 drivers
1 flag boy	1 flag boy	1 slate picker
7 drivers	7 drivers	1 pusher
3 haulage men	2 slate pickers	
2 slate pickers	2 pump men	
1 pumper	1 oil boy	
1 oil boy	2 pushers	

SOURCE: C. G. Duffy to J. L. Salyers, 31 Jan. 1913, WCCR.

jobs of slate pickers might be performed by young lads, and obviously oil and flag boys were children. Outside the mines, tipplemen, dumpers, winders for various hoisting tasks, and workers at powerhouses and powder magazines added further to the diversity of the mine labor force. Also, every mine employed a number of skilled men – carpenters, masons, electricians, and engineers – who worked both inside and outside the mines.

Early studies of mining, company records showing the complaints of company officials about loaders quitting when they wanted, and oral testimony of miners themselves, all point to a rather loose supervision in the mines during the handloading era. Many miners report seeing their section boss no more than once a day and having days pass when he was not seen at all. After studying the issue of "the miner's freedom" in 1925, Carter Goodrich observed: "Coal mining is an industry in which the majority of men are piece workers under very light supervision."[34] At Nuttall, West Virginia, a company town in the New River Gorge area owned by Henry Ford in 1920, the supervisory personnel consisted of a mule-driver boss, two tipple foremen (one at the top of the gorge and one at the bottom), an inside mine foreman (sometimes called a section foreman), and an outside mine foreman (sometimes called a general mine foreman).[35] Usually, all of these foremen worked under a general superintendent of the mines. One former miner who became a foreman in 1939 said he usually supervised ten to twenty men – carrying their time, overseeing their work, and assuring that they paid attention to safety. For his work, he received $170 a month, which he claimed could be topped by a coal loader on tonnage.[36] Unlike conditions in other industries, the hand of supervision seems to have rested lightly upon the miner's shoulder.

Coke ovens could lend even greater diversity to the mine labor force. Mines at Ansted, Elverton, and Kaymoor, West Virginia, or Stonega, Imboden, and Osaka, Virginia, for example, all processed coal into coke. According to one source, "Prior to 1925, Kaymoor's existence depended primarily upon coke production."[37] Coke is a light, porous, cinderlike by-product of coal that has been baked at high temperatures in glazed firebrick ovens – sometimes called "beehive ovens" because of their appearance – for forty-eight to seventy-two hours. Foundries and iron furnaces preferred this efficient and clean-burning fuel until the coming of natural gas and oil. Iron production in western Virginia between 1873 and 1920 stimulated the demand for coke, leading Kaymoor to build a battery of 120 coke ovens by 1901. World War I increased the need for armor plating, which led to 200 ovens at Kaymoor and seventy thousand tons of coke a year in the years of peak production. The Low Moor Iron Company even developed a coke extractor during its years of coke pro-

Drilling the hole. Courtesy of Eastern Regional Coal Archives, Craft Memorial Library, Bluefield, West Virginia.

duction which "became the industry standard" and was adopted by H. C. Frick and company, one of the nation's greatest producers of coke, in the Connellsville, Pennsylvania, district.[38]

The coke process required an assortment of workers, as the following list of the day crew at the Stonega coke yard in 1913 indicates:[39] two chargers, two track cleaners, five cart men, one mason, one helper, one car shifter, one night watchman, five coke machine crew men, and six gin crew men. In 1915, Stonega had 162 men working at its coke yards in Stonega and 177 at its ovens in Osaka.[40] Coke production at Stonega peaked at 32 million tons in 1929, a level to which it never returned thereafter.[41]

From the collective experiences of miners, we can discern a common, if not universal, life cycle of work. As miners' sons reached a certain age – twelve, thirteen, or fourteen was typical, and some began at even

Loading black powder. Courtesy of Eastern Regional Coal Archives, Craft Memorial Library, Bluefield, West Virginia.

earlier ages – they began to work as helpers, trappers, or apprentices under their fathers. Melvin Profitt began to help his dad at odd jobs in the mines at the unusually young age of six in 1910.[42] Russell Matthew, a black miner whose father worked at South Nutall, West Virginia, went to work in the mines after elementary school because he felt it was his duty to help his father. He reported that it was common for fathers to find work for sons in and around the mines.[43] John Luther "Bud" Whittington recalls coming to a coal mine in Kanawha County, West Virginia, with his dad at the age of five in 1900. In 1902 he began in the mines as a helper, carrying his dad's tools; after a short period he worked as a trapper boy.[44] Charlie Blevins, whose family moved from Johnson County, Kentucky, to Borderland in the 1890s, said that his grandfather got a job

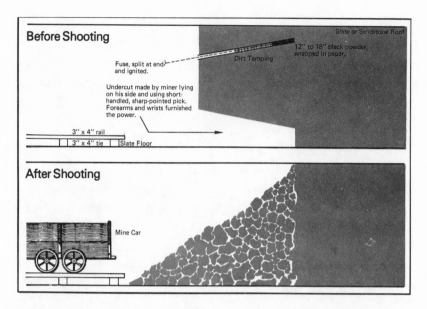

Before and after shooting coal. Courtesy of Keith Dix.

on the railroad at first. "As his boys got older [there were seven of them] he got them jobs in the mines. . . . Pap went in when he was 14, went to this old mine right over here at Borderland, on the Kentucky side." Blevin's father trapped for ten cents an hour.[45]

In the cases where there was more than one son in the family, boys could always work in this boring and lonesome occupation. Ralph Sanders went to work in the mines as a trapper boy in the Kaymoor mine because there were ten children in the family. His brother did the same, and they were paid a dollar a day for ten hours of work.[46] Trap doors were located in the mine passageways to control the circulation of fresh air to the miners. As one former trapper boy described it: "You hear a motor coming or if you're driving ponies, you hear the trip coming, you pull the door open and let them through. That's a job I didn't like, because it's too lonesome to set there all day long."[47] Blevins said about trapping: "When the motor . . . comes through there you have to open a door, which held your air up at the work face. It was your ventilation back in them days. After the motor passed through, you'd shut the door, you see, so that the air'd stay up in the face where miners were working."[48] At the Red Ash, West Virginia, mine, small boys of ten to fourteen years worked leading the mules out.[49]

Such were the ways in which sons of miners became miners themselves, carrying on the family tradition and learning the techniques of

After the shot, Borderland, ca. 1914. Courtesy of Manuscripts Division, Special Collections Department, University of Virginia Library.

mining coal. Chan Forren entered the mines in 1936 at Elverton, West Virginia, in the same year his father died. The mine superintendent allowed the Forren family to stay in the company house with one of Chan's seven brothers responsible to pay the rent. All seven brothers eventually worked in the Elverton mine and lived with their mother. Five of the brothers retired from mine work. When Chan was interviewed in 1980, his son, age twenty-eight, was working in the coal mine at Layland. Chan stated, "Course I've enjoyed coal mining all my life." About his son he commented, " . . . he likes it."[50]

The practice of underage boys working in the mines became widespread even as states passed laws to regulate it before World War I. The difficulty of enforcing age laws was due partially to the unwillingness of

Loading coal. Courtesy of Eastern Regional Coal Archives, Craft Memorial Library, Bluefield, West Virginia.

Coming out of the mine, Borderland, ca. 1914. Courtesy of Manuscripts Division, Special Collections Department, University of Virginia Library.

parents to see them enforced. Under these laws, a boy could work underground if his parents signed a "miner's release" or an affidavit swearing that he was at least fourteen years of age. Some parents lied or attempted to evade the requirement. The Stonega general superintendent, R. E. Taggert, wrote to C. G. Duffy, the mine superintendent at the Stonega mine, on 25 July 1914 after an accident settlement that neither a release nor an affidavit had been completed on the accident victim, Oscar Barnes. Both documents were required. Taggert reminded Duffy that it was his responsibility to discern age before employment. He demanded that he get releases or affidavits immediately on all minors, and if he could not obtain them, the young boys must be stopped from working. He promised to fire any mine foreman who failed to comply.[51] The attempt of parents to circumvent the law continued. The mine superintendent at Roda, another mine of the Stonega Company, was informed in 1929 that he had to stop the boys who were helping their fathers in the lamphouse, even if they were not being paid.[52] It is understandable that boys whose future lay in the mines wanted to begin to learn their craft as soon as possible; it is equally understandable that coal companies who were liable under the laws for employing underage boys wanted to stop the practice. By World War II, the minimum age for underground workers had been raised to eighteen.

Boys who began as helpers, trappers, or doers of odd jobs graduated after a year or so to more responsible work such as working in haulage or outside the mine at the tipple. By the late teen years, one could hope to begin as an apprentice – under one's father or another "buddy" – learning to be a loader, the most desirable of mining occupations in the work cycle. According to Russell Matthew, a black miner who worked at Kay-moor, it took a while before you got to a place where you were entirely responsible for safety and all aspects of the mining process. Then "you were a coal loader" in charge of a "room of your own" with a distinct check number that went on "your car."[53] By his early twenties, a young man could expect to have reached this stage. The years of work as a coal loader – the most desirable phase – might be brief or extended, depending upon a miner's health and physical condition. The closing years of the work cycle might be spent in any number of jobs either under- or aboveground. Jobs as timbermen, drivers, track men, slate pickers, haulage men, carpenters, electricians, and others provided a variety of activity for partially disabled and aging miners. It was possible for a miner to end his work years doing some of the same work he had done when he began as a boy.[54]

Mining coal followed some cultural traditions and carved out others. The working together of fathers and sons and other relatives in the mines, the apprenticeship system of training, and the division of labor were not unlike the practice of agricultural labor, commonly a family endeavor with chores divided on the basis of physical strength. In rural society, there was a man's work and a woman's work, and sons and daughters were expected to learn these from fathers and mothers. But mining coal brought greater divisions in gender. As we have seen, the separation of labor was far more complete at the collieries. Mine labor was not family labor, in spite of relatives who might work together, but men laboring together under extraordinary conditions.

Common dangers and risks characterized this industrial occupation. Mine work engendered a sense of cohesiveness and group solidarity that set coal miners apart, even from many other industrial workers.[55] Mine work was naturally dangerous. Conditions were usually difficult and unpleasant, and they were constantly changing. The roof in one section might be firm and solid; in another, loose slate and fissures called for caution and more timbering. Seams varied in width both from mine to mine and within the same mine. The Taggart seam of the Stonega Company's Derby mine was fifty-seven inches thick; the Marker seam at the same colliery was thirty-nine inches; Dunbar's Taggart seam was forty-six inches and the Marker seam thirty-eight inches. The Imboden seam measured sixty-nine inches. All of these were averages for the year 1947.[56]

Water posed other problems, requiring miners to cut drainage openings or use sump pumps. Constantly changing conditions were vexations, the work exhausting, and the workplace at times cramped and uncomfortable. Fatigue could easily seduce the weary into a disregard for caution and safety. Dangerous accumulations of coal dust and the odorless methane gas might go unheeded and be ignited by a single careless act. Stonega reported cases of slate falls caused by cutter bars striking the roof supports. In another case a miner got ten detonators from the supply store and put them in the same pocket with a shooting battery.[57]

Combine these conditions with the standard practice of not paying miners for setting props under the roof or taking the time to make sure the work area was safe and cleared of loose slate, and the result is one of the most dangerous occupations in the world. On 29 January 1907, Dick Lee, an elderly black miner from Alabama with years of experience, bored and loaded three holes without bothering to make an undercut (commonly referred to as "shooting off the solid") and carelessly tamped them with a small amount of coal dust instead of clay or dirt. The fire from the shot blew out of the hole, ignited the gas and coal dust in the air, and caused a catastrophic explosion at Stuart, West Virginia, mine. The mine owner described the scene:

The sight at the shaft bottom when we got down was pitiful. Over fifty men were lying dead. My transit man for the Stuart and Parral mines, Jesse Arthur, was lying on a mine locomotive with the top of his head blown off. One of the men was sitting with his back against the coal rib, his lunch bucket between his legs, and a piece of bread in his mouth, held by his hand.

On the side of the shaft opposite the side where the explosion originated, a few men lived a minute or so before "afterdamp" got them. One Polish miner had evidently been able to get from the face of his room a hundred feet down towards the entry before the "afterdamp" got him. We found him kneeling in prayer against the room rib. With his hand he had made the Sign of the Cross in the coal dust on the rib.[58]

In an effort to erase the memory of the horrible disaster, mine management renamed the mine Lochgelly.[59] Mine explosions were the most dreadful of events, comparable to major air disasters in the 1980s in the number of lives lost in a single incident. The worst disaster in Virginia's mining history occurred at Pocahontas on 13 March 1884. At 1:20 A.M. the first of five loud explosions rocked the Southwest Virginia Improvement Company's East Mine. The entire night shift was killed. The Norfolk and Western Railway, the parent company, officially announced the dead to number 114 men and boys. Local residents claimed later that up to 150 had died. In the official tally, there were about 40 Hungarian, Italian, and German immigrants and a mixture of young black and white native-born Americans. Company officials had believed the mine to be free of gas and allowed the miners to work with open flame lamps instead of safety lamps. During the evening of the explosion, methane gas built up in the mine, causing the miners' lamps to flicker and go out. Assuming that the cause of the problem was the ventilation fans, the mine superintendent ordered a reduction in the speed of the fans. The buildup of gas continued. About twenty minutes after the fans were slowed, the first explosion came. According to one eyewitness, "The whole valley was illuminated with blazing dust. Pieces of cars, mules and timbers were blown a quarter of a mile away." William H. Cochran, a Cornish immigrant, rushed to the mine's main opening:

I found one body with head and legs blown off. His foot was found 30 yards from the trunk of his body. The other limbs and hand have not been seen. . . . I then entered the main air tunnel, about 500 feet in the air course, and went through a doorway which led into No. 1 East Tunnel. I followed this about 700 feet and came to the bodies of two men. One of them was on fire. The other was at his feet and badly burnt. I had to leave again because of gas that was flowing through the mine after the explosion.[60]

The resulting fires in the mine could not be extinguished, and the company ordered the mine sealed. In the weeks that followed, the families of the entombed miners held public rallies at the local church to pressure company officials to open the mines so they might bury their loved ones. During the course of these protests, a pretty young coal miner's daughter characterized by reporters as the "belle of the village" jumped upon a trough to plead with the crowd: "I have a father in that mine boys. He is dead and I know it. But I love him, and I want to bury his body decently. I will marry any man in this crowd who will lead a party into the mine." When no one responded, she stalked off in frustration, calling the miners cowards. After four weeks, the mine was opened and the bodies brought out and buried.

One of the worst mining disasters in U.S. mining history occurred at Monongah, West Virginia, in 1907 when 360 were trapped underground in a mine explosion.[61] Between 1902 and 1927, mine explosions in the region became commonplace: Switchback (1908 and 1909), Jed (1912), and Eccles (1914), Layland (1915), in West Virginia; Pocahontas again in 1906; Browder (1910) and Happy (1923) in Kentucky; Briceville (1911), Catoosa (1917), and Rockwood (1926) in Tennessee. This requiem of the dead mounted to an average of 100 workers per year or about 2,400 men killed in mine explosions alone over the course of twenty-five years.[62]

No one can deny the calamitous effects these horrific explosions had upon individual mining settlements. Such great losses of life at one time and place shook the entire community. Yet it is also jolting to learn that mine explosions have taken only a fraction of all the miners killed in the history of coal mining in the United States. Mine explosions were dramatic events that riveted the nation's attention. Less highly publicized, but more deadly in the long run, were falling slate and coal, which produced a steady count of death year after year. Between 1906 and 1935, just under 50,000 miners were killed in the United States. Only 8,000 of these deaths, however, were due to mine explosions; 36,000 were the result of roof falls and haulage accidents.[63] The Rockefeller commission in 1980 found roof falls to be the leading killer of miners.[64] Mining was a deadly occupation. Between 1919 and 1924, the Stonega Company averaged 4.09 men killed per million tons of coal mined. This figure was higher than the average for the bituminous fields of the United States (3.54) but below the average for the more dangerous anthracite fields of the North (5.94) and the average of Great Britain (4.57).[65]

Economic pressures in the coal industry and the barbarous response of some operators to place profit above safety had deadly consequences for miners. Pillar extraction is an example of how economic motivations could overwhelm the caution of engineers and frustrate the efforts of mine foremen to reduce accidents. In Harlan County, Kentucky, in the early 1930s, a curious and at first inexplicable phenomenon emerged, which the industry referred to as "bumps." A later investigation by the

Kentucky Department of Mines and Minerals defined a bump as "a sudden violent expulsion of coal from one or more pillars accompanied by a loud report and earth tremors."[66] The investigation revealed other characteristics. Shattering and pulverization of coal as well as the presence of a fine dust, also an indication of pulverization, were commonly noted features. Usually the bump occurred without warning and might also be accompanied by slate falls or upheavals of the floor.

Bumps always occurred when miners, usually in groups of two to four, were at work on pillars. Some of the miners reported an unusual "quieting" of the pillar and a tight and woody feeling just before the bump; others noted no unusual signs. Bumps might expel anywhere from a few tons up to 3,000 tons of coal at one time, thrown off with great violence, taking timbers, track, mine cars, men, everything in its path. Twenty- to thirty-pound steel rails might be bent like pretzel sticks; in one case eight pillars measuring sixty by forty by five feet were completely shattered. Generally, bumps were more likely to occur when the overburden was over eight hundred feet. Theoretically, each coal pillar of standard dimensions was able to withstand the weight of two thousand or more feet of overburden. What the Department of Mines and Minerals found, however, was a practice in pillar removal to leave pillars standing in areas where the coal was thin, due to the presence of sandstone beds or shale in the overburden, and to remove pillars elsewhere in the vicinity. This practice caused a shifting in the weight distribution, which the remaining pillars could not support.[67]

On 9 April 1932, a bump occurred in a Harlan County mine which led to the investigation mentioned above. About 45 tons of coal were expelled, 23 tons in a single lump. Two men working in pillar removal were killed. A mine car and a locomotive were hurled thirty-five feet down the tracks. The end of the car was smashed, and one miner was found inside; the other was found about sixteen feet from his workplace. Standing timbers throughout the area up to sixty feet from the bump were knocked out in what the department considered a minor bump.[68] The first car of coal was shipped from Harlan in 1911, when 26,000 tons were produced from three mines. In 1929, Harlan mined over 15 million tons of coal. As production and the pressures to increase it intensified, engineering departments could not keep up with all the details and conditions of mining, laying the foundation for the occurrence of bumps.[69] Mines in Harlan and western Wise County, Virginia, including the mines of Stonega and Roda, were particularly susceptible to bumps because of the geological terrain.

Bumps were the result of the operators' callous disregard for human life in the face of narrowing profit margins. Ironically, they may have increased the costs of production in the form of claims for accident and death. The Stonega Company produced a five-year study of the costs to the company of fatal accidents from 1929 to 1934, including medical fees, the costs of claim work, expenses of the safety department, and the premiums of catastrophic insurance. During this period, there were 43 deaths, totaling $114,739. Each case cost the company an average of $2,668 or about a penny for each ton of coal produced.[70] There is no indication from this report of how many deaths were directly attributable to bumps. According to Stonega's 1940 annual report, however, sixty bump cases had occurred since 1932, costing the company $43,000 in claims.[71] Actually Stonega was quite successful in reducing fatalities over the years of its operation. Between 1916 and 1920, the company had 66 fatalities and produced 187,426 tons of coal per fatality. The number of fatalities declined, and the tons of coal produced per fatality increased during each subsequent five-year interval until the period of pillar mining. In the five-year period ending in 1935, the company reported 37 fatalities. However, it produced about 70,000 tons less per fatality during this latter period.[72] In 1935, Stonega mined 107 acres of coal from rooms and 104 acres by pillar extraction.[73]

Slate falls, bumps, and other incidents were isolated and unpublicized events that took far more lives than explosions, which were always front-page news. Even less publicized and virtually ignored by historians have been nonfatal accidents. With remarkable consistency over the years, Stonega collieries averaged 96 nonfatal injuries for every mine fatality between 1911 and 1952.[74] These included both "serious," defined as an accident where the worker lost more than twenty-one days, and "slight," losing up to twenty-one days, accidents. In 1952, when the ratio of nonfatal to fatal accidents was 99 to 1, Stonega loaded 15,000 tons of coal per nonfatal accident, and 2.4 million tons per fatal accident.[75] In a typical year, the company lost the equivalent of close to ten days per full-time worker on the average at each colliery because of accidents.[76] Without calculating the potential lifetime earnings of a miner, nonfatal accidents—because of their higher medical costs—cost the company more than deaths. Between 1929 and 1934, they cost Stonega three cents per ton of coal compared to one cent per death.[77]

Occupational ailments and diseases incapacitated and killed an untold number of miners. Untold because coal companies refused to acknowledge any relationship between health and work until 1969.[78] Company doctors treated hernias and hemorrhoids often enough among coke workers, however, to recognize the connection between the strain of pulling the heavy coke and these conditions. These problems were treatable, and usually miners could return to work. Far more life-threatening, and costly were respiratory problems such as chronic bronchitis, silicosis (the result of breathing rock dust), and pneumoconiosis (the result of breathing coal dust, commonly called "black lung"). Yet employers succeeded in avoiding liability even for these obvious and deadly diseases until the 1960s. In spite of medical knowledge as early as the 1920s linking mining to respiratory illnesses in the United States and fifty years prior to that in Europe, operators managed to avoid blame until public pressure forced them to recognize their responsibility for a healthy workplace. For years, operators relied upon the "assumption of risk" argument, which had proved so successful in the courts as a defense against compensation for disabling accidents, until workmen's compensation laws resolved the issue. "Assumption of risk" claimed that all work entailed risks which the worker knowingly and willingly assumed as an acceptable condition of labor. Consequently, the employer was neither responsible nor liable for injuries on the job.

Workman's compensation laws dealt with injuries and accidents on the job. They did not deal with the issue of occupational disease. Only after dramatic events – such as the building of the Hawk's Nest Tunnel in West Virginia in the late 1930s and the Farmington mine disaster of the late 1960s, and subsequent public agitation by reformers – did employers grudgingly acknowledge the connection between respiratory problems and mine work which physicians had proven conclusively over a half-century earlier.[79] No records exist to record the price miners paid for the preservation of this legal fiction.

The awesome toll of death, injury, and disease in the bituminous coal industry cannot be excused on the grounds that coal mining is simply a dangerous occupation. It is true that both operators and miners could have mined coal more safely. But miners did not always use the safety knowledge they had because the system of not paying miners for "dead time," such as the time it took to set roof supports, actually punished those who practiced safe mining. Thus the natural dangers of working underground were magnified by systemic flaws.

What about the operators? Was mine safety determined only by "heartless capitalists?" A historian of coal mining in the Progressive period (1900–1920) argued recently for a better model than heartless capitalism to explain mine safety. Bituminous coal was an intensely competitive and cost-conscious industry. Consequently, he argued, safety was an expense. Only the largest companies could afford to comply with stringent safety standards.[80] However, the experience at Stonega shows that death and injury were also costly – and inefficient besides. In general, regardless of the colliery, mine explosions caused interruptions in production and injured experienced and productive men.

In his evocative study of St. Clair, Pennsylvania, Anthony F. C. Wallace has suggested a theory of decision making to account for the safety practices of all involved in mining coal. Although Wallace's theory applies to anthracite coal, risks and decision making in the bituminous industry are equivalent. In an appendix entitled "The Disaster-Prone Organization," Wallace offers the stimulating argument that, where the decision is between sure loss on the one hand versus the combined probabilities of a greater loss and no loss at all on the other hand, the latter, more risky, alternative is chosen. As applied to collieries, the operators avoided the sure financial loss that would accompany taking all recommended safety precautions and opted for the more risky (and ultimately more costly) alternative of gambling that they could get away with neglecting safety. The decision-making process in this model involves imagining the best possible outcome ("optimum scenario"), ignoring the worst outcome, and considering only those matters in the personal interest of the decision maker. Investors, operators, and miners are motivated to assume risks to satisfy leaseholders, creditors, vice-presidents, or foremen.[81] If applied to the bituminous coal industry, Wallace's model would explain actions such as a miner who ignored setting props, a foreman's decision not to stop the mining process at Pocahontas in 1884 to investigate the flickering lamps, and Borderland's and Stonega's decision to rob pillars – decisions all made on the basis of the cost-effectiveness of taking risks in the mythology of realizing only a better outcome.

Wallace's model is helpful in explaining the behavior of operators. It is somewhat misleading, however, to assume that all shared equally in the responsibility for mine safety. Equality in power and resources to affect mine safety is implied in the Wallace model. In reality, miners, though far from "powerless," clearly did not command the access to knowledge, resources, or power to shape conditions in the mines that the operators possessed.[82] Making the mines a safe workplace, as free from the hazards and dangers of mining as was technologically feasible, was a power that resided primarily if not solely in the owners' hands. Consequently, the burden of responsibility for explosions and diseases rested heavily upon the owners.

The danger of accidents, explosions, and diseases interjected uncertainty and insecurity into life and work in mining settlements. The same uncertainty and insecurity plagued a miner's earnings. The question of how much miners earned in the mines was always a difficult one to answer. Earnings for loaders varied day by day, depending upon the amount of coal loaded. Mechanization and, after unionization, work stoppages affected take-home pay. A brief look at a compilation of wage rates drawn from interviews of former miners will indicate how difficult it is to establish "typical" wage rates, to say nothing of take-home pay.

In 1904, loaders at the Gulf Smokeless Coal Company averaged $3.00 per day and day men $2.00[83] In 1913, the Stonega Company paid its mule drivers $2.25 per day while its loaders received eighty-five to ninety cents per car of coal loaded.[84] In 1915, common labor outside the mines received between eighteen and twenty cents per hour.[85] The Stonega wage rates were markedly higher than those of iron-ore workers at the mines of the Low Moor Company. As noted in chapter 3, Low Moor paid underground workers $1.50 to $1.75 per day during this period. Drillers and timbermen received $1.35 to $1.50. Drill helpers, loaders, and wheelbarrow men got $1.25 to $1.35.[86] During the 1920s, miners reported receiving various rates of pay, depending upon the company. A former miner of the TCI Company at Docena reported a wage of seventy cents per ton or about $8.00 for loaders in 1926. Machine runners got $7.11 and common labor $4.00 per day. Foremen were paid $170.00 per month.[87] At the Wheelwright, Kentucky, mine of the Inland Steel Company in 1926, brakemen were paid $6.26 and motormen $6.81 per day.[88] A black miner at Wheelwright recalls geting forty-eight cents per ton in 1928. Company men outside the mine got $2.47 a day.[89] According to one report, the average monthly wage of 142 black miners in the Kanawha fields of West Virginia in 1929 was $118.00.[90]

Wages in the Great Depression took a nosedive. Miners at Wheelwright who were getting over $6.00 a day in 1926 recall rates of $2.80 per day during the Depression.[91] The Reverend Stuart Frazier, a black miner in Thurmond, recalls being paid $2.84 a day for an eight-hour shift in twenty-six-inch coal during the Depression. Like other miners during these difficult years, he also reported frequent periods when the mines were slack and no one could work.[92] A tipple operator recalled being the highest-paid worker at $4.84 per shift,[93] while another Wheelwright coal loader remembered getting $6.00 per day.[94] All recalled the unevenness and uncertainty of work; all felt fortunate to have found work of any kind. Unionization of the southern Appalachian mines in the 1930s put wage rates on an elaborate and rigid schedule, reduced the hours of work per day, and, thereafter, increased the wages of miners each time a new contract was negotiated. In 1934, Stonega and the United Mine Workers of America reached agreement on a contract to reduce the workday to seven hours and raise the day-shift rate from $4.20 to $4.60 per day.[95] In 1937, the day-shift rate went to $5.60 per day for a seven-hour day and a five-day week.[96] By 1970, miners were receiving at least this amount and more per hour of work.[97]

In real dollars, the average miner was twice as well off in 1970 as in

1940. For example, using 1967 as the base year, in 1937 a day's pay for a Stonega miner was worth approximately $13.33 (based upon the 1937 Stonega day rate of $5.60 times $2.38, the purchasing power of the 1967 dollar). The same seven-hour day in 1970 would bring a miner $27.30 (based upon the average hourly wage rate of $4.54 times $.86, the purchasing power of the 1967 dollar in 1970).[98]

These scattered wage rates, drawn from a variety of sources at different collieries and periods of time, indicate the great variety of wage scales used in the industry. Rates varied from colliery to colliery. Some loaders were paid by the ton and others by the car. Some were paid by the shift and others by the day. Still others were paid by the hour. Even if an average or typical wage rate could be generalized, it would not give us what we really want – the earnings of a "typical" miner. Wage rates simply cannot realistically reflect what miners actually received. Lifetime earnings were also subject to a plethora of factors: injuries, lung diseases, mine closings, market fluctuations, availability of mine cars, work stoppages, the changing of employers – the list seems endless.

Whether former landowning farmers were better or worse off for having traded their horses and plows for picks and shovels is a question that teases with its simplicity while it defies a ready answer. Some were; others were not. It will take much painstaking work with a continuous series of mine payroll records before historians can speak with much confidence on the miner's pay. Even given this kind of record, the problem of labor mobility might frustrate efforts to determine earnings over an extended period. Until such work is completed, individual case histories shed the most light on the question.

Born in Knott County at Emmalena, Kentucky, in 1902, Mae Prater left the farm to marry, moved with her husband to a coal town in 1925, and stayed for forty years. The Praters could claim that the mines allowed them to put two sons through college. Certainly they were proud of their accomplishments, justifiably so. Mr. Prater's crippling accident and early death was a high cost, however. For the thousands who died underground or suffered the agonies of a life with lung disease, the cost was also great. Industrial wages were good, when the mines were open and a miner had his health.

The rural traditions of mutual help and reciprocity continued to function in the coalfields. The Prater family is an example of how families practiced thrift and frugality, occasionally borrowing from others in an emergency, to carve out for themselves the maximum economic security, stay out of debt, and even save for goals like higher education for their children. When asked about their living expenses, Mrs. Mae Prater listed rent at six dollars per month; food, heat, and electricity at twenty-five to thirty dollars per week; and the doctor's fee of two to three dollars per month. "It wasn't too much for the doctor, and our rent wasn't bad," she said. During the years her husband worked in the mines, she stated, they rarely had to borrow money or go in debt. If necessary, "There was some people that lived there we know was able to help us and, really one or two times they did. . . . Sometimes they'd be off from work awhile, you know, maybe they wouldn't work for a few months, and maybe we'd have to. . . . [99] When Ron Daly asked whether her husband was laid off often, she replied:

> Not much, they never had to lay him off unless they just about shut the mines down. Usually he would get some work all the way along. . . . Maybe a few times, I would say two or three times he would be off a little while and wouldn't have work, maybe a month or two at a time, but not much.

Asked whether he took a job elsewhere during that spare time, she answered:

> Well, yes, he would want to and he did a time or two, he worked a little away from the mines, I think, twice, as well as I remember. He worked a little at Carr Fork and a little at Winconsin [sic] while they were down; these were adjoining camps.[100]

When Daly asked if she was able to save money while in the Knott mining camp, she responded: "Yes, we saved a little. . . . We couldn't save too much but we schooled the children and we always managed to have a little extra money, sure did."[101]

At times, this labyrinthine journey through the world of mine work, with all its descriptive twists and turns, may have obscured the larger analytical purpose to relate work and culture. For the weary traveler who may be lost in one of the dark passageways I have explored, and with the indulgence of those who are fortunate enough to see the light already at the end of this tunnel, I want to make some general observations on the contours of work and culture in the mining village.

Although the "typical" company town is difficult to characterize, it would be imprudent to disregard its emblematic features of life. In spite of ideosyncracies of individual settlements, nearly all residents of coal towns shared some common modes of thought, habits, prejudices, values, aspirations, and experiences.

Migrants to coal town in the pioneer and paternalistic periods found an environment very much like a rural community. Chickens, hogs, and cows were common sights, as families depended upon them for food. Vegetable gardens were also plentiful, and hunting and fishing provided additional dietary supplements, as they had for farm families. During the first three to four decades of coal mining, mules were commonly used to haul coal. The livery stable, barns, and blacksmith shop—together wth livestock roaming the grounds—must have given coal towns the smell and ambience of a large farm rather than an industrial district.

In spite of the mobility of mine labor, in some ways because of it, ties of obligation and mutual responsibility remained strong in the company town. Not only did the close proximity of houses and people heighten the awareness of and association with other people—insufficient in itself to reinforce communalism—but the physical setting, together with the dangers and insecurity of mine work, gave residents a group solidarity, a sense of being caught up together in a common fate. Hard times had the same effect.

Coming of age in coal town had its similarities to rural life. Young boys learned from their fathers and then taught their own sons the craft of mining, and all became common sojourners sharing the experience and memories of work from youth to old age. Just as in the farm economy, it was rational to divide the world of work into different worlds. The family as a unit continued to be meaningful. The mining economy depended upon the work of wives and daughters to support the family, whose preservation took precedence over the needs of individuals. This was especially true because the coal industry was so unstable, always subject to shutdowns and periodic unemployment.

The tasking system encouraged group identity, and the dangers of the work required mutual trust and respect in the workplace. Accidents, explosions, and diseases cannot be overestimated in their power to bridge all differences in the world of work, whether those of race, religion, or ethnicity. They were also the source of much uncertainty. One's longevity in the mines could never be taken for granted; nor could one's wages, for that matter. Hard times were endemic to the coal industry and those who worked in it. Consequently, mine culture, like agriculture, was a shared working-class culture. During periods of sickness, unemployment, and death, family and community shared their resources and emotional support.

Nevertheless, working in the mines was also an abrupt departure from the past which later generations would perhaps notice more than the first. Once the decision had been reached to sell the farm and move to the coal town, it was difficult to turn back. The land, the machinery, and the know-how were just too much to recapture. Moving back and forth between logging and farming, for example, was not the same as the move from mining to farming.

Other alternatives also shrank, especially the all-important one of access to secondary means of making a living or supplementing the major source of livelihood. Preindustrial families had been able to rely upon a variety of activities to cover the family. For all of its claims to freedom in the workplace, mining sharply narrowed the workers' choices beyond the mines. Mining in Appalachia produced almost no secondary industry. It was carried on in remote mountain hollows. Raising livestock, hunting and fishing, growing a garden, and borrowing from family and friends all helped. But they could not last forever and were little more than meager substitutes for a steady income. Valuable as it was, the labor of women and children did not provide the same safety valve it had on the farm. Apparently, slackness was the major cause of miners moving from place to place. Aside from mining coal, there was little else to do.

But mobility was not the most important difference between the coal miner and the farmer. After all, the Scotch-Irish of the eighteenth century, southern blacks of the nineteenth century, and southern Europeans of the twentieth century were no strangers to mobility. Mobility has been one of the central themes of the Appalachian, indeed of the American working-class experience. What was unusual, at least for Appalachian families, was not having to move around to make a living, but to be suddenly cut off from the major source of livelihood with no alternatives, not even a move to another coal town. In the face of an economic cul-de-sac, miners experimented with more modern forms of organization, such as mutual benefit societies and the labor union, and simultaneously joined inherited values with the exigencies of industrial life to create a modern working culture characterized by its maleness.

6 And the Union Came

Industrial workers have often formed their own associations to meet their common needs in the workplace. Sometimes these associations have been formed for social reasons. Other types of associations have come in the form of mutual aid societies. Historians customarily refer to these as voluntary associations because they have been organized by the workers themselves who set the terms of membership and run the organizations. Little is known about voluntary associations among coal miners, except for the United Mine Workers of America, about which much has been written.

Borderland Coal Company and Stonega Coke and Coal Company responded very differently to the formation of workers' associations, especially the union. An analysis of their reactions reveals how each company and the union competed to control worker associations and create a work setting in their own best interests. The substantial minority of nonunion workers who refused to join the labor movement at Stonega until they were forced to do so in 1939 suggests the need to reexamine the history of unionism. Violence, first on the part of the operators to prevent unionization, then on the part of unionized miners against strikebreakers and miners reluctant to join the union, has been a constant companion of the labor movement. At times miners at Stonega and elsewhere attempted to rid themselves of the coercive violence of both operators and union organizers. The use of law and police force to prevent violence either by the operators to stymie unionism or by the unionists to achieve a victory has been a major development in labor relations since World War II.

Company records, especially those of the Stonega Company, illustrate the variety of these organizations and how they operated. The Derby Burial Fund, for example, organized by the employees of Stonega at the Derby colliery, required employees to pay an initiation fee of $1.00 and then the same amount each month. If the fund dropped below $500.00, the monthly fee rose to $1.50; if it rose about $2,500.00, no dues had to be paid. Members signed cards giving Stonega the right to make salary deductions to be paid to the fund. According to its bylaws, the fund was governed by a committee of three annually elected members. Any dues-paying member could collect from the fund on presentation of a death certificate for the employee or any family member living in the employee's household. Death benefits were paid according to a schedule, with one amount for a stillbirth and differing amounts for children ages three to seven, seven to twelve, and twelve to eighteen. On the death of a member or spouse, the association paid the maximum benefit of $200.00.[1]

Workers also organized societies that functioned like insurance companies, compensating workers for injury and paying some of the costs of hospitalization for dues-paying members and their families. The Dunbar Relief Fund, for example, paid death benefits but also $10.00 per week for injury until workman's compensation benefits began and $5.00 per week thereafter, up to a maximum of twenty-six weeks. The fund also paid one-half of the expenses of an operation.[2] When the mines closed and miners moved to other collieries of the Stonega Company, they simply joined whatever relief society or burial fund existed there. According to company records, the collieries at Arno, Derby, Dunbar, Exeter, Imboden, Roda, and Stonega had relief societies; Derby and Imboden also had separate burial funds. A Stonega official, writing in 1913 when the issue of these organizations first came to the company's attention, notes that a similar network of organizations was widespread in West Virginia.[3] Presumably, similar organizations were formed all over the southern Appalachian coalfields.

In areas employing larger numbers of immigrant miners, such as West Virginia, volunteer associations combined the goals of mutual aid, ethnic solidarity, and sometimes religious affiliation in the same organization. The Reverend J. Koulake, a Lithuanian priest, founded the St. John Society in Thomas, West Virginia, in 1896. Besides paying sickness and death benefits, its goals were to bring together fellow Lithuanians as Roman Catholics and to promote better understanding between Catholics and other denominations. Membership fluctuated with the coming and going of immigrants in the coalfields until 1938 when the society apparently dissolved, having only six members. At its peak in 1910, it had two hundred members.[4]

The Stonega operators cooperated, albeit grudgingly at first, with the miners' efforts to organize these associations. Eventually they came to see their value both to the workers and to the company. In 1913, when Stonega's miners implored the company to permit a payroll deduction of twenty-five cents per month from a miner's salary to be placed into a burial fund, a company official objected on the grounds that compulsory deductions are "always undesirable"; new employees, when informed of the deduction, would immediately conclude "that there was a lot of people dying or getting killed at Stonega," and this would present "an unfavorable impression."[5]

Much later, in 1934, another company official revealed how attitudes had evolved toward voluntary associations. The official began his letter by noting that the UMWA had made a great effort to gain control of the Imboden society and handle its money, which Stonega had managed to keep in the hands of the mine superintendent. While the local vice-president disavowed any interest in running relief societies, he nevertheless acknowledged that they had been "an excellent proposition from the workman's point of view" and saved the company considerable money.[6]

Benefit societies signaled the adaptation that preindustrial families had made to new conditions of work. When their borrowing from family and friends, along with other traditional, time-honored forms of mutual support, proved inadequate to meet the needs of down-and-out families, miners organized their own organizations for this purpose. The fact that they did so has to qualify the conclusions of contemporary activists who complain about the historic "tradition" in Appalachia of nonjoiners. Nor did these associations, new and modern as they were, spell the end to traditional forms of aid. In the 1930s, for example, oral history chronicles the efforts of mining families to deal with hard times in the forms of "depression suppers" where potluck meals brought together groups of families. A more notable form of association, however, was the labor union.

Periodically, beginning in 1912 in West Virginia and continuing off and on until the 1930s, the coal operators and labor organizers battled one another for the hearts and minds of coal miners. Both sides, armed to the teeth on occasion, resorted to violence and intimidation in their efforts to win over the workers. Under such circumstances as these, freedom of choice became a hostage to fear and irrationality. In the 1910s and 1920s, the operators put up a fierce battle to keep the union from organizing their workforce. Union organizers met force with force until the West Virginia coalfields were turned into a battleground. During the 1930s and the later years of the union movement, both the operators and the union leaders combined to force the "closed shop" upon the mine labor force, making the "choice" one between joining the union or leaving the mines altogether. It was an extraordinary turnabout in the space of less than two decades.

The trade union was another form of worker association designed to meet the needs of modern labor. Although it evolved into a paternalistic organization, especially after the 1930s, initially it sprang from needs different from those that had generated the mutual benefit societies. Its impetus arose from the weakened condition of industrial labor in a capitalistic society where the operators controlled both the market for labor and the conditions of work. It had an obvious appeal to the labor force, as would any organization that came promising improved conditions of labor and higher wages.

More has been written about the union movement than perhaps any other aspect of coal-town life. Indeed, labor activism has been the central focus of the writers, journalists, and social scientists of the twentieth century who have written about the southern Appalachian coalfields. "Bloody" Harlan, the Mingo "war," Cabin Creek, Paint Creek, the Matewan "massacre," Baldwin-Felts agents, the march on Blair Mountain, labor spies, evictions from company houses, yellow-dog contracts, tent colonies – all these and more are terms that constitute the lexicon of observers who have made West Virginia a cauldron of labor unrest. Most recently, filmmakers produced a movie on the incidents surrounding the Matewan shootout on 19 May 1920.

Labor historians, understandably, have studied unionism, not its absence. They have examined the "seemingly endless procession" of strikes, lockouts, and evictions. They have ignored the interstices of nonunionism while compressing the history of the period into a series of episodes that move from strike to strike. Areas where nothing happened and years of inactivity have gained little attention, presumably since they are of little significance. The union movement, which may have had a marginal impact upon the lives of thousands of ordinary miners, has achieved primary or exclusive importance in the history of mining settlements. Coal mining has been particularly susceptible to these tendencies, perhaps because so much has been made of labor incidents, especially in southern West Virginia.[7]

The brutish behavior of some of the mine guards, the pathos of evicted families living in tent colonies, and the exploitation by the owners have generated strong feelings of empathy for the union and its cause. Likewise, the harsh conditions under which coal miners worked – in the early period, some of the worst that industrial workers faced in the late nineteenth and early twentieth centuries – have invited the sympathy of later generations who, since they have never experienced anything comparable, have failed to set the experience of miners within the context of workingmen's realities and the perceptions of the age, and who therefore see the union only as the arbiter of justice.

At best, the appreciation for the plight of miners has clouded some issues of potential importance. For example, the potential historical connection between early nonunionism and the apathy of miners toward the union today has remained unexplored. The exaggerated emphasis upon strikes and violent confrontations between the operators' police forces and the strikers has equated the history of coal miners with the history of labor discontent. At its worst, such a view begs the question whether all miners were alienated by the conditions of industrial capitalism. The understandable empathy shown for the miners has left unexamined the issue of nonunionism as a legitimate inquiry.

In fact, in spite of the attention given to conflict, nonunionism was widespread enough to challenge as misleading the equation of the history of coal miners with a mass movement of class-conscious workers rising up as one against an oppressive and exploitive labor system. A brief reexamination of union activity in West Virginia – presumably a hotbed of labor radicalism, to judge from the accounts of labor historians – between 1880 and the Great Depression reveals two things: long spans of relative inactivity broken by briefer periods of intense industrial conflict; and a substantial, if indeterminate, number of miners who refused to join the union even during an age of notorious labor repression.

For example, during the period from 1880 until the famous Paint Creek–Cabin Creek labor conflict of 1912, workers did protest conditions of work, but such protests were sporadic, infrequent, unorganized and local. The UMWA was organized in 1890 but was unable to organize West Virginia's miners until shortly before the Paint Creek strike. In that famous conflict, one historian estimated that 7,500 miners worked in the fifty-five mines on Cabin Creek and forty-one mines on Paint Creek, and they supported a total population of 35,000.[8] Yet Thomas L. Felts of the Baldwin-Felts Detective Agency, who had no self-evident reason for underestimating the number of miners, set the number employed at the time of the strikes at 3,000 for Cabin Creek and 2,000 for Paint Creek, for a total of 5,000.[9] The labor historian of the southern West Virginia coalfields spoke of a walkout of "thousands of nonunion as well as union miners in the Paint Creek district" who were "joined by 7,500 nonunion miners on Cabin Creek, Kanawha and Fayette counties."[10] From these conflicting accounts it is impossible to gauge the precise number of miners, to say nothing of the extent of union and nonunion sentiment. More needs to be known, especially the ratio of miners and sympathizers to the total labor force.

Years of relative inactivity followed until 1920. During this period, labor organizers continued their effort to unionize the miners and the operators theirs to prevent it. In addition, World War I provided some protection to organized labor and boosted the strength of the UMWA. Yet in 1919, the UMWA claimed a membership of only 60 percent of the labor force in West Virginia. Since union organizations may inflate membership figures for obvious reasons, a safer estimate might be about 50 percent. In spite of the maladroitness and heavy-handedness of the operators in the Paint Creek district during the strike, despite the boost of the war period, and despite the allegedly oppressive environment in the company towns, nonunion sentiment remained high in the state.

The years 1920 to 1922 witnessed another labor upheaval, this time in Logan and Mingo counties on the Kentucky border. Again, accounts make it impossible to calculate a union-nonunion ratio. At the peak of the confrontation, an estimated 5,000 to 7,000 miners faced several thousand opponents along a front line that stretched across both counties before the miners capitulated. Then followed another long period of relative calm and waning support for the union. Union membership plummeted to only several hundred by 1932.[11]

Thus, even a cursory reexamination of the labor movement in the heart of pro-union territory produces questions about nonunionism and gives an entirely different impression from that of labor historians. From 1880 to 1912, from 1913 to 1920, and from 1923 until the Great Depression, West Virginia was relatively free of strikes and violent labor unrest. In other words, during a fifty-year span, there were four years of strikes, lockouts, violence, and labor militancy, but forty-six years of relative calm. Such a history does not appear to justify a conclusion that strikes during this period were:

> collective and militant acts of aggression, interconnected and conditioned by decades . . . of social change, economic exploitation, and oppression . . . products of decades of evolving attitudes toward and about work, life, existence, unionism, employers, law and order, social and economic justice, the state, the community, and the meaning of America.

Nor could one conclude: "Miners vented their discontent in almost unceasing efforts to unionize the mountain coal fields." What about the thousands of miners who did not participate in the labor movement? What explains the absence of strikes and violence in other mining areas, and in southwestern Virginia or eastern Tennessee?[12]

Miners in the handloading era were prepared by rural conditions of hardship to accept what today might be judged to be primitive conditions of life and work. They expected to work long hours, to perform hard physical labor, to live in modest frame houses. Such was the plight of working men and women everywhere in America in the late nineteenth and early twentieth centuries. Most were happy just to have a steady, well-paying job. Especially for the first generation of industrial labor fresh from the chronic misery of rural life, a very low level of expectations gave operators wide latitude in the treatment of their workers.

Nevertheless, the labor union had susbstantial appeal among miners.

The important expressions of nonunionist sentiment should not be allowed to obscure the pro-union sympathies among mining populations of southern Appalachia, especially in light of the obstacles miners faced in expressing their feelings. The forty-six years of apparent calm may have been years of building resentment against the operators and the laying of plans to overcome the stubborn resistance of anti-union forces. It took more than mere determination to join the union, particularly during the turbulent post–World War I years, when coal operators resorted to brutal suppression of labor activism. One of the major causes for the appeal of the union was probably the vehement anti-unionism of the operators themselves. Their severe reactions to attempts to organize their workers alienated miners and made a mockery of their own expressions of paternalism. In this environment, the very existence of nonunion sentiment becomes even more intriguing.

Overbearing resistance did not exhaust the reasons for the appeal of the union, of course, even if it was one of the most significant factors. Also important was that the union provided one of the few chances miners had to save their jobs after World War I. Coal mining had experienced phenomenal growth during the war. In six counties of eastern Kentucky, for example, the war transformed mining into the major source of employment for a majority of the population. The bubble burst in 1923 when bituminous coal production in the United States peaked. Between 1923 and 1927, 200,000 miners left the U.S. coalfields. Southern Appalachian producers hung on until 1927 when production began a decline that sent the region's major employer into a depression from which it never recovered, at least not in labor demand. Many placed their hopes in the union as the only means left to preserve their livelihood.[13]

Those hopes proved misplaced, however. The union supported mechanization, for example, which displaced even more workers. Then, in the 1930s, the union, struggling to gain a foothold, joined the forces of repression itself when it negotiated labor contracts that demanded membership in the union as a condition of employment, stimulating another round of nonunionism perhaps, this time among the very miners it hoped to organize.

The history of unionism at Borderland Coal Corporation and Stonega Coke and Coal Company during the 1920s and 1930s exhibited two developments in response to the postwar union drives. For financial reasons Borderland had always been grudging in its commitment to paternalism. When the union drives began in 1919, however, Borderland launched an anti-union policy that may have been second to none in its militancy. Part of the explanation for Borderland's vehement reaction lies in the attitudes of the company's founder, Edward Stone. In addition, the Borderland collieries lay in the targeted area of UMWA organizers. Stonega, on the other hand, had always relied heavily upon paternalism to cultivate a contented labor force. When the union drives began in the West Virginia region, Stonega, which never became a target of union organization, could react more benignly, retaining substantial good will among its miners.

Borderland Coal stands out in this study as a company that battled the unionization of coal miners. Its owner, Edward Stone, led the charge. Unopposed to the union affiliation of his Stone Printing Company workers in Roanoke, Virginia, probably because the printers were scarce skilled workers, Stone fought the UMWA with unwavering determination until it led his company into bankruptcy. Perhaps it is an overstatement to associate Borderland's financial ruin entirely with its antilabor activities; nevertheless, even Stone had to admit that the financial costs were substantial – as we shall see. An entertaining but revealing document in Borderland records entitled "Unions," dated about 1921 or 1922 and signed by Stone, outlined his opinions on the subject. He began by proclaiming his belief in the legitimacy of unions, such as the United States of America, Cooper Union, Western Union, the postal union, and the union stockyards. But "if they trespass on the law or rights of others – disregard the laws and the constitution, they must pay the penalty." Ghandi was in jail, Stone said, because he went against the law.

After having trivialized the issue, he confronted it directly by asking about labor unions such as the UMWA, to which he responded to his own question: "They have rights, of course – certain rights." These ended, he elaborated, when they placed loyalty to the union above that to country and law. One way of recasting Stone's logic might be: the union was lawful so long as its actions were lawful. Of course, since the union had no legal identity until New Deal legislation was passed, logic led directly to its illegality. On the issue of legality, Stone objected to other practices of unions:

> Our men were told by the Union Agents that if they did not join the Union a strike would be called when the Union had a sufficient number of members, and that the men who did not join the union would then be out of a job. They were threatened, intimidated, shot at in their homes, and at their work, and the result was that many of the men joined. We told the men, however, that if they joined the union, *under these circumstances*, we would have to let them go, as we had not the slightest intention of signing a contract with the Union.[14]

Stone also objected to labor unions on the grounds that a contract with a union was unenforceable, "not worth a hill of beans," because unions were not incorporated and therefore could not be sued for breach of contract. If they decided they didn't like a previously agreed-upon contract, they could strike regardless, something usually referred to as "outlaw strikes." Stone believed that a corporation should have a right to refuse to contract with the union – the same right it had with regard to any other individual, organization, or business – if the contract was unsatisfactory, had no basis for enforcement, or provided no means of recovery when it was violated. He presented a litany of grievances, many of which were drawn from incidents at Borderland:

> When we decline or refuse to sign their agreement or contract, they frighten our employees; shoot at them when they are going to or coming from work; shoot at them in their homes, dynamite its [the company's] Power House, attempt to blow up its Bridges and Coal Conveyor, and then attempt to lay on our shoulders the burden occasioned by the deaths, destruction, living in tents, and all the other ills that follow; all of this is beyond my comprehension.[15]

Between 1915 and 1932 Stone pursued a variety of tactics to prevent the unionization of his Borderland miners and to destroy the UMWA. Apparently believing that one unlawful act deserved another, he stopped at little short of murder to keep the union out. The use of what Stone and his manager referred to as "secret service agents" or Baldwin-Felts men continued throughout these years. He first contacted Thomas Felts in 1911 about the costs of using detectives and was quoted a cost of $350 to $450 per month, depending upon the services provided. Stone advocated raising the issue at the next meeting of the Coal Operators' Association, a group of operators on the Tug River. He felt that, for less than a penny a ton, the operators could well afford to hire Felts's men in order to keep tabs on labor organizers. By 1916 he had five to six secret-service men "in the field" and remarked that "we are beginning to get some reports." The reports fingered not only outside organizers but miners at Borderland who were helping the union. Stone used the reports to identify and then fire them.[16]

Industrial espionage became complicated at times. For example, in 1915 a secret-service report revealed an all-day session the agent had spent with a group of union men who played cards by a fireplace in a Kentucky cabin while they talked unionism. The agent, a double himself working under the guise of a union organizer, reported warning the men about company spies – who acted as union organizers – sent in by the coal companies to infiltrate the union. About two weeks later, the same agent reported to Borderland the efforts of union organizers to get the requisite number of twenty miners to join the union and pay their dues so a charter could be granted. The names of the men who paid were given, and the agent reported that the leaders must be gotten rid of, although it would be hard to discharge them since they were considered the best on the job. According to the agent, "You have to get in the mines and work with the boys to secure facts these days." The following month L. E. Armentrout, Stone's on-site manager, sent the secret-service reports to Stone with the note that he had arranged to discharge the named individuals. A month later Kelly Ackers, a native-born white, was fired and evicted.[17]

World War I temporarily interrupted the efforts of the UMWA to oganize the southern West Virginia coalfields. With the coming of the Armistice, the union renewed and intensified its efforts to bring mine labor in the region under the union banner. This was not just a goal of the UMWA; the miners and even the operators of the "central competitive fields" (i.e., Pennsylvania, Ohio, Indiana, and Illinois) supported the unionization of southern Appalachia. Miners in the North disliked the higher wages of nonunion labor, a strategy the southern operators used to remain unorganized, and operators believed that nonunion labor allowed operators to respond to market fluctuations more readily by temporary wage reductions, thereby giving them a competitive advantage. In 1919, southern West Virginia became the target of these efforts to unionize. Equally determined were the operators of the southern fields, men like Edward Stone who enjoyed the flexibility and cost advantages of nonunion labor and defied anyone to come between him and his employees.

Thus, the battle lines were drawn in 1919 when the UMWA sent its organizers southward to sign up the miners. They were met with Baldwin-Felts men and other armed individuals paid by the coal operators to keep out labor organizers. In the twelve months following August 1920, on separate occasions, thousands of armed miners faced hundreds of mine guards as the violence escalated. Firings and evictions increased as the operators used these weapons against union sympathizers. Two famous shootouts, one on 19 May 1920 at Matewan which killed eleven men, including the mayor and seven Baldwin-Felts men, and an ambush – allegedly staged by Baldwin-Felts men – on the steps of the Welsh courthouse, which killed Sid Hatfield, the sheriff of Matewan fame, inflamed the confrontations. After the Matewan shootout, the UMWA called for the miners to strike. The strike dragged on for twenty-two months, in spite of the operators' ability to restore the mines to prestrike production levels within six months, mainly through the use of strikebreakers and nonunion miners.[18]

During the time of these events, Borderland took the lead in combating the union drive with firings and evictions from company houses, with labor spies, and with court injunctions, pushing one case all the way to the U.S. Supreme Court. On 5 May 1920 the company posted a notice at its collieries:

> This is a free country and this company is not going to dictate to its employees whether they shall or shall not join a union, but for your information and for the information of your friends, we wish to state positively that no union men shall be employed by this company. . . .

Unmoved apparently by the contradictions in their notice, Borderland's officials concluded by asking all who wanted to join the union to quit and leave the company. When miners would not, Stone had them evicted. The UMWA responded with tents set up for the evicted families. Nearby operators did the same. In September 1922, between twenty-five and thirty tents filled with strike families from various collieries in the vicinity could be seen within three-fourths of a mile of Borderland.[19]

Evictions were always nasty affairs. They led to the Matewan shootout, for example. At the moment of eviction, the miner lost both his home and his job and was in no mood for a surly Baldwin-Felts man ordering people around with the family possessions. On 22 October 1920, John Gee of Borderland claimed he was shot by one of thirteen Baldwin-Felts men who "invaded" his home and threatened his family during an eviction. Ultimately, evictions like Gee's were challenged in the courts, leading to a West Virginia Supreme Court of Appeals decision in 1924 in *Watt Angel v. Black Band Consolidated Coal Company*. In the decision, the court took note of the ideal that "a man's home is his castle." On the basis of this theory, the court pointed out, gunmen had been imported into the state in defense of the evictees and committed murder "in self defense." The judges decided in favor of the operators that this theory was indefensible because the house was part of the company's plant. If necessary, the court decided, the company could use whatever force it deemed necessary, including knocking down doors, tearing out windows, or even tearing down the house during evictions.[20]

Baldwin-Felts reports were valuable documents, not only because they revealed Borderland's tactics to avert unionism but because they simultaneously exposed the clandestine tactics the UMWA used to achieve the opposite end of unionizing the workforce. For example, according to one informant — who the union organizers believed to be one of them — when the union men got word that wages were about to be reduced in the Tug District, they asked the informant to "feel out men about loading these big cars for the price they were getting" and "get men in line" for chartering a local. (The union required miners' signatures as evidence that a local chapter was desirable.) A foreigner at one of the mines was

Don't Spend All Your Earnings

Form 19 10M 8-22

Put some aside for possible sickness or misfortune.   Don't run the risk of loss by fire or thieves; deposit your surplus earnings with this bank where it will earn three per cent. per annum, interest and principal payable on demand.   Write to-day for booklet giving full information about opening an account.

POLISH   Wysyłamy pieniadze, sprzedajemy szyfkarty.
HUNGARIAN   Pénzküldés, hajójegyek és közjegyzői okmányok.
ITALIAN   Biglietti di passaggio e Vaglia per Italia.

THE NATIONAL BANK OF COMMERCE
WILLIAMSON, WEST VIRGINIA

No.............................   Borderland, W. Va., ...192.....

Mr..

IN ACCOUNT WITH Borderland Coal Corporation

LIABLE FOR ANY SUBSEQUENT INDEBTEDNESS

DR.			CR.		
To Account in Store			By Hours ....@......		
" Scrip			" " ....@......		
" Powder...................			" Cars ....@......		
" Rent......			" " ....@......		
" Coal			" Water..........@......		
" Smithing			" Yds. ....@......		
" Lights..................			" Props...........@......		
" Cash			" Ties.............@......		
" Doctor			" Caps...........@......		
"			" ....@......		
" Sundries			"		
" Insurance......			" Cash		
E. and O. E. Total.			Total...............		
			By Balance Due Workman....		

RETAIN THIS STATEMENT

CUT THIS RECEIPT OFF AND PRESENT IT AT THE PAY WINDOW

NOT TRANSFERABLE WITHOUT ORDER ON THE BACK
If this receipt is lost after signing, notice must be given in writing at our office before pay day.

Work No..........................   Borderland, W. Va.,........................192....

Name..

RECEIVED OF Borderland Coal Corporation

....DOLLARS
100

($..................) in full of all claims from..Inc.

WITNESS AT SIGNING:

....

....   (Sign here)...............................

WOODROW—CINCINNATI 84556

Miner's account, Borderland, ca. 1920. Courtesy of Manuscripts Division, Special Collections Department, University of Virginia Library.

Borderland, ca. 1921. Courtesy of Manuscripts Division, Special
Collections Department, University of Virginia Library.

BORDERLAND

PUT YOUR NAME ON THE

OR ELSE

BOLSHEVISM   UNIONISM
SOCIALISM   TERRORISM
ANARCHISM   BULLETS

Ask any one of thousands who have refused to sign Union Contracts, or those who have been beneath the heel and domination of "Unionism."

Not the half of the activities, "direct action," intimidation, etc., of the Union and its sympathizers at Borderland has been told.

Unionism is all right, theoretically, perhaps; so is Socialism, theoretically; but, practically, it doesn't work; and "work" here has a double meaning.

After signing a Union Agreement the real trouble, petty annoyances, unfairness born of supposed power, begin.

"Heavy, heavy hangs over your head," all the time.

If one signs an Agreement for, say, one year, and then does not want to renew it, he is branded as "non-union," "rat," "scab," "unfair"; is boycotted and suffers from all the annoyances Union Agents and their sympathizers can inflict.

Which is quite different from what happens between business people when they do not sign or renew a contract.

Power takes its morality from the results of its use. If the power of trades unionism means that a man cannot work without the approval of a union, no matter what its motto for the future, no matter what its record for the past, no matter who its champions, trade unionism cannot survive in the United States.

—LAW AND LABOR.

Borderland tract, ca. 1920. Courtesy of Manuscripts Division, Special Collections Department, University of Virginia Library.

Tract No. 4.   Jan. 1st. 1923.

TAKE CARE OF THE COMPANY'S HOUSE—MAKE 'IT YOUR HOME— KEEP IT CLEAN— PLANT FLOWERS— MAKE GARDENS STAY ON THE JOB— WORK SIX DAYS IN THE WEEK MAKE FRIENDS WITH YOUR BOSS-MAN AND YOU WILL SUCCEED—

READ WHAT THE BIBLE SAYS ABOUT THE BUSY-BODY AND THE FELLOW WHO DOES NOT WORK.

„For we hear that there are some whhch walk among you disorderly, working not at all but are busy-bodes in other peoples' business. Let as many servants as are under the yoke count their own masters worthy of all honor, that the name of God and his doctrine be not blasphemed."—I Tim. 6:1.

All work is important; stick to your work and stay on the job. Let every man and woman say: 'I am doing a great work, so that I cannot come down. Why should the work cease while I leave it, and come down to you?"—Nehemiah 6:3.

Whatsoèver thy hands findeth to do, do it with thy might; for there is no work, nor device, nor knowledge, nor wisdom in the grave, whither thou goest. This we command you, that any would not work, neither should he eat."—II Thes. 10:11.

IDLENESS IS HELL—THE DEVIL'S WORKSHOP.
KEEP BUSY.

MODERN EDUCATIONAL TRACT AND LECTURE BUREAU

P. O. Box 82.   —O—   Kimball, W. Va.

Borderland tract, ca. 1923. Courtesy of Manuscripts Division, Special Collections Department, University of Virginia Library.

Form 100-B

CONTRACT

In order to preserve to each man the right to do such work as he pleases and for whom he pleases and the right to payment in proportion to service rendered, to preserve the natural and constitutional right of individual contract, to preserve to each individual the fruits of his own labor and to promote the interests of both parties

hereto *Stonega Coke + Coal*

Big Stone Gap. Va

employer, and *J. C. Phillips*

employee, agree as follows:

That so long as the relation of employer and employee exists between them, the employer will not knowingly employ, or keep in its employment, any member of the United Mine Workers of America, the I. W.W. or any other mine labor organization, and the employee will not join or belong to any such union or organization, and will not aid, encourage or approve the organization thereof, it being understood that the policy of said Company is to operate a non-union mine, and that it would not enter into any contract of employment under any other conditions; and if and when said relation of employer and employee, at any time and under any circumstances, terminates, the employee agrees that he will not then or thereafter, in any manner molest, annoy or interfere with the business, customers or employees of the employer, and will not aid or encourage anyone else in so doing.

Witness the following signatures, this the *18*

day of *April*, 192*9*.

STONEGA COKE & COAL COMPANY

B E Pace

Superintendent.

Employee *J C Phillips*

Witness

O. F. Falin

IN DUPLICATE   Form 100-A

APPLICATION FOR POSITION AS _____ Date _____

Name _____

Nationality _____ Age _____ Weight _____

Height _____ Color _____ Eyes _____ Hair _____

Scars or Deformities _____

Married _____ Single _____ Children under 17 _____ Over 17 _____

Next of Kin, Name _____

Address _____

Where last employed _____

How long _____ Why quit _____

Where previously employed _____

How long _____ Why quit _____

Ever work for this company _____ When _____

How long _____ What capacity _____ Why quit _____

Mining experience _____ Other work _____

FOREIGNERS state where born _____ Date _____

Date of arrival in U. S. A. _____ Are you naturalized? _____

Where did you get first papers _____ Date _____

Second papers _____ Third papers _____

Can you read or speak English _____ Other languages _____

REMARKS _____

I am not now a member of the United Mine Workers of America, the I. W. W., or any other organization of mine workers, and will not, during this employment, join or affiliate with any such mine labor organization, because I believe the preservation of the right of individual contract, free from interference or regulation by others, and payment in proportion to service rendered, to be to my interest, to the best interest of the public and of all industry, and I enter this employment with the understanding that the policy of the Company is to operate a non-union mine, and that it will not knowingly employ anyone belonging to such Union, or organization, and would not give me employment under any other conditions.

SIGNED _____ Applicant.

WITNESS _____

APPROVED _____ COMPANY _____ MINE.

"Yellow dog" contract, Stonega, 1929. Courtesy of Westmoreland Coal Company Archive, Hagley Library.

targeted by the union organizers as "King Bee among the foreigners." Names of other "good union miners" circulated among the organizers. Two white men from Indiana came to Williamson, an independent town about eight miles from Borderland, and attempted to rent a basement apartment in the black section of town to use as a headquarters for the mailing of application blanks to the various mining camps in the district. Another report noted a white man and a black man working the McDowell County area. The black man was described as "very intelligent" and using the cover of an insurance agent. He carried with him a map of all the coal-mining camps of southern West Virginia. Card playing and gambling sessions often served as ruses for union organizing. Meetings could be held, and the company would suspect only gambling. The double life of a spy for the company working in the guise of a union organizer must have been difficult, as one agent reported:

> I am using my best efforts to make good with both sides, the Company and the miners. I am working every minute the mine runs [sic], loading as much coal as any miner working in the mine. My work seems satisfactory to the mine foreman. On the other hand, I am making many friends among the miners. I get out and play cards with them, visit with them and eat and sleep with them. Please handle this matter carefully – I hope without having me fired. I like it here.[21]

Borderland became the target of pro-union violence as a result of its determined anti-union stance. During the long months of the UMWA strike between 1920 and 1922, "union gunmen" fired at men at the drift mouths on several occasions. In June the Number Two colliery was "shot up." The next month another shooting from the banks of the Tug River into Pike County was reported; "union gunmen" also attacked Number One. Two weeks later, about thirty-five shots were fired in the direction of nonunion men who were working at the tipple. The company called in deputies with dogs but could not find the culprits. Other random shootings followed. In late July, the Borderland pump house was dynamited. The next month, a box of dynamite destroyed the engine room at Number Two. In December a house burned. Mrs. Williamson, the boardinghouse keeper, claimed it was set on fire by union men who had threatened arson if "they continued to keep nonunion boarders." Finally, the UMWA called off the strike in October 1922, and the violence abated.[22]

Borderland, like other coal operators in the Tug River District, paid its labor spies and financed its anti-union activities through bookkeeping practices. In 1921 Stone wrote to Armentrout advising him to keep the company books "in a more secret way." He suggested having the bookkeeper report to the cashier and the cashier to the treasurer. He also suggested separating general and administrative expenses from the rest of the annual financial statement and having them handled in the treasurer's office. A problem surfaced, as further correspondence revealed, during the twenty-two-month strike period, when a labor spy was hired by Majestic Coal, another Tug River operator, and paid in kind for his services through the company store. The bookkeeper, who was not privy to the arrangement, learned of it and, like a good employee, dutifully reported that the company store manager was giving a miner goods out of the store without a record of charges. According to Stone's manager, Armentrout: "During the strike period, I suppose every man in charge of a mine along the river had some similar arrangement." As for Borderland, Armentrout took care of his informant's pay through his own expense account.[23]

When required, Armentrout was not averse to lying about Borderland's use of informants. In 1920, the UMWA produced a pamphlet entitled *Borderland and Bullets* in which Borderland was accused of hiring Baldwin-Felts "thugs" and firing at union organizers. Armentrout responded with a signed affidavit:

> I further certify that I have been manager of the Borderland Coal Company, later changed to the Borderland Coal Corporation, since 1903, and for the past five years vice president, in charge of operations, and during the entire time this plant has been organized, we have not had any Baldwin-Felts thugs or Gunmen in our employ, or on our property, and I further offer a reward of $100.00 (one hundred dollars) cash to anyone that can prove otherwise.[24]

Borderland's use of labor spies continued during the 1920s, in fact until 27 January 1930, the date of the last reference to such activity in the company's records. Some of the reports were signed by T. L. Felts himself. Spies continued to monitor the efforts of union organizers, which had been scaled down considerably due to the defeat of the UMWA in southern West Virginia and the union's court battles. In 1925 Armentrout reported to his Roanoke boss that his informants were monitoring the movements of union organizers, but he was unconcerned because Borderland now had contracts, most likely yellow-dog contracts, with 98 percent of its miners, and union activity was under a court injunction.[25]

Stone did not stop at labor spies, however, in his efforts to prevent unionization. On 22 July 1920, he wrote to Armentrout about the Thompson submachine gun. He indicated that "a pretty big man" had advocated that he should get a machine gun to stop the strikers from shooting at the employees. Stone continued:

Of course, none of us want to get into that sort of work any more than is absolutely necessary, . . . but when our employees are willing to work, and those who are unwilling to work are making "pot" shots on them it seems that there ought to be some way to protect the employees.[26]

The following April 1921, toward the end of the extended twenty-two-month period of violence in Mingo and Logan counties, the Southern Auto-Ordnance Sales Company answered a Borderland inquiry about the Thompson gun with two circulars advertising its special qualities: "There is only one way to hit a target with 100% accuracy. That way is to *spray the target.* We can spray with .45 calibre U.S.A. steel jacketed bullets at the rate of 1500 shots per minute." The price of the gun was $225. The circular self-servingly suggested that one gun was not enough. "The thing to do is to get each bank, the chief of police of each town, each manufacturing establishment, each cotton mill watchman, and each municipal government to provide these guns for safe and complete protection." With ten of these guns, the company claimed, the county would be "fixed." Stone subsequently inquired about the range of the gun, whether it fired consecutively, and what attachment was needed to fire one thousand rounds continuously. He believed that, if these questions could be answered satisfactorily, "I have no dout your agent could sell a dozen or more guns in this vicinity." Nothing indicates whether Stone ever purchased any of the guns. Later, Armentrout wired Stone from the Vaughan Hotel in Williamson, West Virginia, and asked for a price on two hundred explosive shells and "a one pounder." He asked his boss to respond in code, using the words "trap" and "birds." On 24 March 1922, Stone wired: "It seems exceedingly difficult to secure the birds you inquired about. Expect info soon." Thereafter, company records become silent on such efforts.[27]

Stone also pursued the UMWA in the courts. In October 1921, during the strike that led to firings, evictions, violence, and tent colonies, Borderland sought a temporary injunction as part of a bill for a permanent injunction against the UMWA and its president, John L. Lewis. The judge first attempted to secure Lewis's agreement to cease all efforts to organize the nonunion coalfields of Mingo County, West Virginia, and Pike County, Kentucky. Lewis refused. So the defendants, Ora Gasaway and W. D. Van Horn—members of the executive board of the UMWA—were enjoined from any further attempts to unionize miners in the Williamson-Thacker field of West Virginia and Pike County. The checkoff system of dues collection also had to cease. The injunction did not prevent the UMWA from paying funds to members living in the tent colonies or to unemployed miners.[28]

The case of *Gasaway and Van Horn v. Borderland Coal Corporation* was appealed, first to the district court, then to the Illinois Seventh Circuit Court of Appeals in Chicago. The district court decided that the UMWA and the operators of the central competitive field (the coalfields of Pennsylvania, Indiana, Ohio, and Illinois) had entered into a conspiracy to violate the Sherman Anti-Trust Act. The court recognized the rights of the West Virginia operators to remain nonunion. The central competitive field operators, hoping the court would decide otherwise, had claimed that nonunion operators maintained a competitive advantage. The attempt to unionize, the court said, was accompanied by "unusual incidents of violence and exhibitions of force; and matters progressed until a state of war existed in West Virginia." The court claimed to have evidence that the UMWA bought firearms and ammunition and financed violent activities out of the dues and checkoff system of deductions from miners' wages. The district court upheld the injunction of the lower court and granted a further injunction against the tent colonies. The case went on appeal to the circuit court.[29]

The circuit court upheld the district court ruling in all matters, except the abolition of the checkoff system. The case then entered the federal courts where, apparently, it died in 1922 when the UMWA abandoned its strike and the tent colonies folded. UMWA officials reported that relief work had cost the union $25,000 per week at the height of the two-year strike and $11,000 per week in the final months. James Woods, vice-president of Borderland and congressman from Virginia's Sixth Congressional District, reported the UMWA was "disintegrating," a view which Woods claimed Lewis had expressed privately. According to Woods's one-sided view, the demise was not the result of antagonism to the principal of unionism but because of "the high handed, drastic and unlawful methods that this particular union adopted to force its arbitrary will upon the country."[30] Union officials gave no estimate of the legal costs involved in pursuing their goals through the courts.

For Stone, the enemy was down but not out. He initiated a brief effort to sue the UMWA for expenses entailed in the injunction proceedings. In 1922, Stone took up the matter of a suit with Woods, who served as legal counsel as well as vice-president at Borderland. Stone hoped to mobilize the Tug River Coal Operators' Association, composed of companies in the Tug District. He explained his intentions to the assistant district attorney of West Virginia, who informed him that a Chicago appeals court would likely reverse any lower-court decision against the UMWA, an opinion offered to Stone by the League for Industrial Rights, one of several companies with which Stone corresponded in his anti-union campaign. Stone also felt that unions should be required to incorporate and report to the Federal Trade Commission or the Interstate Commerce

Commission, just like a business. Perhaps a suit would raise this issue. In the end, he decied that a suit would be too costly, especially since he anticipated having to fight it all the way to the U. S. Supreme Court, at Borderland's expense.[31]

Stone, who had once gloated that the strike in the Tug River District cost the UMWA $2 million, saw his own company slip into bankruptcy in 1932–33. Part of the explanation was the general slump in the industry after 1924 and other economic circumstances peculiar to small coal operations like Borderland. However, a significant factor in the company's demise was the cost to Borderland Coal of fighting the UMWA in the early 1920s. At Stone's request, Armentrout calculated the company had spent $300,000 in its campaign against the union. In a letter to the National Association of Manufacturers in 1925, Stone wrote the following to appear in a circular to be published by NAM:

> Our company, the Borderland Coal Corporation, stood "in the breach" of the last strike that centered around Matewan and Williamson in West Virginia, the cost to our company being something like $400,000 outside of the money expended by and through the Associations and other organizations. We might have been able to recover some or all of this through court proceedings, but . . . after two or three years of strikes, after continuous running, but no profit worth mentioning, the opinion is that the nonunion operators of West Virginia needs [sic] support from every possible source.[32]

Stone fought the UMWA to the bitter end. In 1933, Borderland was in a kind of receivership with its financial affairs being handled by a committee of three men. The treasurer of the committee, L. Franklin Moore, told Stone that labor troubles were over and that the company would have to deal with the union as a result of New Deal legislation if it wanted to stay in business. Stone took issue with the advice and refused to deal with the UMWA, unless the government forced him to do so. He remained convinced that miners did not want to join organized labor.[33]

The history of labor relations at the Stonega Coke and Coal Company was far less tumultuous and ended in the company's acceptance of organized labor. Little is known about labor relations in the early years of SC&C's history. In the company's 1917 annual report, officials took note of the growth of organized labor in the region. In Harlan County, Kentucky, the UMWA was reportedly "making inroads," with one colliery already organized. Near Raven, Virginia, a local had been organized. SC&C officials feared that conditions were going to be "intolerable" until the question was definitely decided and would continue to be "intolerable if recognition is granted." Yet the company did little to avert unionism beyond signing all of its employees up under yellow-dog contracts. The process began in the late summer of 1922 but "was not pushed vigorously until the month of October. By 1 December, the company had completed a contract with each of its employees. The violence and rancor that accompanied the union movement in West Virginia seems absent from the mines of southwestern Virginia, however.

Another hint that the situation was different at SC&C comes from the recollections of the company's former miners. L. F. Minor did not remember any efforts to organize a union in Wise County before 1934. He described the tactics of union organizers mentioned over and over by others in the coalfields, miners and operators alike: a man comes in that nobody knows too well, talks to a few men, attempts to get names on a list, and continues to build the list on the theory that, the more names he can get, the greater the likelihood of adding others. According to Minor, this process eventually led to a strike at the Imboden colliery which continued for a year. Nevertheless, no strikebreakers were brought in, and the mines continued to operate. Why? Because not all the miners observed the strike. Beyond a few fistfights, there was no violence, either. The same levels of tension do not seem to have existed in southwestern Virginia as they did further west, and nonunionism was apparently respected among the Stonega men in the early 1920s.[34]

Fred Gaddis recalled the Stonega colliery as having organized, but not until 1933. SC&C fought the unionization of miners at its collieries with the customary firings and evictions, but in a limited and selective way. Not all who joined the UMWA were treated this way, only the more radical miners such as the outside organizers and those local miners who became organizers themselves. Gaddis also noted a difference at the various collieries of SC&C. Not all of them exhibited the same levels of discontent. At the Stonega colliery, he recalled, the miners were quieter than those at Derby. The evictions were at Derby, not Stonega. When asked to explain the difference, he responded that a number of men objected to the union and that the "whole lot" at Stonega seemed to be loyal to the company for some reason. "I don't understand what it could have been now." The strength of nonunionism at the various collieries of SC&C became even more obvious with the UMWA drive in the 1930s, this time under the protective umbrella of New Deal legislation.[35]

At the Imboden colliery, as at the other mines of SC&C, a serious drive toward unionization began in 1933. About forty years later, Lloyd Vick Minor remembered the drive in terms of the beating of an old man, a Sunday-school teacher with a family and a wife who was in a wheelchair. The man had been "scabbing" at the time, and the union men were determined to put an end to that. Conflict in general escalated at Imboden during this period. State police were called in to keep the peace. They made searches for knives and guns and otherwise tried to stay out of the conflict, unless someone was killed. Union men, organizers from Pennsylvania and West Virginia, "jumped" Minor at the drift mouth one evening and beat him up, too. "Most of 'em were . . . pretty rough characters."[36]

SC&C continued to make life difficult for the organizers in various ways, including the courts, as the following examples illustrate. T. V. Lester, "a very radical agitator," was injured, denied a claim for compensation, fired, and evicted from the company house at Derby. When he retaliated by boring a hole in the base of a small shade tree in the yard of his company house and putting salt in it, he was prosecuted and fined. D. Coldiron attempted to organize workers at the Osaka colliery and was arrested for trespassing. Earl Bowers at Roda assaulted a nonunion man and was arrested, tried, fined, and dismissed from his job. He appealed his case – with uncertain results. In September 1933, during a strike at Derby, which appears to have experienced more conflict than the other collieries, wives and daughters of the miners attempted to picket the drift mouth and were restrained by policemen Cummins and Young. The women charged the officers with assault. The policemen were defended by the company, and "a sympathetic magistrate" fined them ten dollars, which was appealed. The company's annual report of 1933 took note of the labor troubles during the year:

A number of other questions have arisen in connection with all of this labor trouble and I have consulted with the different officials and employees of the Company with reference thereto, and during the period of the strike consulted with the Commonwealth's Attorney and the Sheriff and the Superintendent of the State Police.[37]

The union drive at SC&C continued for the next six years before it was completely successful, even under the protection of New Deal legislation, which by now gave unions the legal right to organize and represent workers. During this time, conflict between union and nonunion supporters continued at SC&C. Ultimately, labor unrest and the union's right to bargain collectively produced strange bedfellows, aligning the company and the union leaders on one side against the nonunion miners on the other. The conflict was worse where the divisions were deepest, such as at Derby. There in 1934 the union managed to get 290 miners to sign cards giving the company permission to deduct union dues from a miner's pay; 207 refused. At other collieries, union sentiment was stronger. At Arno, 143 out of 152 signed checkoff cards; at Imboden, 239 out of 259; at Roda, 530 out of 645; and at Stonega, 110 out of 140 at the mines and 7 out of 71 at the coke yard. Overall, 75 percent of the miners signed checkoff cards. But at the end of the year, the company's annual report noted the continuation of strong nonunion feeling:

> The Stonega Coke and Coal Company still has a very large number of employees who are eligible to belong to the United Mine Workers of America, but who have not yet joined; it is also true that a very large number of loyal employees have joined the Union simply because it was the line of least resistance, and kept them and their families from being heckled by enthusiastic and radical members of the Union.[38]

Holding the miners in the UMWA proved troublesome, also. In 1936, John Saxton, the District Twenty-eight president, wrote to J. D. Rogers, an SC&C vice-president, to enlist the company's help in disallowing members of the union to withdraw their checkoff authorization cards after they had signed, "because the Union needs some protection in the disciplining of the men." Saxton argued successfully that, if the miners were allowed to leave the union whenever they wanted, then every time the union decided against them, they would bolt. Saxton threatened to file a grievance if SC&C refused to enforce the checkoff. The union president promised to reimburse the company for any loss of dues money in the case of anyone who sued for back pay. Rogers replied that Stonega would attempt to checkoff (collect dues from) members but not investigate and decide who was a member, which would embroil the company in a legal controversy with the union and the miners. Rogers also argued that, if a miner wished to return his card, "I think it fair to assume he has ceased to be a member" of the UMWA. "Surely you agree that we should stop making deductions." But the union did not agree, and the checkoff became a part of the Appalachian and Virginia District Agreement between SC&C and the UMWA.[39]

Immediately after the agreement went into effect, a miner sent a letter to the payroll clerk notifying SC&C not to make any further checkoff because he had sued to prevent it. The letter reached J. L. Camblos, the general counsel at Stonega, who reminded the determined miner of the contract with the union, which had an expiration date of 1 April 1937. SC&C was bound to abide by the terms of the contract unless a court decided otherwise. The case was dismissed in court.[40]

Some miners protested being forced into the union. In June 1936, eight-five miners signed an injunction to stop the checkoff from their pay "because of a breach of the agreement on the part of the Roda Local with each of the undersigned, and that false and fraudulent misrepresentations have been made . . . in order to induce them to sign the checkoff." The injunction was sought after the Roda superintendent, at Vice-

President Rogers's request, notified the miners that they could not cease to become members according to the terms of the 1937 agreement. The defendants in the request were SC&C and the UMWA – versus the Roda miners. To older miners who had witnessed the company resort to firings, evictions, and yellow-dog contracts to combat unionization, it must have seemed a world turned upside down.[41]

Conflict between union and nonunion miners continued into 1937. It became especially bad when the old contract expiration date rolled around on 31 March. When the old agreement expired, a new one became effective on 2 April, but it was not settled until 17 April. During this interval, union miners staged strikes and would not permit nonunion employees of the company to work. According to Stonega's annual report: "A very definite effort was made to organize the collieries 100 percent union with the idea of then enforcing a closed shop." Day by day the tension mounted, and "violence was prevented only by extreme precaution on the part of the management at the several collieries." Threats and intimidation forced a construction crew working on a tipple at Stonega to quit. One member of the crew was followed to the bathhouse and assaulted there. At Roda, three pumpers, two of them nonunion, were afraid to enter the mine after threats, and "the company was forced to permit union men to attend these pumps during this period of inactivity." Union pickets, stationed at the mine entrances, walked their posts with pick handles and "other visible weapons." Vice-President Rogers went to union District Twenty-eight headquarters at Norton to protest the violence and unlawful conduct, to no avail. The sheriff of Wise County promised to assure that both union and nonunion men who wanted to work could do so. But, when called upon to curb threatened violence at Roda, he came, took one look, and left. For the two-week interval until the new agreement was signed, "the Company, its non-union employees and its property were entirely at the mercy of this lawless union element."[42]

Even the signing of a new agreement did not end the conflict. Following the signing of the contract on 17 April, all union miners struck and refused to allow the mines to operate "until all non-union men signed up 100%." Such "outlaw strikes" were illegal under the terms of the contract, but the union simply fined every man one dollar per day of the strike. The union miners usually stayed out several days and then returned to work. For example, Dunbar closed on 20 April; Derby 20 to 24 April; Imboden, Roda, and Stonega 21 to 24 April. This unstable situation continued for the two years of the agreement until April 1939 when the contract expired.

The years 1937 to 1939 turned out to be pivotal in the confrontation between union and nonunion supporters. On 17 April 1937, the day the new contract was signed between Stonega and the UMWA, E. P. Humphrey, the Stonega president, notified Harry Meador, the general superintendent of all the Stonega collieries, to notify all company personnel that the Wagner act had been upheld by the Supreme Court.[43] He directed company officials to take a neutral stand in the conflict between union and nonunion forces. In January 1937, before this announcement, Stonega had 2,489 miners eligible to join the union. But only 1,494 were paying dues. In other words, 995 men, or 40 perent of the labor force, were still nonunion. In January 1938, the figure was down to 769 nonpayers, or 30 percent of the labor force.[44]

Under the terms of the 1939 contract, the UMWA was recognized as the exclusive bargaining agent for the miners. Included was a provision "that as a condition of employment all employees shall be members of the United Mine Workers of America" except those designated as management personnel. At the time the new contract was signed, Stonega had approximately 600 men (28 percent of its work force) eligible for membership but not yet members. Stonega gave them until 1 July to join the union. Even though "this order caused considerable dissatisfaction," all but 2 men capitulated and joined.[45] The final breath of nonunionism had been squeezed out of the mines, and the closed shop settled over them until it was made illegal in 1947 under the terms of the Taft-Hartley Act. By then, unionism had a firm foothold, and few wished to return to the bad old days of labor conflict.

The UMWA gradually assumed some of the petty paternalistic functions of the company, such as distributing Christmas treats to children, decorating trees, and handing out candy and other treats. The company cooperated by making deductions (in the form of dues: $5 in 1950, for example) from the miners' wages for these favors.[46] The union also assumed most, if not all, of the functions of voluntary associations. The relief societies of Dunbar, Exeter, and Arno ceased to operate in the 1930s. So too did the Wentz Colored Community League, a society formed at an unknown time for the purposes of "burying of the dead" and "care of the sick" as well as improving attendance at churches and the general improvement of the community at large." [47] In 1946, the UMWA Welfare and Retirement Fund was created. A levy of five cents per ton of coal promised to bring in $25 million per year. One fund was established for retirement benefits; another for medical care, hospitalization, and burial assistance. Members of the Roda Relief Society voted to liquidate after the establishment of the Welfare and Relief Fund and to transfer its funds to the union fund. The Dunbar Relief Society dissolved in July 1949 and distributed its funds on hand to the membership.[48] The Exeter Village Organization, on the other hand, a dues-paying organization "to benefit the citizens of the Village of Exeter," continued to operate as late as the early 1950s.[49]

"And the union came" might be the best way of describing the culmination of years of struggle and conflict. Both the operators and the miners finally welcomed an end to labor friction, which the closed shop brought. W. B. Turner, Sr., who began mining at Docena in 1929 and stayed until 1966, attempted to remain neutral as the UMWA worked to organize the miners. When a strike was called, he remembered staying at home out of fear of getting beat up. He concluded:

> Well, I think they finally realized that the company really would gain by signing a contract and going ahead and recognizing it and working, because they had some order then, when you didn't have a union you had more than one faction and you had disorder all the time because the men were actually fighting one another.

Fred O. Gaddis, who began work in the mines in 1931 at age seventeen and retired in 1973 – he worked part of this time at the Osaka mine – also recalled the 1930s and his efforts to remain neutral:

> Well, I don't know. I got strattling a fence there. I didn't – see, we never had any organized labor in this country, and we didn't understand what it was all about. And had a whole lot of thugs, both sides did, and a whole lot of us were kinda leary about taking sides with either side. . . . the fact of the matter is I still yet going to school, and the company I thought had treated my dad fairly good. About 40 cents an hour back in those days. You could eat. But then in 1937 you got a closed shop, and everybody that worked in the mines had to go in the union. Sign the checkoff they called it. Dues. So then, that stopped so much friction then.

D. B. Oglestree, a miner who came to Docena in 1926, became a union man "after I had to. . . . I had work and had a family and I didn't want to get messed up. So I want the easiest way around." Local men were not as bad "as the outsiders coming in here and trying to make this bunch join the union. . . . most of 'em was bully fellows anyway. Rough bunch." For Oglestree, having to join the union at least offered the benefit of ending the years of tension and conflict.[50]

The mines of the Virginia Iron and Coal Company in St. Charles, Virginia, were organized in the summer of 1933. M. W. "Bud" Clark, who helped to organize 535 members of Local 6376, the first union local to win a strike in Virginia's coalfields, remembers the union coming suddenly, without violence, once VIC decided it was inevitable and agreed to accept a union contract. The union soon claimed 3,400 members and nine locals in St. Charles. However, Bill Ricker, a retired miner, and Junior Oliver, now retired, believe that union strength and success in the southwestern Virginia coalfields have been maintained through the use of violence. In spite of Virginia's right-to-work law, passed in 1947 under the protection of the Taft-Hartley Act, Ricker and Oliver claim police used to look the other way at striker violence against strikebreakers. According to Ricker, "Back then, strikers knew how to deal with workers who crossed picket lines. They'd go to their house and pull them out and whoop them – whoop the union into 'em." Both Ricker and Oliver feel it is harder to win a strike now. "They're letting them walk all over them. They don't do it right. They should get up in the bushes and shoot the hell out of them."[51]

Clearly, the actions of both the union and the operators contributed to the turbulent history of the movement at the individual collieries. In locales where the union targeted an area and sent in outside organizers, such as the Tug River District, operators like Edward Stone put up a fierce resistance, and the trouble often escalated. According to John Luther, a former miner at Thayer, West Virginia, the union would send in its men, and the company would send Baldwin-Felts detectives; the coal miners would, in turn, get their high-powered rifles and set up on the side of the hills and try to pick off the Baldwin-Felts men. "There was so much meanness going on when they didnt' have a union that the company finally gave in to stop it." The Borderland Coal Company fits this model of reaction to the union movement, except it went bankrupt before it gave in. As a company, Borderland modeled its approach after its director Edward Stone, who, from his time as a scrappy copyboy in the newspaper office, had seemed always to be spoiling for a good fight.[52]

SC&C waged a different campaign. Dedicated to contentment sociology, it fought unionization, but with far more restraint and evenhandedness. Stonega encouraged more voluntarism, more freedom for miners to create their own workers' associations, than did Borderland. No evidence of voluntary associations was found in Borderland's company records. Both companies practiced paternalism, but SC&C's was more thoroughgoing and long-lived. Stonega officials exhibited more patience with unionism and reconciled themselves to its coming wheras Borderland fought it to the bitter end. Stonega also benefited by having less pressure from outsiders sent to the area by the union. Its paternalistic concern toward its workers established much goodwill toward the company. Indeed, the flourishing nonunionism in the southwestern Virginia coalfields demonstrated considerable loyalty to the company.

Voluntary associations, whether mutual benefit societies or the union, also revealed the gaps in paternalism, areas of industrial labor where the company assumed little or no responsibility. In 1900 it was common for industry to deny any responsibility for a safe workplace. The courts backed the industrialists by agreeing that, upon hiring, the worker knew the risks of mining. The miners' acceptance of the job was an acceptance of the risks entailed in digging coal. Companies were even more reluctant to assume liability for occupational disease. Until 1969 coal operators refused to even acknowledge its existence. Out of necessity, miners organized to deal with the crises of sickness, accident, and death.

In the union, the miner confronted a great dilemma between freedom and power. Without an organization of workers, the individual miner was at the mercy of the coal operator and the inequities that industrial capitalism could visit upon the powerless. Within a worker's organization like the union, he was empowered by the collectivity of workers. Consequently, the UMWA had a magnetic appeal to helpless miners. It produced greater equity in the workplace and forced the operators to consider their workers in more humane terms. That so many miners joined the union in the face of operator resistance is a measure of its appeal.

Yet the miner's empowerment came at the expense of his individual liberty and control over the organization that claimed to represent his interests. When the operators resorted to rough-and tumble tactics to keep their miners loyal to the company and out of the union, the UMWA organizers believed they had to use similar tactics to win the struggle. Caught in the middle of the struggle was the miner. Just as it required conviction to join, it also took a special person of independence and courage to stand up to the company, the union officials, and even fellow miners to demand the preservation of the absolute freedom of choice. Much more needs to be known about these nonunion men.

UMWA membership in the United States in 1989 stands at only 65,000, active miners down from the 500,000 peak of World War II.[53] It is common to hear the steady decline of union strength explained in terms of the corruption of recent union leadership and the dissatisfaction of the rank and file with their leaders. Perhaps modern anti-unionism owes something to the treatment of nonunion mine workers in the 1930s. Just as the excesses of operators like Edward Stone created converts to unionism, similar excesses of the UMWA organizers may have fed a legacy of nonunionism and even anti-unionism. Technological and economic changes have also contributed to conditions where unions have become "an endangered species."[54]

Regardless of the reasons for the decline in union membership, little joy should be taken in the erosion of union strength. The history of neglect in the coal industry for the health, safety, and welfare of miners and their families and the role of the union in restoring to miners some influence over their workplace demonstrates the importance of the union.

The company town was the habitat of the miner and his family. It is now time to examine this social setting where miners, bosses, and their families lived. The union hall and the corporate boardroom were places where decisions were usually made on behalf of mining families. Certainly it is important to understand how outside forces shaped the world of mining populations. Yet our understanding of life, work, and culture in these towns would be incomplete without hearing from the miners themselves – finding out how they felt about life in coal towns – and without observing the social and economic relationships that actually transformed the towns into active communities.

7   The Company Town: Images and Perceptions

Popular images of company mining towns are universally negative, as anyone familiar with the literary treatment of them will attest. The towns have been described in government studies, newspapers, novels, scattered historical accounts, even pictured in films, and it is not surprising that all have portrayed the "typical town" as a filthy, crowded, and exploitive environment dominated by autocratic coal bosses. What is surprising is that the oral histories of many mining families contain numerous statements that challenge prevailing images. For example, Shirley Young Campbell, who lived in three separate mining communities in the 1920s and 1930s, said: "We had fun in the coal camps. My father was a mine electrician, so the pleasure we found can't be attributed to the fact that we lived in 'one of the big houses on the hill,' because we didn't. . . . Life in a coal town was not always drab or gloomy, as some people may think."[1] Campbell's couching of her convictions in apologetic terms indicates the distance that exists between the perspectives of mining people and outsiders. Repeatedly, oral histories confirm that mining families feel "misunderstood."

The purpose of this chapter is to examine these descriptions and to account for conflicting perspectives on life in the company town. The nature and content of government studies, the persumption of writers that modernization was universally alienating, and a corresponding disregard for the perspectives of the residents themselves have created a formidable sterotype. The disdainful and sometimes contemptuous views of outsiders stand in sharp contrast to many miners' perceptions. Whether the company town was universally good or bad is in the eye of the beholder and matters less than how mining families themselves perceived the company town and, ultimately, how this perception may have shaped their response to industrial life.

Keep in mind that mining families were not reacting to some ideal world of the historic imagination in their evaluations of life in these towns. Their alternatives were not limitless, but bounded by factors of knowledge and resources and conditioned by cultural values like the stable ideal. They may have believed that America was a land of opportunity – I suspect that most did – but they knew the reality of their own limited means and, with a stoic optimism, played the cards that they were dealt.

Examples of the coal-town stereotype include the following descriptions drawn from two separate government studies of mining towns. The first is taken from the Boone Report of 1946, the second from the Rockefeller Report of 1980. According to the Boone Report, the "average" camp had

> monotonous rows of houses and privies, all in the same faded hues, standing alongside the railroad tracks close to a foul creek; or camps like ones farther up the valley, with their scattered houses on stilts, perilously perching, with their privies behind them, on steep hillsides.

A generation later, the Rockefeller commission studied the American coal miner. By 1980, company towns had closed, and the commission members had no firsthand knowledge of company towns. Nevertheless, the study restated the popular image even more emphatically. Historically misleading, accepting the very stereotype it sought to demolish, and not a little patronizing, the report noted that one of the most prevalent images,

> accurate 30 or 40 years ago, when coal companies operated company towns and maintained a kind of feudal relationship with their workers, is that of a downtrodden worker whose life grinds along on the edge of poverty and injury, whose wife is a gaunt and craggy figure surrounded by dirty-faced, ill-clothed children.[2]

Government investigators routinely measured quality of life in the company town on the basis of northern, urban, middle-class standards of housing, sanitation, and leisure. Historically, coal towns never measured up to the "national" standard. For example, in 1925, in the first major federal study of coal towns, the U.S. Coal Commission produced a five-volume study of 880 coal communities in the United States, 167 of which were "independent" towns and 713 "company-controlled" towns, with data on the physical environment and sanitary conditions. The report ranked the company-controlled communities as good, average, or poor based upon a weighted scale, giving the most credit to housing, water supply and distribution, and sewage and waste disposal. Running water, indoor toilets, and a system of garbage removal weighed heavily in the rankings, in spite of the absence of these conveniences in most areas of the rural South. Such factors accounted for nearly two-thirds of an individual community's rating. The rating system was analogous to that of the U.S. Public Health Service whose sanitary surveys the Coal Commission used.[3]

In 1946 the Boone Report enlarged the negative images of company towns with photographs of sanitary conditions in the best and worst camps. A supplementary section entitled "The American Coal Miner and His Family" also contained photographs of the day-to-day life of a "typical" mining family, including miners' homes and surroundings in some of the worst-looking camps to be found. Other photographs showed the miner seated at the kitchen table with his simple fare or sitting in a galvanized washtub taking a crude bath. The survey was done by a group of military officers from the U.S. Navy headed by Rear Admiral Joel T. Boone. The officers spent four months "in the field" inspecting sanitary facilities and dwellings of miners at 260 mines in all major areas of the bituminous coal industry to ascertain the structural quality of houses and the adequacy of sanitary facilities and water supplies.

The Boone Report's standards of judgment were those of the National Housing Agency and the U.S. Public Health Service. Accordingly, all dwellings were supposed to be subdivided into at least two areas, one for cooking and dining and one for sleeping. They should also have fresh potable water; refrigeration; a stove for cooking and heating; safe, artificial lighting; window areas of at least 10 percent of the floor space; proper ventilation; and sanitary garbage and sewage disposal. Housing that did not correspond to these requirements was judged inadequate. In 1947, just as was the case with the earlier study, many of the dwellings in Knott County, Kentucky, in Blount County, Tennessee, and in numerous other areas of the rural South would not have passed the test of "standard" housing.[4]

In 1944, Melba Kizzire, a black miner's daughter, came with her father to the company mining town of Docena, Alabama. She recalled her memories of Docena and what she had left in rural Tennessee:

> We came from a farm in Nyota in Blount County. In Nyota, we lived in just an old wooden house, and here we had it wallpapered, we had running water – it was cold, but we had running water. We had electricity, and we had our sanitation provided for our nice house, our churches, our teachers.... I lived in a wood – a log cabin home in the hills of Blount county, and I came to a brown, painted house. Like, you know, there was paint on *all* four sides and the top. First time I'd ever lived in a painted house. All the rooms were wallpapered with what I thought was the most beautiful wallpaper I had ever seen.... The floors were covered in linoleum, and I had been able to see the chickens through the floor where I lived. I mean it was primitive. And the schools had flushing johns. First time I ever saw a flushing john. First time I ever saw a telephone was when I came here. And I had a lot of firsts wen I moved here.... The houses were warm, had a fireplace in every room.... And to me it was breathtaking, all the wallpaper.... It took me a week to – I was stunned for about a week. It was like I had gone to heaven you know.[5]

To put it in the baldest of terms, counting the number of outdoor privies would not have occurred to mining families as the measure of quality of life in a coal town. Actually, it was not all that unusual for government reformers and writers in America to focus upon the physical setting of the mines. As the following comment on British mining settlements of the nineteenth century shows, a similar process of image building went on in Europe:

> In the traditional mining village or small town, the physical appearance of the place – pit-head buildings, pit-heap, rows of terraced houses, tawdry commercial and public buildings – is immediately striking, and tends to fix an image in people's minds. And indeed for this reason the mining settlement has attracted widespread condemnation, morally by writers and practically by planners seeking to change or erase. Yet surely what is significant for the sociologists is not the surface appearance, the bricks and mortar, the sheerly physical – although these are the most obvious features – but the pattern of economic and social relationships which are developed and which justify describing settlements as mining "communities."[6]

These government studies have provided a wealth of information about coal towns. Upon their completion, the studies became a standard themselves, widely consulted and quoted by those interested in the subject. The clinical and detached manner in which the information was presented lent to them an aura of objectivity and authenticity. Certainly they are indispensable statistical guidebooks, not just to southern Appalachia but to coal communities in both the anthracite and bituminous fields. Anyone interested in the company town would do well to study the reports. Without them, much less would be known about life in the coal towns. However, reformers' standards of judgment differed from those of rural folk of the South who had migrated from conditions inferior to those they found in the company towns.

The difference in perspectives is obvious too with regard to other middle-class ideals. Mine culture did inherit a rural, agrarian attitude toward time; it did not see the necessity of organizing every minute. Such an attitude corresponded with the less acquisitive and materialistic values of rural culture. Simply put, time was not money, at least not primarily. Casual conversation or "visiting" was not a waste of time. Visiting served several ends, including relaxation and enjoyment, exchanging news and gossip, and acquainting community members with one another's needs and problems. Such attitudes did prevail in a rural familial society of folk who lived close to the edge of economic marginality and who therefore needed to maintain instrumental relationships as a strategy for survival.[7]

Such views did not lead adherents into regressive or antimodern economic attitudes or behavior. Clearly, when such things became attainable, many of these people embraced the benefits of modernization in such forms as a Sears and Roebuck washing machine. Radios were also popular with miners. Certainly miners were acquiring consumer tastes as wages put more and more possessions within their economic reach. Gradually, mining families adopted middle-class values. Except in the case of the Rockefeller Report of 1980, however, the miners were not asked their opinions of whether housing was satisfactory, their life more fulfilling, or even whether they felt exploited.

The Boone Report took a disapproving view of the miners' habits of leisure. The major recreational pursuit, the survey noted disdainfully, was "just sitting and talking." In the reproving eyes of outsiders, miners and their families wasted many hours visiting their neighbors, having picnics and family reunions; or the men would just "hang around" the company store, "another popular meeting place." What these miners needed, the naval officers condescendingly noted, was more "organized recreation," more "time of gainful leisure."[8]

Moreover, government reports are static descriptions of typical towns which were themselves neither static nor capable of being reduced to a real model. As I have shown, towns moved through phases of development from their founding to closing. In addition, some operators took pride in well-maintained towns; other paid less heed to living conditions.

Writers have also contributed to the stereotype of the company town. Winthrop D. Lane provides a glaring example. In 1921, Lane, a reporter for the New York *Evening Post* described coal towns in the Guyan River Valley of Logan County, West Virginia, without ever leaving his railroad car. After traveling to other camps in West Virginia, he facilely concluded that life in mining towns in West Virginia was "essentially dreary."[9]

Meanwhile, others have been bemused with the alienation of the miners. Labor historians have emphasized the power of the operators and the powerlessness of the miners to shape their own lives and destinies. A focus upon labor strife implicitly condemns the company town. Also, labor history has stressed such towns' most oppressive features, especially the scrip system, the company store, and the company house.[10]

Many mining families accommodated themselves to life in the company town. The most surprising and least anticipated revelations during this study were the positive expressions of former miners and their families about their mining-town experience.

When Lula Lall Jones was asked if she had anything to add to the comments she had already made in an interview about life and work in a mining town, this black miner's wife responded:

No, I guess that's all. But I know that we had a good time around Rock Lick. . . .
Had anything we wanted, bought anything we wanted to. . . . And the people around
there was just like . . . a bunch of family, just families. If you had something I
wanted, you let me have it. . . . We lived as just one big bunch of family.[11]

Jones remembered how the sharing even extended to clothes borrowed
to attend church, if your favorite outfit was in the wash. Her comments
reflect a vibrancy of community life not usually associated with the
company-dominated coal towns of southern Appalachia.

Most striking about former miners and their families are their positive
recollections of life and work in a company town. Striking because the
historical and literary treatment of coal towns surveyed above points toward mining populations alienated from their culture, living in conditions of squalor and disease, and laboring under the hegemony and social control of "coal barons" or absentee capitalists. Could anyone be
satisfied in such an environment? Mae Prater, who described herself as
not in the group of those who "liked it [life in the camp] real well" but
among those who "liked it well enough," did not express an extreme position
but a realistic appraisal – commonly heard among former town residents –
of one whose alternatives were limited. Furthermore, recollections like
hers came not just from those living in what historians usually refer to
as "model towns," which composed less than 2 percent of coal-mining
towns and affected a tiny fraction of all who lived in the southern Appalachian coalfields, but those from a variety of settings in southern
West Virginia, southwestern Virginia, eastern Kentucky, and northern
Alabama.[12]

Christine Cochran, D. B. Oglestree, and Melba Kizzire grew up in
the coal town of Docena, Alabama. Cochran described the miners as content because mining was "a nice way to make money." It was to the
miners of Docena what the gold rush was to Californians. Oglestree, who
first arrived in 1926, reflected in 1979 upon his first years:

It was real nice. . . . They kept them [the houses] up. They painted them about
every two or three years. They had a nice school up there. And the company furnished teachers. And . . . I don't know, it was real nice, nicer than it is now.

After an incredulous interviewer, obviously in the tow of the popular image of coal towns, asked – to the great amusement of his subject – "Really?"
Oglestree continued:

Yes sir, (laugh), and you had to keep it nice, you couldn't let your yard get messed
up. If you did they sent a man around to clean it up and then made you pay for
it. . . . I liked that part about it because nobody couldn't . . . just let their yards,
ya know, get messed up, like some of them now.

Melba Kizzire, a black miner's daughter, who described Docena earlier, spoke with great poignancy about the town. When asked what struck her most, she responded that

> it was and *is* a very good place to live and bring up a family. People seldom leave. When the older people die out their children take over the homes. . . . The close friendships that I have made for 35 years in the schools and in the churches. . . . And I want my children to grow up in this atmosphere and I'm bringing up my grandson in this atmosphere. . . . And what I came into 35 years ago, I relived this Christmas, which is hospitality, southern hospitality, that could only be learned by living under the hardships of a coal mining community.[13]

Celia Chambers and Dometrius Woodson lived in the coal town at Kaymoor, West Virginia. Because of the rugged terrain, Kaymoor was more isolated than other camps. It was really two towns, Kaymoor Bottom, located at the foot of a steep cliff, and Kaymoor Top, located on top of the cliff. Celia was one of thirteen children from Buckingham County, Virginia. Her brother got a job at Kaymoor, and when she visited him there she met her future husband. They were married in 1926; he was forty-four and she sixteen years of age. They moved into a four-room company house in Kaymoor Bottom, next-door to Celia's brother. They raised two boys, one a nephew and the other an unrelated child, and stayed for twenty-seven years. According to Celia:

> I like it very well. We made a good living down there. We raised hogs, chickens, garden and everything. We got along fine down there. I really was sorry when we moved out from Kaymoor. But after the mine blew out [she may mean "closed"], we had to leave. . . . We had a nice church down there.[14]

Celia said her husband loved to work. He was a good man who never drank, not even coffee or tea. He was the janitor at the church. They had a large garden where they grew corn, beans, cucumbers, and pumpkins. Her hardworking husband fenced "way back up to the top of the mountain" so they could have chickens and hogs. After her husband died, Celia moved to Chicago and for thirteen years was a live-in housekeeper, until 1963. Woodson was equally happy at Kaymoor, where he was a coal miner most of his life, happy "because that's all I know."[15]

Thelma Rotenberry, Jane Taylor, and Carry Mae Marcum lived in company mining towns of southwestern Virginia. Between 1910 and 1937, Rotenberry lived in Arno, Virginia, a company town of SC&C, where her father worked in the mines; Thelma taught school in the area for forty-two years. True, she said in response to my having repeated to her much of the stereotype, the houses were mostly double, two-story dwellings, all of the same design and built side by side in long rows without indoor plumbing. However, many of the other houses in the surrounding area

had no indoor plumbing. Her father rose to the position of superintendent, sent five of his six children to college, and bought a small farm with
his earnings at Arno. "We were taught to live economically and to moder-
ate our life style to be in harmony with other employees, the coal miners
for whom we had great respect," recalled Thelma. She remembered many
families sending their children to Appalachia High School and then on
to neighboring institutions of higher education – the girls to Radford
College, Martha Washington, or Virginia Intermont, and the boys to
Virginia Polytechnic Institute.

Thelma believed that the management of Stonega provided many services for their employees: a well-stocked commissary with food, clothing,
and furniture which the company "never made . . . compulsory," although
her family "was clothed and fed through the years at the company store;
a movie theater "within walking distance of most homes"; and a company doctor for which "each employee paid only a small fee of one dollar
per month and . . . could obtain medicine and medical service anytime
they deemed necessary" (delivery of a baby cost ten dollars). Thelma concluded her letter to me with the following comments:

> My life as a child and young adult spent living in the coal fields was a good one
> and I'm proud to have experienced this mode of life which has passed. People were
> friendly and concerned about each other. . . . I hope you will portray life in the min-
> ing towns in South West Virginia in a more favorable light because I believe this
> is justifiable. Many of us who have spent so many years of our lives in the coal
> mining towns resent being portrayed as low class citizens as well as deprived.[16]

Jane Taylor lived in Roda, another town of the Stonega Company, in
a later period – after indoor plumbing had been installed – having moved
there in 1943. Her father was a payroll clerk, and her mother and father
ran the Roda Post Office. She was only two years old when they moved
to Roda; she graduated from Appalachian High School in 1958. Jane
described the years she spent in Roda as "idyllic" and elaborated:

> We didn't feel deprived – we just didn't know things could be any better. Therefore,
> we were a happy lot and did all of the natural, carefree things that children are sup-
> posed to do. . . . I suppose it was a curious place to live: warm, understanding,
> friendly, but an anomaly too as the blacks had their place to live, the Hungarians
> their place, the Italians theirs, etc., but we all got along. We never threw words
> of race at each other. We were welcome in each other's neighborhoods. We helped
> each other. And played with each other. And cried with each other.[17]

Carry Mae Marcum lived from 1933 to 1954 in the company town of
Pardee, a town of the Blackwood Coke and Coal Company, where her husband Doyle was a miner. In 1954 they moved to Big Stone Gap, where
her husband finished his working years as a miner for the Stonega Com-

pany in 1966. Altogether, Doyle worked fifty years in the mines, having begun at the age of twelve. They raised eight children and had two sons get degrees in engineering at Virginia Polytechnic Institute, something of which Carry is justifiably proud. At Pardee, the family lived in a three- or four-room house with electricity, an outdoor well and pump for every four or five houses, and outdoor privies. However, Carry was quick to add, "We were better off than those back in the hollows on poor farms." In the coal town, they raised three or four hogs each year, had their own butter and eggs, and Carry sold milk to the management employees at Pardee. Many miners had gardens in the hills. Carry recalled a variety of leisure-work activities common to working-class culture, including apple pickings, bean stringings, corn shuckings, cannings, and hog killings. Pitching horseshoes, organizing baseball teams, shooting marbles, and scouting in the bigger areas were pastimes. Periodically, the church had an all-day meeting with "dinner on the grounds" of the cemetery and "much preaching and singing." Listening to news or "Amos 'n' Andy" on the radio were other forms of entertainment, she recalled. She looked back upon her life in coal camps as "sweet and good" and concluded, "I'd go back and live the same life again and not make many changes."[18]

Cora Frazier, a schoolteacher in the mining camps of eastern Kentucky during the 1920s, recalled that the miners lived "really well." The children were clothed and fed well, the houses were all kept in good condition, especially at Neon, Kona, and Millstone. Teachers in the company towns she lived in received a hundred dollars per month compared to seventy-five dollars for county teachers. The Great Depression changed all of this. Marvin Gullet, also of eastern Kentucky, admitted the work was hard, that work conditions could be difficult, but miners came from a tradition of hard work on the farm: "People at that time was content with their living because the people was all satisfied. They didn't want to leave." The Rockefeller commission echoed many of these comments when it quoted the wife of a Harlan County miner:

> I really liked it in the coal mining camps. It was just one big family. All the houses were sort of close together. Everybody knew each other. If you had a problem, they had it. Everybody went to the same church. Everybody had the same occupation. We all had the same things in common. Nobody considered themselves better than others because they all made the same. I think everybody got along better.[19]

Later, in the last years of the company-town era, the Stonega Company conducted an opinion poll of its miners. Rarely do historians enjoy the luxury of having the subjects of their work questioned about their attitudes. This is especially true for ordinary men and women, the so-called "inarticulate." In 1951, however, SC&C, which employed the majority of miners in Virginia, contracted with an outside agency to conduct a poll of its workforce. The pollsters randomly selected and interviewed 137 miners of the Stonega Company, all members of the United Mine Workers of America. The miners were interviewed in their homes in the company towns of Roda, Imboden, Stonega, Derby, Glenbrook, and Pine Branch, and were promised anonymity. At the time of the survey, SC&C had 3,181 on the company payroll; three-fourths of those lived in fourteen communities selected for the survey. A total of thirty-eight questions were asked, five of which were "essay" questions.[20]

The extent to which miners had come to embrace the benefits of modernization can be inferred by looking at their possessions as indicated in the poll. Out of the approximately 130 miners, most (123) had radios, electric regrigerators (107), and electric washing machines (106). Fewer (57) had cars, books (52), sewing machines (38), and pianos (5). Not only do these possessions show that miners had become consumer-oriented, they also indicate that those who were able to persist as mine workers did quite well.

According to the opinion survey, the Stonega employees had a high regard for the company and their work. Miners felt that their work was well planned and organized (103 out of 135) and safe (127 of 132) and that top management was interested in them (116 of 127). In general, they were satisfied with their work (131 of 135) and preferred to keep their present job (113 of 135). Living conditions in the (by now) aging company towns were not as satisfying, but even so, surprisingly few still considered it a bad place in which to live (13 of 121). A stunning 84 percent rated Stonega as good, 16 percent as fair, and no one rated it as a poor company to work for.[21]

Only in one area did miners appear uninformed: the overall operation of the company. Few could answer how many tons of coal the company mined in the previous year (1 guessed two million, another three billion, and 30 did not attempt an answer), the number of stockholders in the company, or the names of the officers of the company. Only 18 could name the President, E. B. Leisenring, Jr., of Philadelphia. Very few (3 of 133) had ever seen a company financal statement, though many (107 of 130) expressed a desire to do so.[22]

The Stonega miners did have complaints, of course. They complained about the condition of the tracks, the lack of cars, and rock in the mines. In the town of Stonega there were complaints about the flooring, ceiling, and the size of houses. At Roda miners wanted bathrooms and complained of uncollected trash, the lack of house repairs, and poor water. At Imboden and Exeter they talked of the poor quality of the water; also, uncollected trash, camp life, bad water, a cold house, and swampy low places drew complaints from at least one person each. At Derby they felt the need for bathrooms, a playground, and more frequent trash removal. And at Pinebranch they wanted additional recreational facilities. Some criticised management for allowing rural people as casual labor.[23]

A number of complaints centered upon relations between the company and the United Mine Workers of America. Miners criticised management for hiring rural people in the mines who came in and did most of the "wildcatting," that is, an unorganized walkout of miners for petty reasons. Apparently, casual day labor was more prone to this sort of activity because of its impermanent status and relative independence. Both union and management came in for criticism: "The management let the unions get too strong a hold in the beginning." "It looks like the union runs the company." "The miner might be more sympathetic toward a company who seemed to want to better their conditions, even if it didn't meet John L. Lewis's demands. . . . Satisfied miners are better workers." "Unions, when they have a grievance, seem to go about everything wrong. All they know how to do is to strike and don't think of talking to management." Unions should "stick to the contract." "Lots of times the men are more at fault than the company." "Quit wildcatting."[24]

As these complaints demonstrate, miners took a rational, independent, and self-interested position between management and the union. The feeling was almost universal that both management and labor should work together for the good of all, control their tempers, work out disagreements and avoid the costly wildcats and lengthy grievance procedures that had come to plague the industry by 1951.

A common concern of miners in the survey was their public image. The public had an image of miners as "wild men," and many felt "it would be wonderful to convince the public that miners are a decent, law-abiding and respectful group of citizens." For this reason, 130 out of 136 miners wanted the company to publish a newsmagazine in which employees and their families would have a chance to contribute ideas and articles, and in which news about employees and their families and about the company would be published. A significant number (120 out of 180) even volunteered to take part. As a result, *The Stonegazette,* a company tabloid newspaper, was published in 1951 and lasted for an indeterminate period. In addition, nearly all (126 of 128) expressed an interest in a weekly radio program over a national network devoted entirely to the coal industry. Such a program would allow miners the opportunity to express their own views and would provide information on conditions in the industry. The results of the survey indicated, therefore, that miners were concerned about negative images and vitally interested in presenting themselves in a more positive light to the public, especially in the local area.[25]

Town of Exeter. Courtesy of Westmoreland Coal Company Archive, Hagley Library.

Town of Keokee. Courtesy of Westmoreland Coal Company Archive, Hagley Library.

Town of Stonega. Courtesy of Westmoreland Coal Company Archive, Hagley Library.

An examination of photographs of the company towns in this study provides some visual evidence that the miners' perceptions of being better off were justified in many cases. The towns of Keokee and Exeter reveal neat, well-kept houses on fenced lots located at some distance from the railroad and coke ovens. The lots included areas for gardens, and the roads provided easy access to churches, schools, and the company store. The town of Imboden also had well-maintained houses, but the lots seem smaller, and the railroad tracks are closer to the houses. The town of Stonega was situated in a narrow valley and, although the housing seems well maintained, it bordered the tracks and extended in an elongated line down the valley without any sense of a town center. Borderland provides an example of small houses that were poorly constructed and maintained and located adjacent to the tracks, with limited town facilities. In 1985, I visited Docena and found residents still living in the houses they had formerly occupied as miners. The town was designed around an open center with spatial separation from the mines and tipple facilities. Schools, churches, and the company store bordered the open center, which was used as a recreation area.

The attitudes expressed in these oral histories and the Stonega opinion survey stand in sharp contrast to the popular images of coal towns. Must we conclude from these sources that mining families were incapable of understanding their own social situation? It would be foolish and arrogant to make such a claim and to ignore the commentary of hundreds of miners. David Potter has reminded historians that the advantage of hindsight can really be a disadvantage in understanding how a situation appeared to the participants. The task of the historian, and one of supreme difficulty, is "to see the past through the imperfect eyes of those who lived it.[26] Should we conclude that company paternalism befuddled miners and their families into a languid acceptance of the status quo? Miners were rational people who accepted paternalism as something in their best interests. Out of this intersection of self-interested operators—who wanted a dependable labor force—and self-interested miners—who had their own agenda for their life, work, and culture—emerged a work culture that both parties had a hand in shaping.

The contradictions between miners' perceptions and observers' views is more readily understood by examining the historically conditioned biases of both groups. Government investigators and writers were products of middle-class life and culture who could not easily identify with their subjects. Coming from more privileged backgrounds, they tended to focus upon the amenities of life, which they had taken for granted as the American standard. In this view, spacious and comfortable homes,

Town of Imboden. Courtesy of Westmoreland Coal Company Archive, Hagley Library.

running water, convenient garbage and sewage disposal, and education were the measures of success and achievement. Implicitly, the yardstick used to exalt the achievements of middle-class culture to a national standard simultaneously both condemned the other America that failed to meet the standard and, implicitly, exonerated middle-class bureaucrats from any responsibility for social and economic inequality. In the middle-class view, status was simply a matter of individual achievement. Middle-class writers, more critical, sensitive, and introspective, still found it easier to criticise the operators than the national government or the "free" enterprise system for creating the conditions of national neglect that had produced appalling poverty and inequality in the South and conditioned the working class to believe that escape was merely a matter of individual merit and effort.

As for the miners and their families, life and work in coal towns must be seen in relationship to living and working conditions in the rural South at the time. Low wages, inferior housing, the scarcity of medical and dental care, rural isolation and loneliness, and the general hopelessness about the future of farming gave coal-town residents a perspective on their situation different from that of persons outside of this experience. Preindustrial Appalachia was no golden age of pastoral bliss, at least not for the transplanted, not for Mae Prater's family of Knott County, Kentucky, or Melba Kizzire's of Blount County, Tennessee. Such are the reasons why "analytical primacy" should be granted to the participants' perspectives – how they saw their own social situation, conditions of living, circumstances of work, and their measures of fulfillment and achievement – rather than using the yardstick of either an ideal world or irrelevant middle-class standards.[27]

Still, it is not necessary to deny the oppression that did exist in the company town, both above- and underground, in order to affirm that the company town has been stereotyped. David Corbin interviewed scores of miners who complained of entrapment through the scrip system, monopolistic company-store practices, price-gouging, disregard for the safety of underground workers, eviction from company houses, blacklisting, and a wide range of other antilabor practices.[28] The Borderland Coal Company, as I have shown, was a model of labor repression in the Tug Valley of West Virginia. In this chapter, I have presented much evidence of accommodation. The boundaries of resistance and accommodation are more difficult to discern. Evidence of alienation is readily available, whereas accommodation is subtle and obscure. Yet both must be recognized and explained. Clearly, the rural world from which mining families migrated figured largely into their assessments of and reactions to the company town.

Resistance and accommodation were both responses to conditions in the company town. Recognizing the existence of nonunionism is only a first step toward a full understanding of these conditions. What labor historians must provide is a more satisfying explanation of why some miners resisted while others did not. How are resistance and accommodation related to the formation of a mine work culture? What role did the composition of the labor force play in periods of "quiescence and rebellion"? Is there a generational perspective on life in the company towns that would explain patterns of accommodation and resistance?

During their free time, mining families provided the most intimate view of mine culture – in the form of leisure activities. Perhaps more than in any other arena of their lives, miners at play were able to create their own world.

8   Leisure

Race, ethnicity, sex, age, and marital status were structural components of every coal-town population. Sometimes they merely described the composition of the town. At other times, as when they intersected with cultural ideals, company paternalism, or the physical requirements of heavy industrial labor, they influenced or caused changes in the social environment. Saloons characterized the earlier years when drinking and gambling – by young single males, who dominated the first generation of mine labor – were common. As the operators launched their search for more family men, the sex, age, and marital status of the towns changed dramatically. As families, coal-town residents spent their spare time in theaters, billiard parlors, bowling alleys, or in more familiar activities like baseball, picnics, and visiting. Theaters, bowling alleys, playgrounds, and dance halls were rare in the pioneer phase of development. During the immediate prewar years, they mushroomed as the operators sought competitive advantages in a scarce labor market.

Gradually, a mine work culture evolved that was not a creation entirely of either company paternalism, preindustrial values, structural components, or the demands of mine labor, but a combination of all of these ingredients. Fundamentally, it was a male-dominant culture.

In the coal towns for which I have information in West Virginia (Kaymoor, Thurmond, Elverton, Glen Jean, South Caperton, Rock Lick, Concho, Thayer, Elmo, and Quinnimont), eastern Kentucky (Wheelwright and Yellow Creek), southwestern Virginia (Arno, Dunbar, Exeter, Imboden, Keokee, Osaka, Roda, Stonega, Borderland, and Pardee), and northern Alabama (Docena), miners participated in an extensive social life. Varied though it was from town to town, some forms of leisure were so common as to be almost universal. Visiting, exchanging news and gossip at the company store, picnicking, going to the movies, and playing baseball are some of the most frequently mentioned activities, widely practiced even in the most isolated towns.

Baseball was the miners' sport. Sports played a leading role in mining areas of nineteenth-century England, too, especially organized football, or what Americans call soccer. It was the miners' sport in British working-class communities as baseball was in the United States. British mining villages had their own teams, colors, and songs. Even if a remote village did not have its own team, miners would identify with a nearby team. The feeling was often intense. Extra police had to be called in for games involving close rivalries. Contemporaries noted how the mood of the entire village depended upon whether the soccer team won or lost. Some even claimed that it was successful in weaning miners from the bottle. Baseball served similar purposes in the coal towns of Appalachia, although it probably contributed to as much drinking as it discouraged. Mae Prater recalled with pride the colors of her father's baseball uniform. Coal companies became involved – as a public-relations ploy – in the recruitment of players and the success of the teams.[1]

Between 1920 and the 1950s, industrial towns throughout Appalachia and the South had baseball teams.[2] In southern West Virginia, "nearly every coal town had a baseball team." Teams "were in county leagues, some in a United Mine Workers league, some in black leagues, and some in no organized leagues at all."[3]

In the larger towns of Williamson, Bluefield, Beckley, and Charleston, players were Class D professional in the Mid-Atlantic League. Some coalfield players went on to major-league teams and stardom. The famous Stan Musial of the St. Louis Cardinals played for Williamson in Mingo County; others – like Buford Tudor, who played for twenty years in Raleigh County – turned down contracts to play in Class D because it paid only fifty to seventy-five dollars a month, and they were making more in the mines. In the 1930s, Raleigh County had two county leagues, a UMWA league, and "a more loosely-organized league of all black teams." Black teams were organized in separate leagues, but they did play white teams. They also played over a wider geographic area than white teams did.[4]

Before World War II, the Sunday-afternoon baseball game was a major social event in coal towns. Hilton Garrett, a black former miner from the town of Wheelwright, Kentucky, answered the question "What did people do on holidays back then?": "Well, most of the time, they have a ballgame. That's what they mostly had, a ball game on a holiday." Garrett believed it was common to recruit miner-players from other places and give them "a real easy job to do." Such favoritism was more common for whites, who enjoyed "special privileges. . . . They didn't do nothing for the colored." Everett Hall supported Garrett's claim that the company hired some miners because they were baseball players. The Tennessee Coal and Iron Company (Docena) had thirteen white and fifteen black amateur baseball teams.[5]

In 1916, Stonega boasted the champion baseball team of the Coal Fields League. Kaymoor's well-known team played in Kingston, Scarbro, and Glen Jean against the miners' teams from those towns. Dometrius Woodsen of Kaymoor said that coal operators used to hire miners in Kentucky who were good ball players and bring them to Kaymoor. The operators lured good players from neighboring mines with offers of higher pay, better schedules, lighter work above ground, and afternoons off for practice. Over five hundred people attended the Sunday-afternoon games of teams like the New River Giants and the Raleigh Clippers.[6]

The Reverend Stuart Frazier, a black minister from the West Virginia coalfields, recalled Thurmond as a town with a lot of restaurant, beer parlors, and baseball teams. Ada Jackson of Concho remembered the Concho miners going to Ames, Glen Jean, and other places to play baseball. The women of Concho also had a softball team, which played in Thurmond and elsewhere. Usually women attended the games with children; some cooked large meals of fried chicken, potato salad, and hot bread to feed out-of-town players between the game and the long train ride back to their own towns. Chan Forren of Elverton said he went to Thurmond nearly every weekend to play baseball. He continued:

> If you was a good ballplayer, you'd get a job anywhere. I mean these superintendents, these mines would hire you if you was a good ballplayer. Because that was about the only sport that people had to watch, and . . . the coal companies would sponsor ball clubs, and buy them uniforms and everything. So about all of them did have ball clubs and they'd come to Thurmond, or play their neighbors up the track or down the track. . . . everybody backed their baseball teams. . . . That's where they had a lot of fun on Sunday afternoon, watching those ball teams, and drinking beer and moonshine.[7]

Some of the same forces that transformed coal-town life in general also account for the decline of baseball. The Conclusion treats these forces in detail, but three must be mentioned here. Unionization in the 1930s, World War II in the 1940s, and the closing of the company towns in the 1950s greatly weakened the sport of baseball in the coalfields. When the UMWA organized the miners, the coal operators ceased to sponsor teams, buy uniforms, and organize leagues. Without company backing, the number of teams dwindled. World War II siphoned away many young players, and when the men returned, they no longer had the same interest in baseball. In the 1950s, the closing of the company towns virtually ended the sport. With the demise of the company town, the baseball team lost its identity, support, and spectators. The automobile and television also played a role, as they did in changing other aspects of coal-town life, by providing alternative forms of recreation.[8]

Visiting constituted another favorite pastime of miners. Men spent a considerable amount of time together as did women. Visiting is mentioned in numerous interviews of women who were residents and is common in the interviews of men. Mae Prater indicated that women frequently got together after the men had left for the mines and the children for school. Men gathered to play guitars, banjos, and fiddles. At Roda, thirty miners formed an active, uniformed band that gave concerts in homes. According to an Imboden miner, many miners wanted a banjo or guitar, but only a few were lucky enough to have one. Card parties in homes were occasions for gathering to sit around, drink coffee, play cards, and, most of all, talk. Reuben Barnes of Docena talked of family days and get-togethers, such as reunions or picnics. Unlike more modern society, with its highly organized recreational activity of a decidedly spectator nature, working-class leisure offered more casual and participatory forms.[9]

Visiting took place in a variety of settings and circumstances. Church socials, picnics, Saturday-night dances, playground encounters, baseball games, union or company get-togethers, movie theaters, bathhouses, school yards, run-ins at the country store, even the mines themselves – virtually every place where mining people came together could become an occasion for visiting. Marvin Gullet reported that, on days off, men sat around the commissary steps and talked to one another. Joseph Tony of Big Stone Gap recalled:

> Well – when they weren't a working the people would gather up around the commissary and on the porches and then they'd have places on the road tracks – where the mining camps were or at these shops – men would go out and play set-back, play for matches – is what they'd play for. They'd talk. They'd do a lot of talking in the mines. When you was working with a man and you'd run into somebody you knowed and then two or three would get together.[10]

In addition, there were the more purposeful events such as apple-pickings, bean-stringings, and a host of other work-sharing sessions. Baptisms, weddings, funerals, and other church celebrations brought them together for still other purposes; but, whatever the occasion, visiting was a central feature of life and work in coal towns.

Men, and sometimes women, found relaxation in hunting and fishing. Many interviews mentioned this form of leisure over and over again. T. B. Pugh of Thayer, West Virginia, recalled going up on top of the mountain to hunt raccoon at night; favorite game for day hunting were possum, rabbit, squirrel, and groundhog. Fishing in the surrounding rivers and streams brought satisfaction as well as food to others. Leisure of this type was very much in keeping with rural habits and folkways and offered endless opportunities for visiting.[11]

Mining people also listened to the radio, read magazines, and went to the movies. In 1951, the public opinion survey of the Stonega Company (discussed in the previous chapter) chronicled these activities. In spite of the public image of miners as backward, the survey indicated a broad contact and familiarity with popular culture. Most had radios and favored such programming as preaching or religious services, news, and "hillbilly" music— in order of importance. Miners listened to the "Grand Ole Opry" on the radio, enjoyed Dale Evans and Betty Grable as their favorite entertainers, rated *Gone with the Wind* as their favorite movie, and subscribed to *Life* magazine. Other favorites, along with a variety of comic books, included comedy and detective radio programs, stars of movie westerns and country music, adventure movies, and a variety of specialized and general-interest magazines.[12]

Sometimes leisure came to the miners. Stonega, for example, sponsored a black gospel quartet that went from town to town and sang at union and company get-togethers. Sometimes vaudeville shows, like the *Fox Sunshine Comedy*, came out of Washington, D.C., to the Virginia coalfields. At Docena, a group called the "Fa, So, La Singers" performed at the camp. Minstrel shows also visited the coalfields and nearby towns. The Silas Green minstrel show came from New Orleans on a railroad car, set up a tent, and played on Saturday nights. They paid twenty dollars to use a local lot, charged fifty cents admission, and got large crowds.[13]

Sometimes miners left the coal towns for leisure. Miners' wives and daughters took shopping trips to nearby towns and larger cities. Maybelle Harris of Kaymoor, for example, would walk to a nearby town, cross a swinging cable bridge, and catch the morning train to Charleston, returning in the evening to Kaymoor. Playing baseball teams in other towns was common, and often entire families traveled to watch. Train transportation between the many coal towns along the New River in southern West Virginia meant that many forms of leisure activity were merely a short ride away. While Keeney's Creek, because it was a small operation, had only a company store, nearby Elverton had a movie theater which Keeney's Creek residents attended. Nuttall, also close by, had a movie theater, a store, and a church.[14]

Towns like Thurmond and Glen Jean offered still other possibilities. Trains that traveled Loup Creek touched many coal towns, and Thurmond was "sort of a terminus." The Dunglen Hotel in Thurmond was the Las Vegas of West Virginia. Coal operators often met there with buyers for the company stores, salesmen, businessmen, and miners. Card games, gambling, drinking, and other forms of activity were readily available. According to a former porter: "You could get anything you wanted, and some people got lots of things they didn't want." The rich used the higher floors, and "street people" were not allowed on them. On weekends, the trains stopped every two hours. At Glen Jean, an ornate opera house was frequented by operators. Miners were more often seen at the saloon,

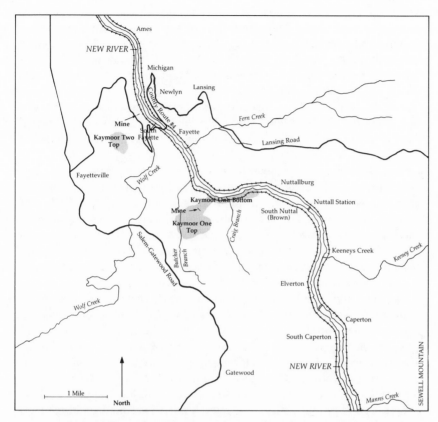

Towns in the New River Gorge of West Virginia. Courtesy of Eastern National Park and Monument Association.

drugstore, or ball park. The opera house was built by Bill McKell, a Scotchman who also owned a railroad, and operas were actually performed there. Chautauqua players and singers also visited Glen Jean and put on plays. Thus, miners were not always confined to the leisure activities of their own settlements.[15]

Drinking was an activity in the coal towns that disturbed some, like Mae Prater, and was always present in some measure. It is impossible to gauge the extent of this activity, but it was more often associated with the young and unattached miners than with family men. As might be expected, some drank to excess, others in moderation, and still others not at all. In various areas, illegal whiskey, called moonshine, was readily available. An Elverton miner, for example, said that moonshine could be easily gotten in the nearby hollow where mostly blacks made it. Scrip was used to buy it, and then the makers would take the scrip to the company store to buy the sugar and corn for the mash. Celia Chambers of Kaymoor claimed that most made it themselves because it was cheaper than buying it. She continued: "I had lots of friends down there and a lot of them were Christian people and didn't indulge that stuff and I didn't either. That is the way it was."[16]

Opinion varied among the operators whether to encourage or discourage drinking. Justus Collins, who operated the Superior Pocahontas Coal Company, reported in 1909 that one of his colliery managers, one P. J. Riley, was attempting to get the county court of McDowell to reverse itself and issue a saloon license. In spite of Superior owning one-half interest in the saloon, Collins "never relished the idea" of using the saloon to control labor, which was Riley's intention. In 1912, Collins received a report from a Baldwin-Felts agent that it was costing his company as much as seven dollars per carload to produce coal because the night shift was carrying whiskey into the mines and doing a lot of sleeping on the job. Then too, quarrels, fights, shootings, and other acts of violence were often associated with excessive drinking.[17]

Schools, dance halls, lodges, churches, movie theaters, and especially company stores were major centers of social life. Besides containing the grocery store—or the "commissary" as miners called it—the company store in many towns combined under one roof a variety of activities. Reuben Barnes, who came to Docena in 1926, recalled the company store as housing a white social club with a dance hall upstairs. Downstairs were a concession stand; pool tables; a store with hardware, dry goods, groceries, and patent medicines; and a library. Docena even hired a "social science director." One day per week the clubhouse was off limits to men, and the pool and game tables were reserved for women. Normally, the building opened at 7:00 A.M. for miners to buy cigarettes, candy, or ice cream; shoot pool; read a book; or play a game. It was "just a general meeting place during the week."[18]

Some forms of leisure suggest the encouragement of the operators, especially those forms customarily associated with middle-class families. At Docena, for example, the company store served as a meeting place for the more organized groups, such as Boy and Girl Scout troops, Brownies, and a story-hour circle, something that would have impressed the gainfully leisured. Edith Shoemaker, whose father came to Docena in 1908, recalled Saturday-night dances with live music and one festival called "Dance of All the Countries" where students from each classroom would dress up and stage a dance for the country it represented. For her the commissary was "a well remembered place." Belinda Mardis, a black miner's wife, had fond memories of Whist parties and games at the commissary in "our own little socializing department."[19]

Mining families in the Stonega fields appreciated the facilities for leisure, and Stonega officials responded with additional efforts. L. F. Minor recalled that, when he came to Imboden in 1908, he found school buildings at every colliery. Children did not have to "go away from the place to school." School buildings often served leisure as well as educational purposes since they could also be used when school was not in session. In addition, there were tennis courts, croquet fields, ball grounds, grandstands, and ball teams. In the 1915 Stonega annual report, company officials noted: "People living at the plants where we have built theaters and equipped them with moving picture apparatus have appreciated them." At Keokee, the company remodeled an old power plant, a building sixty feet long, forty-three feet wide, and with a twenty-five-foot ceiling. A ten-foot-wide stage was built at one end with an arrangement for curtains. At the rear a fifteen-foot-wide area was partitioned for a ticket office, machine room, and stairway to the gallery above, probably for segregated seating. Christmas Eve marked the formal opening. The next year the company did the same at Stonega. In 1917, Stonega built playgrounds at several of its large collieries on an experimental basis. When they discovered that adults liked them too, they decided it was a good idea. The annual report noted: "Men well up in years and in many cases women came out, joining in the games and every evening when the weather was favorable, large audiences were at the playgrounds participating in the amusements as spectators or in conversation with their friends." Thus, the company vowed to enlarge the playgrounds in 1918 and to build others. Stonega also built bathhouses for its workforce. By 1921 every colliery had one. Not centers of leisure, they nevertheless brought miners together before and after work and served as places of casual conversation.[20]

Church and related activities occupied the time of a smaller number of mining families (see chapter 10). Stonega, with a total 1916 population of 2,470 (500 of whom were black), or 456 families, had a Catholic Church with two resident priests; white Methodist, Presbyterian, and Baptist churches; a Hungarian Presbyterian church; and black Baptist and Methodist churches. According to Mae Prater, church attendance was small because mining families had so many more alternatives for socializing than farm families did. This does not necessarily mean that mining families failed to take religion seriously. In fact, Prater revealed her deep religiosity at the end of her interview. Moreover, the preference of mining families for religious programs on the radio speaks to their widespread interest in religious matters. Nearly always, when the subject of religion

COLORED
FIRST AID CONTEST
AT
Andover, Virginia
FRIDAY, AUGUST 8th, 1924

TWELVE TEAMS--6 MEN EACH
of Stonega Coke & Coal Co. Employees will compete.
A prize for every team also special prizes.

Contest Will Be Held at Stonega Ball Ground beginning at 1 p. m. sharp

Music by Brass Band.   Speaking by "Bob Clay" of Bristol.
Foot Race $5.00; Relay Race $9.00; Wheelbarrow Race $6.00; Singing Contest $15.00.

BALL GAME
DUNBAR vs. STONEGA

Over $400.00 given in Cash Prizes to only Colored Employees of Stonega Coke and Coal Company.
All people present at 1:00 o'clock p. m. will receive a number, three of which will draw prizes.

Refreshments and Eats Served on the Ground by Stonega Methodist Church.

MAKE YOUR PLANS TO COME

Andover handbill, 1924. Courtesy of Westmoreland Coal Company Archive, Hagley Library.

COLORED
CELEBRATION

AT

Andover Ball Field

SATURDAY, August 8, 1931

ATHLETIC EVENTS

Greasy Pole	$ 5.00
Greasy Pig	Keep the Pig
Wrestle Royal	$10.00
Women's Race	$ 3.00
Tug-of-War	$15.00
Boy's Sack Race	$ 2.00
Men's Relay Race	$ 5.00
Wheelbarrow Race	$ 4.00
Dancing Contest	$ 5.00
Base Ball	$40.00

Music By The DUNBAR BAND

Andover handbill, 1931. Courtesy of Westmoreland Coal Company Archive, Hagley Library.

EMANCIPATION CELEBRATION

at Stonega Ball Ground
Tuesday, August 8th, 1922
Under Auspices Mt. Olive Church Organization

Public Speaking, Barbecue, First Aid Contest, Ball Game, Athletic Events. "Bob Clay," of Bristol, will deliver an address in the afternoon.

The Stonega Coke and Coal Company will give in cash prizes over $200.00 for teams from their various collieries competing in First Aid Contest.

Also cash prize of $25.00 to winner in Base Ball Game; $5.00 to winner in 100 Yard Dash, and various other cash prizes in Athletic Events to be announced later. All these contests are open to any colored employee of the Stonega Coke and Coal Co. The church invites you to join them in making this a big day. Make your plans to come.

Appalachia Printing Co. Appalachia Va

Stonega handbill, 1922. Courtesy of Westmoreland Coal Company Archive, Hagley Library.

FREE SHOW

At_____

COAL MINERS and FAMILIES!

SEE THESE MOVIES!

Black Bullets   Railroaders Always

Hear Interesting Talks By

Three Wounded Veterans

Former Coal Miners

Listen To Them   *Talk With Them*

General Public Invited

Help combat Absenteeism in Coal Mines. Fight
the War on the home front.

**These Shows Arranged by the U. S. Army in Cooperation
with the War Manpower Commission, United Mine Workers
of America, and the Coal Operators Associations**

Buy Bonds

Stonega handbill, 1943. Courtesy of Westmoreland Coal Company Archive,
Hagley Library.

came up, those being interviewed mentioned a church, either in the coal town or in a nearby town. Christmas pageants, youth socials, groups for men and for women, all of these activities and more occupied the time of mining families interested in participating.[21]

As we noted in the previous chapter, when outsiders viewed the coal town they saw the physical structure: the rows of simple weatherboard houses, the outdoor privies, the water and sanitation problems, and little else. Outsiders had no appreciation for the great variety of leisure activities that engaged miners; some forms, such as visiting, government reformers viewed as little more than ways to "kill time."

Although it appears that traditional forms of leisure dominated, the coal town did incorporate newer forms of leisure activity, what the middle class entitled "gainful leisure." Such pastimes as garden and bridge clubs, literary societies, and scouting organizations emerged on a small scale. Unlike home visitation or even baseball, these activities were more likely to bring together members of varied social groups. Beyond mentioning the organizations, however, oral histories and company records give little evidence of social mixing across lines of race and class, regardless of the activity, and they give substantial proof of race segregation and class division in all areas of town life.

The heterogeneity of the coal-town population – blacks, whites, foreigners – was a potential source of social tension. In the pioneer phase of development, the higher concentrations of young, unmarried males and the prevalence of drinking and gambling added to the chances that disagreements would lead to outbreaks of violence. World War I and the growth of families diminished the frequency of gambling and excessive drinking. The war also brought greater homogeneity as large number of immigrants left the towns. Social distance between the black mining population and the dominant white culture was preserved through residential segregation and racial separation in leisure activities.

In addition to having separate baseball leagues, as handbills reveal, black miners had separate holiday celebrations. Black miners at Stonega, for example, observed an annual "emancipation celebration" which they held on 8 August each year. It featured a barbecue, a baseball game, athletic contests, first-aid contests, drawings for prizes, and public speeches. Presumably, other ethnic minorities and whites had their own unique celebrations too, although no public notices were found in the records of the Stonega Company marking the occasion, unlike the case with blacks.

Coal towns also had separate rescue teams, one for black and another for white miners. First-aid or rescue-team meets were held on an annual basis throughout the coal fields. The teams faced mock disasters and were judged according to the way they handled the disaster and their response time. These contests – as much social events as rehearsals for disaster – were racially segregated affairs.

Leisure in the company town was sexually as well as racially segmented. Males engaged in certain forms of activity, females in others. Drinking, gambling, organized baseball, and less formal athletic contests at company functions, for example, were male activities; rarely are women mentioned in connection with them. Quilting, bean stringings and other work-related activities, church socials, and drop-in home visits were examples of the kind of socializing routinely associated with women. Going to the movies, bowling, reunions, and picnics were often family events that brought together people of different ages and sexes. Nevertheless, even in these family occasions, men and women customarily divided – men in one area and women in another – to socialize and talk about their common life experiences, especially work.

Hard physical labor performed by men was an overwhelming reality in the coal town. It molded virtually every aspect of life, including leisure, into a workingman's culture. Males were the chief breadwinners, and their economic superiority clearly translated into a preeminent concern for their health, welfare, and contentment. Women played a crucial, but supplementary, economic role. It is not surprising, therefore, to see photographs of coal-town men and women socializing on the steps of the company store or at company picnics with the men clustered together in one location, the women in another. Voluntary associations, like those described in chapter 6, provided benefits to men and women, yet because they were related to the work of men, these quasi-social organizations were male dominated.

If the interaction of structural components and cultural values provided the basis of the work culture, popular culture reinforced its composite content. Mining families embraced the figures of popular culture after World War II who celebrated the ideals or dealt with the common problems of hardworking people. Men and women like Dale Evans, John Wayne, Minnie Pearl, Roy Acuff, Red Foley, Ernest Tubb, Cowboy Copas, and Jimmy Dickens are well-known examples of actors and singers whose movies and music routinely re-created the joys and sorrows of sweated labor. Preaching or other religious services on the radio – the favorite radio programs of Stonega's mining populations – together with such literature as comic books, western novels, love stories, and hunting and fishing magazines – the major categories of literature found in miners' homes – all emphasizd the values of a culture of hardworking men and women. In turn, the work culture of the coalfields provided not only much of the raw material for lyricists, writers, and filmmakers but a ready audience for their renditions of it.

9 The Company Store

The company store was the social and economic nexus of the company town. No town was without one. It was usually located beside the railroad tracks. The same cars that carried the coal out of the town brought in the town's supplies. Groceries, furniture, clothing, boots and shoes, window and door screens, buckets, nails, drugs, black powder, miner's lamps, refrigerators and washers, radios, garden tools, ice, and household gadgets were just some of the great variety of items available in the company store. Haircuts and hairstyling, movies and bowling, shoe shines, sodas and ice cream, and – as technology developed – gasoline and tune-ups for automobiles, as well as laundering and dry cleaning, were just some of the many offerings at these service and recreation centers. Lodges and meeting rooms, dance halls, and libraries were other uses of the stores' space. Of course, not every company store offered all of these goods and services; some were more comprehensive than others.

Day by day, a constant coming and going of people enlivened the stores activities: women appeared early in the moring to pick up a quick item for breakfast or in the afternoon for something for supper; children came after school for a soda or ice-cream cone. These and other visits kept the company store at the center of activity. Women met and talked about their children, about who was sick or well, what they were sewing or what they were fixing for supper, how their gardens were doing, the weather, problems with a neighbor, how many eggs they were getting, or whom the dog had bitten. Annie Kelly noted that, without refrigeration, she had to stop at the company store daily; she went every morning. "That's what us women done for one thing – all meet at the store and compare how smart our children was, and what they had done or said the day before." She continued to reminisce: "We talked while we were waiting to get waited on. It wasn't like it is today where you went around and picked up what you wanted. You had to tell the clerk and he went and got everything."[1]

Men might brag about the fish they had caught, plan a hunting trip, or talk about the number of tons of coal loaded that day, about a close call in the mines, the foreman, when the mine would close or reopen, or the pain in their chests or backs. Or, as Christine Cochran of Docena noted, men might just go and sit all day, eat crackers and sardines, and talk. News, gossip, information, talk – small and big – were all exchanged in this setting. In 1947 the Boone Report captured this social world in the following way:

> The company store is the mecca for everyone in every coal camp. Even when the store is closed, the men gather there in their free time, frequently after working hours, and on Sundays and holidays. It is a common sight in summer to see miners, and often the women and children in the community, sitting or squatting on the porch or steps of the store, relaxing in idle talk. For the wives of the miners the visit to the company store offers the nearest approach to relaxation and diversion. . . . Here they learn and dispense the local news, read their mail, and meet their friends, as well as buy their groceries and supplies. To Management, the company store may be strictly business, but to the miners and their kin it is commissary, club room, and bulletin board rolled into one.[2]

In other words, company stores were centralized places of communal life and affiliation. No other place in the company town brought as many people together in one location. Certainly not the churches, which were not well attended. The lodges, ball fields, dance halls, and other places of leisure and amusement, just like the church, attracted people, but these were planned encounters with a purpose, not the chance meetings of a variety of town folk across social, ethnic, and racial lines.

Like the country store in the rural areas, the company store was a crossroads where differences of race, class, and gender were ritually acted out in the daily gathering of people from the community. For example, most stores were segregated, even in towns like Docena that had a black majority. Company managers, foremen, and clerks shopped here along with miners, it is true, but undoubtedly there were as many expressions of patronizing friendliness as there were genuine acts of kindness. Friendships across class lines were probably unusual. After all, some miners' wives and daughters worked as maids and housekeepers in the homes of management. It also seems unlikely that ethnic minorities who sometimes lived in separate housing sections of the town would have been treated as equals when they came together with the majority at the company store. As for women, they shopped for the family and talked with other women in the course of their daily routine.

Mining residents, however, viewed the company store not in terms of the way social interactions betrayed their prejudices and conventions or pointed up their social status – these they no doubt took for granted – but as a place of enjoyment, conversation, recreation, entertainment, a lively and interesting environment which changed daily with the coming and going of people, mail, and freight. If there was one spot in the town to relieve boredom, one theater of uncertainty and mystery, one imaginary connection to faraway places, it would have been the place where

Keokee company store, ca. 1915. Courtesy of Westmoreland Coal Company Archive, Hagley Library.

the trains arrived and departed, bringing with them passengers and freight. Such was the case even for management. According to a former payroll clerk of the railroad company town of Quinnimont, West Virginia, there was a custom called "highballing": town residents would gather on the platform where the trains arrived around noon on Sundays merely to watch the people coming and going. It was a place "to see and be seen."[3]

The coal-town store was also the official arm of the company. The administrative offices of company management occupied the upper floors. In 1915 the old company store burned at Stonega, and the company built a new, 2,586-square-foot facility. On the second floor were the store warehouse; a large furniture and clothing display room; and the offices of the plant superintendents, the lumber department, the telephone exchange, payroll clerks, the store manager, and the inspector of mines. In these offices men made a few decisions, carried out many more that had been made by vice-presidents, met the big bosses who made infrequent visits from company headquarters, prepared reports and accountings, and main-

Exeter company store. Courtesy of Westmoreland Coal Company Archive,
Hagley Library,

tained records of the miners and their families. For each mine worker,
time and attendance records, number of days worked, number of cars
loaded, and mine safety records were scrupulously kept. Company clerks
recorded deductions for rent, lights, coal, the doctor's fees, powder, sun-
dries, and any advances of scrip with equal care. Many company stores
had payroll windows where miners might line up on a Friday afternoon
to receive their two weeks' wages, minus any deductions for rent and
utilities, the doctor's fee, and scrip advances. Most company stores had
a scrip system.[4]

Scrip was a form of currency issued by the coal company through the
company store. A miner's wages might be paid in scrip, and once paid
in that form, the scrip could not be converted back into U.S. currency,
but instead had to be redeemed in merchandise at the company store.
It was issued in paper, plastic, or metal and came in a variety of denominations. TCI produced copper tokens in pennies, nickels, dimes, quarters, halves, and dollars with "T.C.I." imprinted upon each token. Edith
Shoemaker recalled hard cardboard or plastic forms of scrip which the
miners called "clacker," after the sound it made when it came together.
It might also be issued in paper similar to U.S. currency in various denominations. By one count, there were twenty thousand coal-company
stores in the United States, Mexico, and Canada that issued scrip at one
time or another.[5]

It is through the scrip system where miners could fall prey to the
worst the company town had to offer – outrageous prices, a monopoly on

Roda company store. Courtesy of Westmoreland Coal Company Archive, Hagley Library.

essential food and supplies, and crippling debt. Allegedly, miners were paid only in scrip, and because only the company store would redeem it, they were forced to pay "monopolistic prices" for their purchases. Prices ran several times above those of local independents, it is said. Miners were charged "outrageous deductions" for items like a burial fund, doctor fee, and "other services," something one writer called "audacious robbery," while another alleged it held miners "in peonage" because miners ended up "ow[ing] their souls to the company store."[6]

Mine labor at Stonega, however, was not victimized through the company store. And evidence of miners avoiding entrapment elsewhere is widespread. Many miners understood the potential for exploitation and avoided owing their souls to the company store.

Payment of wages exclusively in the form of scrip does not appear to have been common. Birdie Kyle, who grew up on Cabin Creek, West Virginia, and later worked for Senator Jennings Randolph, wrote: "How I remember the mixed feelings we had about coal company scrip." In a family of twelve children,

> we 'drew' a lot of scrip. . . . Scrip could make you schizophrenic. You had to decide between two evils: drawing scrip and having no cash on hand – or not drawing scrip so that Dad could draw a payday, by trying to stretch the groceries and home-canned food in the meantime. Usually our family, due to its size, lost the scrip battle.[7]

NOT TRANSFERABLE

N° 2507   Date........................., 195........

To **THE SPRUCE RIVER COAL COMPANY:**

Please deduct from money due me the sum of

TEN   DOLLARS

and pay same to **J. E. BALLARD,** Jeffery, West Va.

(Sign here)..No....................

Witness:..

Unspent portion redeemable in cash by employee on pay day when due.

Company scrip. Courtesy of Eastern Regional Coal Archives, Craft Memorial Library, Bluefield, West Virginia.

In some coal towns, perhaps, miners were forced to draw their pay in scrip, but the present study turned up no instance of this mandatory requirement. Neither Stonega Coke and Coal, Borderland Coal, Low Moor Iron, nor the operators of Wheelwright paid wages exclusively in scrip. Most miners recall drawing scrip upon demand on payday or, if needed, between paydays as an advance against future wages.

If the operators intended to entrap miners in a web of debt through the scrip system, miners seem to have thwarted them by using it judiciously. Admittedly, it would have been easy to have become overextended, and some did, because the coal companies encouraged easy credit. Lloyd Vick Minor said that the company was good at extending credit, whether it was for something as small as groceries or as big as a car. Scrip was like today's credit card; it did not seem to be like money. As Christine Cochran noted, it was like a charge account, and "we were happy with that and the company was happy to get back all of the money that they paid the miners for digging the rich coal." Yet miners recognized the inherent dangers. L. F. Minor pointed out, for example, that one negative feature of taking scrip instead of cash was the loss of freedom and independence to shop at other stores outside the company town. Of course, there were those who had difficulty managing their affairs. In the words of Carry Marcum, "some had to go get an issuance of scrip before they could eat breakfast."[8]

Miners used the scrip system of credit for sundry purposes. Stonega advanced scrip to miners who were temporarily unable to work due to injury but had not yet received their checks from workmen's compensation. Miners were not even required to sign a promise to repay the company out of their compensation checks. Yet the company suffered no losses, in spite of such lenience. Stonega also advanced scrip to any miner who carried insurance that included sickness benefits. This flexible system of credit was put to still other uses. According to Irene Hicks Skaggs, if a miner got in a pinch and needed money but felt he could not get it, other miners might go to the office window, draw scrip on their accounts, and give it to the needy miner. An Elmo, West Virginia, miner's wife claimed scrip was used mostly for clothing and furniture, rarely for food. At Stonega, tools and safety shoes were explicitly approved for credit purchase in 1938. On rare occasions, perhaps, a miner might get a cash advance. One miner proved rather creative in his use of company credit. At Justus Collins's Winding Gulf colliery, the superintendent reported that "a colored man" came into the office and asked for eighteen dollars in cash. He had drawn eighty-eight dollars the Saturday before to buy "his woman" a suit and cloak. He wanted the eighteen dollars to "take her somewhere," reassuring the superintendent that he "could make it easily in two days and pay it back." The superintendent commented fastidiously: "These are the people who should buy bonds."[9]

In spite of the miners of legend who "owed their souls," evidence suggests that "debt peonage" was rare at the company stores. An analysis of the records of the Stonega Company, for example, found that outstanding debts at the stores averaged less than 2 percent of sales between 1910 and 1947. The payroll clerk in 1932 found only forty-two men at Stonega in debt: twenty-five owed over a hundred dollars; twelve over two hundred dollars; and five over three hundred dollars. Correspondence in company records indicates that Stonega kept close watch over indebtedness and attempted to keep it under control.[10]

Moreover, miners regularly received considerable proportions of their earnings in cash. After 1900, store deductions amounted to 30 to 50 percent of the mine payroll in selected mines of Virginia and West Virginia. In other words, miners here received 50 to 70 percent of their earnings in cash, after deductions for rent, doctor fee, fuel, blacksmithing, powder, and store purchases on credit between paydays. These figures do not reflect racial and ethnic differences. A study in West Virginia found that blacks returned 72 percent of all their earnings to the company store, foreigners about 33 percent, and native whites 51 percent.[11]

Records from the Fenwick mines of the Low Moor Iron Company in Covington, Virginia, for the year 1902 show that the average iron worker received a wage of $28.00 per month. Rent was $2.00; doctor's fee, fifty cents to $1.00; and previous scrip advances to be deducted averaged $7.12. Even at this very low wage, average take-home pay in cash, after paying all expenses – including previous scrip advances – amounted to $18.11. The exploitation in these cases was not in the scrip stystem but in the poor wages. It defies explanation how miners could have lived on such paltry sums, if they received this amount month after month. Yet somehow even iron-ore workers, who were usually paid less than coal miners, managed to avoid the temptation of excessive indebtedness.[12]

Payroll accounts of the Crozier Coal and Coke Company, which operated company towns in West Virginia at Turkey Gap, Elkhorn, and Dott, showed an employment of 418 workers. In August 1910, deductions totaled $6,289.30 with a balance due to employees of $10,117.17. Thus, the average employee might have received $24.20 after deductions for expenses like powder, rent, and lights, as well as doctor, smithing, and stable fees. With minor exceptions, all the workers showed a balance due to them. In these cases, the oppression was in the form of long workdays and workweeks. Coke-yard men worked 10-hour days, six days a week. Some coke loaders even reached 18-hour days. In other cases, for tipple men and company men in the mines, for example, the workweek was reasonable, less than

160 hours for the month. Regardless of the hours and wage rates, few of the men were indebted to the company store.[13]

Discounting of scrip presented a problem both for miners and for operators in the coalfields until laws were passed to regulate it. The operators wanted scrip to be redeemable in merchandise only at the company store. But the miner who had drawn scrip might want to spend it as he pleased. So the practice of discounting arose whereby the miner would sell his scrip coupons to anyone who would take them, whether other miners, local people, or merchants, in return for cash. Usually he sold at a discount. Robert Hicks remembers buying $1.00 worth of scrip for seventy-five cents or a $5.00 coupon book for $3.75. Local businesses also engaged in discounting. Chan Forren recalled a pawnshop operator, Jim Martin, who would pay seventy-five cents on the dollar for scrip and then redeem it at the company store for ninety cents. In 1918, when the U.S. Supreme Court ruled that scrip was transferable and redeemable in cash, local merchants began to take scrip in payment for merchandise at one-fourth its value and then demand cash on presentation at the company store. The Virginia Coal Operators' Association successfully lobbied for a bill in the state legislature the following year to make scrip nontransferable upon issuance. After the passage of this bill, the Stonega Company had no one who tried to purchase employee coupons at a discount and redeem them in cash. A similar law was passed in West Virginia. Some companies there complied and others did not. If the coal company was using metal coins or tokens instead of paper or coupons, upon which it was easier to imprint the words "Non-Transferable Redeemable in Cash on Payday to Whom Issues," companies simply paid the penalities rather than go to the expense of purchasing new coins. In 1925, the majority of the operators in the Pocahontas fields made no change; the Winding Gulf and Superior companies ordered new coins.[14]

Coal companies faced stiff competition from many sides: mail-order houses, local stores, vendors, and even other company stores in the same vicinity. Initially built out of necessity where local merchants did not exist, by World War I the company store faced many competitors who flocked to the burgeoning centers of population to set up small businesses. Miners ordered out of catalogs and had their purchases shipped in on the train. At Docena, an ice wagon canvassed the company town, selling blocks of ice to mining families.

Local farmers in the vicinities of Kaymoor and Borderland brought produce and vegetables to the edges of the company towns where they set up small stands on certain days of the week. In 1922, the Kaymoor Number Nine store, located on the line of the Chesapeake and Ohio Railroad, grossed about forty-three thousand dollars in business – not a bad year. But its income was limited because it shared its business with Sears, Roebuck and Company; Montgomery Ward; National Suit and Cloak Company – all mail-order houses – as well as local businesses such as Kanawha Cash Grocery and the Great Eastern Bargain House at Sewell, West Virginia.

In addition, competition was keen among the stores of individual companies. Towns in the "isolated" New River Gorge region averaged only a mile apart. Dewey Osborne of Wheelwright, Kentucky, answered the question of where he bought his furniture by saying, "Anywhere you wanted to buy it." The company store had it, or it could be bought and sent in by train. Wiley Pennington, who also worked at a Kentucky mine, said he shopped anywhere he wanted. Robert Hicks from Wayland, Kentucky, spoke of going to Andy Martin's grocery, where he even used scrip, so long as he spent a whole book at once. Ada Wilson, a black miner's wife from Concho, West Virginia, shopped in nearby Oak Hill where she was also able to use scrip, even though she felt the company store had "just as nice stuff as it was up town."[15]

At the Winding Gulf colliery, Superintendent George Wolfe opposed store operators in the town of Davy bringing merchandise to the miners at the colliery by team because they were reducing "our business." He proposed to Justus Collins, the owner, that he be allowed to fire two good and steady miners who owned property in Davy and "never spend a cent of their earnings with us." Wolfe had gone so far as to ask attorneys for a court injunction against the two men to keep them and any other employee who rented a company house from making purchases outside and having them delivered to the company town. Collins, however, who had a reputation for being heavy-handed with his workers over labor matters, demurred in this case and sided with the miners. He disagreed that forced trading at the company store would be a good idea:

> My policy, stated many times, is that if I was employed by a Coal Company at a certain stated wage, and that Company in any manner, shape or form undertook to coerce me to trade at its store, paying higher for goods there than elsewhere, that more hell would be put in me in a minute that could be gotten out in a year.

Collins went on to explain to his manager that he originated the tenant house contract and the right to evict miners solely to exercise the right at strike time "to keep out undesirables," not to force anyone to trade at the company store. He noted that people in the town of Beckley who were not even employees traded at the company store of the Raleigh Coal Company. He admonished Wolfe not to antagonize his employees, but since he had already gone so far, to "confine yourself to defining trespassers" as a way of saving face.[16]

Wolfe would not give in and in a subsequent letter refused to accept his boss's interpretation of his actions, preferring to state them in his own terms. Wolfe continued his querulous campaign, arguing that he was not trying to compel anyone to trade at the company store, just keep the teams off the property. If deliveries were allowed, he felt he could not be competitive because: flour cost $6.30 a barrel, and "they will deliver for $6.50; feed cost $1.50 and "would be delivered for $1.65; it cost us seven and one-half percent to do business, and we couldn't compete." He reminded Collins that he had a store stock of $14,000, on which he had netted $11,000 the previous year. As for the Raleigh Coal Company, he felt that store was not comparable – they were much larger" ($80,000 in stock), "bought in bulk, and paid cash on the spot."[17] He finished his case by appealing to Collins's anti-union bias. He told of J. G. Bradley, manager of the Elk River Coal and Lumber Company, who used a five-strand barbed wire fence, ten feet high with only one gate, and a twenty-four-hour guard to keep trespassers away. Wolfe pointedly reminded Collins that Bradley worked nonunion, even though union mines surrounded him. His net store profit was 12 percent, and he had no outside teams coming onto his property. "Absolute rule seems to me to work out better," he concluded. But the boss had spoken, and the matter rested.[18]

Collins understood, as the operator who had to hire and keep a labor force, what Wolfe, with his narrower interest in showing a company store profit, could not grasp – namely that the labor market was competitive, and the company store had evolved into a service to entice workers. So what kept the company store in business after World War I?

Only the competition of labor and the lower "transaction-costs" of providing credit explain the store's persistence, according to a recent economic study of company stores. According to this theory, the company already possessed the credit information it needed on each miner. It did not have to involve itself, therefore, in costly credit searches each time it extended credit to a miner. Through the scrip system it could virtually garnishee a worker's wages to collect on a debt without having to go through the courts. In short: a company could get its money without a costly lawsuit, had the power to extend or limit credit as economic times demanded, and saved on the borrowing costs of money by using scrip.[19]

The train gave the miners additional freedom and independence from the company store. The automobile's impact was slow to be felt because of the mountainous terrain of most coal towns and the lack of good roads. But train service was dependable, regular, and accessible. Far from being isolated in mountain hollows, miners enjoyed greater accessibility to the outside world in coal towns than had been the case on the farm. The train made this possible by bringing goods, people, and mail on a consistent schedule even to the remotest of settlements.

For example, at Nuttalburg during the 1920s the train arrived four times a day, bringing mail, freight, and passengers and leaving with the same cargo. Residents of the town could catch the early morning train at 7:15, spend the day in Charleston shopping, and return at 6:15 in the evening. Even Kaymoor, located in a narrow passageway through the New River Gorge, had two trains a day, at 11:00 A.M. and 5:00 P.M., taking passengers to Thurmond or Charleston, where most traveled for major shopping. Ada Wilson claimed that thirteen trains came and went from Concho each day, and it was a rather simple matter to go to Charleston and back in the same day; others went to Cincinnati, and occasionally Ada journeyed to Chicago. Residents of Ligon, Kentucky, welcomed three passenger trains each day, one in the morning, one at noon, and one in the late evening. To get from Ligon to Hi Hat cost ten cents in 1924 by train, but by car it was a very difficult journey, which Wiley Pennington made once in the family Plymouth by following the creek beds; there were no roads. The train was the only way in and out of Wheelwright, unless one rode a horse. Two passenger trains daily served Martin, Wayland, and Allen: The 5:20 A.M. returned at 1:00 P.M., and the 1:00 P.M. returned at 5:00 P.M. Fewer than ten people owned a car at Wheelwright by the end of 1926, the year the first automobile appeared in the town. The first paved road was not completed until 1935.[20]

Nevertheless, the miners who did trade with the company store, whether by choice or necessity, may still have been overcharged. If so, might not former miners be able to tell us if there was a general pattern of price gouging in the company stores?

Recollections equivocate over whether prices in the company stores were higher or lower than in the surrounding areas. D. B. Oglestree of Docena believed prices were higher but that the higher quality of the merchandise justified them with name-brand items and nothing cheap or shoddy. Frank Bonds recalled the prices in Docena to be slightly less. A former payroll clerk at Quinnimont, West Virginia, a railroad company town, said bread that cost the store eight cents a loaf was sold for ten cents; meat had a 25 percent markup, dry goods 40 percent; and furniture had the highest markup, 70 percent. Celia Chambers of Kaymoor said that merchandise was higher in the company store, but after one paid transportation costs from Oak Hill, the company store was cheaper. Besides, "They had very nice stuff in the company store and you get anything you wanted there."[21]

More exact comparisons of the company store with local merchants are available in government studies. An analysis of figures from studies of the coalfields by the U.S. Immigration Commission in 1908 and the U.S. Coal Commission in 1922 show prices at company stores to have been higher in the New River and Kanawha districts of West Virginia than in nearby manufacturing districts like Charleston. However, the higher prices in isolated areas could be due to the higher transportation costs of getting merchandise into these areas. Or they could be due to monopolistic practices. Which was the case is unclear. One study, which calculated store profits, failed to support a claim of exploitive pricing in the company stores of southwestern Virginia. Net store profits at the Stonega mines hovered between 10 and 15 percent of sales from 1910 to 1915 and averaged about 6 percent for the years 1916 to 1929 and 1937 to 1947.[22]

Even if company stores did not overcharge, ensnare miners in an inescapable web of debt, or retain a monopoly over the coal-town trade, they do appear to have been profitable enterprises. A guaranteed return of 6 percent at a minimum was a handsome figure that most nineteenth-century businessmen would have been happy with. Ten to 15 percent was excellent. Company stores had clear advantages over most business enterprises and may not have, therefore, had to gouge miners to remain profitable. They had a dependable if not captive supply of customers. While it is true that not everyone did all their shopping there all the time, still the base of customers was sufficient to make a good profit. The stores also enjoyed the advantage of frequent train service to bring in supplies Just like modern enterprises, they also used differential pricing, i.e., very high markups on some items, like furniture, and more modest markups on other items, like food. Finally, the fact that a company store siphoned much of the payroll of the company back into the company's coffers while at the same time making a profit was a business arrangement of manifold importance, even at low returns.

It should also be noted that some towns had multiple commercial enterprises; the company store was not the only money-making establishment. Some towns had nearly as many businesses as one would find in a small independent town. In the 1920s, for example, the town of Keokee had four general merchandise stores, a meat market, a hotel, an ice-cream parlor, a jewelry shop, a barbershop, an opera house, a swimming pool, a golf range, and even a concert band.[23] Indeed, this kind of economic diversification probably allowed some companies like Stonega to survive the boom and bust cycles of the coal industry.

On the face of it, the instrumental power of the company store – located as it was in remote areas and offering the benefits of convenience and easy credit – seems formidable. But the store's power and control over the mining population was blunted by the rational behavior of miners and the business acumen of company officials who understood the limits of their control in a tight labor market. Labor scarcity and a highly mobile labor force during the first two decades of the twentieth century meant that coal operators could not be successful with the stick approach in garnering labor; they had to consider the carrot. The George Wolfes, the managers who believed that miners had to be forced with guns and barbed wire to deal at the company store, may have achieved some fleeting monopolistic control through company stores outside the range of this study, but it is doubtful that it would have lasted very long in a competitive market situation.

Finally, the dual functions of the company store, as both a social center and a province of company authority, however limited, deserve further study. Since company paternalism was mediated through the company store by providing forms of recreation, a center for social discourse, and various services, the store could easily be overlooked by the miners as an instrument of manipulation and social control. Miners, who appreciated its convenience and benefits, were likely to ignore its rapacious and deceptive practices. "Biting the hand that feeds you" was something to which miners from hardscrabble backgrounds were understandably averse. Consequently, company stores in the early days, one expects, would have been able to get by with more than later generations were willing to accept. Perhaps this explains the disagreement among miners over pricing practices. In any case, miners brought to their dealings with the company store the same realism and practicality they exhibited elsewhere, and in doing so, they limited the hegemony of the store and the operators over their lives.

10 The Company Church

In 1933 Elizabeth R. Hooker summarized "the church situation" in the coal towns in the following words:

> Many coal camps have either no churches or very weak ones. This situation is owing to several conditions. For one thing, there is a social gulf between company officials and white-collar employees with their families, on the one hand, and the miners with their families on the other; so that neither group readily joins in a church or Sunday school started by the other. Again, there is a lack of local leadership. In many cases the personnel of the company group have no interest in churches. Miners that perhaps took an active part in religious work in their former country communities, here feel shy, jaded and without responsibility for the religious welfare of a community where they may not have taken deep roots and which they may soon leave.[1]

Hooker expressed alarm at "the general indifference to religious things," at how "the evils of gambling, hard drinking, violence, and sensuality are all about." She scorned "the second hand car" as a final reason for religious indifference.[2]

Aside from its prudery, the report offers some astute observations on the state of religion in the coal towns, especially the causes for the lack of religious participation. I shall return to these matters later in the chapter, but first I want to examine the development of coal-town religion as displayed in the towns of this study. Why would coal operators support an institution like the church when there was no economic benefit to be gained from doing so? To what extent was Hooker correct that organized religion in the coal towns lacked widespread support? The very idea of a "company" church suggests that coal operators had at their disposal a powerful instrument of social control. The ability to exercise this control would be limited, however, if mining families did not attend churches in significant numbers. Were mining families diligent attenders or lax in their support of the church, and why did either situation come about?

The company church was a product of the same forces that gave rise to schools, recreation halls, movie theaters, poolrooms, and other leisure and recreational facilities – namely, the early labor shortage and the desires of coal operators to attract and retain miners. It was a part of the

ideal of contentment sociology, predicated upon the belief that a satisfied laboring population would be stable and productive.

Occasionally, company records expose the economic foundations of contentment sociology. On 7 August 1916, the manager of the Winding Gulf
colliery wrote to the owner, Justus Collins, telling him how "crazy" he
thought it was to keep building houses when Winding Gulf already had
twenty-six empty dwellings and five new ones under construction. A better policy, he suggested, would be to do something to make people more
satisfied and thereby increase the tonnage loaded. Wolfe's recommenda-
tion was to build more places of amusement and relaxation. Consequently,
he had arranged for the construction of a movie theater and a poolroom.
But he also desired to encourage churches. Miners had raised $500 for a
church, and "according to the contract we must provide $500." Wolfe
pointed out that Winding Gulf was the only operation in the region without a single church for whites; most had two or three churches. "We have
no form of amusement and people quarrel, bicker and fight constantly."[3]

One possible explanation for the Winding Gulf colliery's delay in church
building compared to other collieries of the region is that Collins feared
labor trouble in his camps if churches were allowed to establish themselves. Nine years before Wolfe's letter, an anonymous miner had written
to Collins about conditions in his camp at Davy, West Virginia. Besides
referring to bootlegging in a "joint" over the company store by a
"darkey," the miner mentioned an incident he felt should also be cause for
the owner to visit the camp and "straighten things out." It involved a sixty-
five-year-old preacher who had come to preach a revival. He preached all
week and began to talk to miners downtown. The issue of wages arose,
whereupon the preacher stated that he did not believe in strikes but considered the wages of miners to be too low. The boss's wife, Mrs. Cooke,
invited him to dinner. She seems to have considered the minister's comments on wage rates inappropriate. After the meal she invited him into
an adjoining room. A Mr. Riley knocked him down with something, and
the bookkeepers and store clerks jumped on him and beat him up. He
suffered several broken ribs and multiple bruises. According to the anonymous miner, the incident upset local church people; some began to buy
guns, and a lot of miners threatened to quit the mines.[4]

Methodism and the Baptist faith became the chief denominations in
the coal towns of southern Appalachia. The major era of church building
coincided with the departure of many immigrants from the coalfields.
Poles, Italians, and Hungarians created the need for Roman Catholic
and Lutheran churches; with their departure from the coalfields during
World War I, Protestant white and black miners formed congregations.

In 1930, a U.S. Department of Agriculture survey of 117 counties in Appalachia counted 14,423 churches, or 187 per thousand square miles. If evenly distributed, there would have been a church every 2.3 miles. Compared to the United States as a whole, there were nearly twice as many churches per thousand inhabitants in the Appalachian region. To the question of why there were so many, the survey answered that the many isolated, narrow valleys without roads required churches to be located close to the residents. As for denominations, about 40 percent were Baptists, 33 percent Methodists, and the remainder, except for a small percentage of non-Protestants, were Presbyterians, "Christians," Perfectionists, and members of other Protestant sects.[5] Most congregations were small, one-fourth having fewer than twenty-five members and over one-half with fewer than fifty.[6]

Given this distribution of denominations in the Appalachian region, and in the South as a whole, it is not surprising that the same religious groups prevailed in coal towns. According to one study, 80 percent of all black miners were Baptists, and about 16 percent were Methodists.[7] The coal town of Wheelwright had Methodist, Baptist, Church of Christ, and Church of God churches.[8]

Roman Catholic churches were uncommon, except perhaps in nearby larger towns.[9] The USDA Report of 1935 took note of a similar absence of rural worship centers for Jews and Catholics.[10] When an Austro-Hungarian Catholic miner, Steve Tomko, was told by a Catholic priest that it would take two to three months and fifty dollars for his future wife to become a Catholic, Tomko and his fiancée decided to be married by a Baptist preacher. Later Tomko concluded, after his reading of the Bible, that he could no longer remain a Catholic, in spite of having already baptized two children as Catholics.[11] Similar difficulties may have caused others to convert to the dominant Baptist and Methodist faiths.

The Stonega Company assisted in various ways to help miners establish congregations. Usually, miners interested in forming a congregation would agree orally to deductions from their wages to support a minister. The company would then contribute another small sum to guarantee a monthly wage. In 1904, Stonega guaranteed a Presbyterian minister $60 to $75 a month to serve a congregation of miners and the following year offered to contribute $25 monthly toward the salary of a Catholic priest.[12]

It was not difficult to secure ministers. Many wrote to SC&C inquiring about the possibility of serving in the coal towns. Their interest was due to the low salary and burden of work in rural areas. About 1910 in southwest Virginia, one dedicated pastor in the mountains preached at two services each Sunday, held three weeks of revival annually, and received an annual salary of $13.20. He and his family lived in a two-room cabin on thirty acres of rented land. He exchanged his labor with a neighbor in return for the use of a horse to plow his fields. On Sundays he walked to his churches, which were about five miles apart. Another pastor in the same area worked in a grist mill and received a salary from his part-time churches of $30.[13] According to a 1913 survey of fifty-four hundred Southern Baptist churches "with quarter-time pastors," the average annual salary was $378, "but some made less than $30 per year." Weather and fluctuating farm prices sometimes meant that pastors often failed to receive even the salaries they were promised.[14]

In Appalachia generally, the average yearly salary for a pastor was $624 (allowing $200 as the cost of a parsonage), and 40 percent received less than $500 a year. Of those who were full-time pastors, one half had four or more churches, a figure three to four times the national average. No wonder over one-half of the rural ministers had other work, mostly as farm laborers. A tradition of unsalaried ministers in parts of the rural South contributed to the low average salary and the desire of ministers to seek other congregations.[15]

In 1906, the Reverend W. E. Patton, a Baptist pastor from Mendotta, Virginia, wrote to request to live rent-free in one of Stonega's dwellings. He was denied on the basis that he had not been regularly "called" by one of the congregations on the premises of the company. A new church was in the process of completion at Osaka with the understanding that a general election of the congregation would decide the sect of the preacher. Stonega officials held out the possibility that Patton might be able to receive a call from the Osaka congregation.[16] In 1909, the Reverend C. R. W. Kegley wrote to offer to baptize the children and otherwise serve "the Lutheran Hungarian people." He was informed that he could come, but only a few members of this denomination were at Stonega.[17] At the time of these requests, Stonega already had eight preachers and two missionaries, "all who get some assistance from the company."[18] One of these was the Reverend Julius Balogh of Pocahontas, Virginia, who came every fourth Sunday for two or three days to serve a small Hungarian Reformed congregation.[19] At Docena, black congregations depended upon preachers who also worked in the mines and served congregations simultaneously for "a quarter, dime, nickel, scrip, a hen, a piece of ham—anything."[20]

Company officials also provided lots and aided in the construction of churches. In 1906, the president of SC&C authorized the spending of $1,200 to build and fence a parsonage for the Catholic priest at Stonega.[21] In 1908, the Virginia Coal and Iron Company conveyed to the Roman Catholic bishop of Wheeling a lot at Stonega for the use of the Catholic congregation there.[22] At Exeter, another company town of the Stonega Company, a four-room tenement without partitions and with benches built around the walls was built to serve as a church. When the schoolhouse was completed, it replaced the tenement house as a church.[23]

Coal-town churches were typically segregated facilities. Following the Jim Crow system of segregation, the Stonega Company aided in the building of separate black churches. In 1906, it deeded a lot to the African Methodist Episcopal Zion Church with a designation that the site was to be used only for church purposes, not for "labor agitations and undesirable entertainments." A violation of the deed would result in the return of the lot to the company.[24] A Baptist-Methodist Union church and "a colored church" were built at Stonega under an arrangement whereby the company donated $300 to each church contingent upon the congregation's raising another $300.[25] Once congregations were established, SC&C made small annual donations to Sunday School programs, usually $5 to $10 in the form of credit at the company store, where members of the congregations would receive merchandise at 10 percent over cost.[26]

In spite of the accessibility of institutional Protestantism, miners apparently were irregular church attenders. J. C. Blume was not even aware that the New River Gorge mining communities had churches.[27] Wiley Pennington, a former miner in Ligon, Kentucky, said very few miners attended church in the towns of his memory.[28] When asked if she went to church, Mae Prater responded: "when I could get to. When I raised the children I didn't have much chance to go, but I would go sometimes and take them." The interviewer probed the issue further:

> Interviewer: Did many people go to church?
> Mae Prater: Not too many really. They sure didn't. There wasn't too many that would go too much.
> Interviewer: Why do you think that was so?
> Mae Prater: Well, I just don't know whether they was just too busy or just wasn't interested. . . . Most of the women were out on Sunday, they just cook dinner, you know, and took it easy, didn't do too much, and didn't go much either. Some of them now, after they got cars, they would get out and ride around, maybe go to church, do a few little things.[29]

A former pastor at Docena, Dr. E. L. McFee, connected the laxity in church attendance among the miners he served to the nature of mine work, which made them fatalistic. McFee served the Docena and Edgewater Methodist churches between 1939 and 1941 as a substitute or "student-supply" pastor while attending Birmingham Southern College. He preached at Edgewater two Sundays per month and at Docena the other two. He lived at home in Birmingham but often stayed overnight in the homes of mining families. The Docena church had fifty to sixty members out of a community of several thousand. McFee reported that they lived very well, spent money, and bought cars, but seldom attended church in good times. At times of depression, death, injury, sickness, or shutdowns, church attendance increased. The nature of mine work – dangerous, irregular, and uncertain – encouraged them to "live for today." He found miners to be "good spirited," "likeable," "very enjoyable," "fine people with character," and "hard working," but "the church simply did not command any large percentage of the number of people in the community."[30] Fatalism seems less important as an explanation for poor attendance than other factors, however.

The laxity of church attendance is intriguing in the coal towns of this study among a population of mountaineers who had migrated from a region with a plethora of rural churches and a legendary religiosity. According to the Reverend S. R. Emerson, Alabama's state chaplain to its prisoner-miners in 1910, few of the state's twenty thousand miners attended church because of the association of the pastors as "company men." About the same time, a Methodist minister, the Reverend W. P. Blevins, told a district conference meeting in the mining town of Dora, Alabama, that miners did not like to attend church with company men. These comments echo Elizabeth Hooker's earlier observations.

Another explanation for religious "backsliding" was the impact of modernization upon church attendance. Mae Prater noted, for example, how limitations on free time constrained women to stay at home on Sunday. She also noted how churches had to compete with other activities for the miners' attention. In 1907, the Reverend W. P. Blevens addressed a district conference of the Methodist Church in Dora, Alabama, decrying the reality of fewer converts in mining camps than in foreign mission fields. His remarks, summarized by J. Wayne Flynt, stressed that

> mining communities needed institutional churches devoted exclusively to miners, with reading rooms, games and tables, a small gymnasium and baths, a night literacy school, a glee club, and religious services two evenings a week conducted "as often as possible by a miner in the interest of miners."[31]

Yet the church failed to respond to these social needs in the industrial town. Feeling the church had abandoned them, the miners abandoned the "company" churches.

The number and variety of social activities in the company town kept the church pews empty and bedeviled the efforts of clergy to fill them.

In rural areas, churchgoing had always served social ends as much as it fulfilled spiritual needs. According to Asa Spaulding, a black farmer's son in the Carolina Piedmont, visiting as much as praying characterized the rural church. People who worked six days a week, whether in agriculture or in mining coal, were glad to see Sunday come because it was such a great social occasion.[32] In the coal towns, the church lost out to visiting, the train station, Sunday baseball, the saloon, and a host of communal functions like picnics, reunions, gospel sings, informal music sessions in homes, and holiday festivals. In these gatherings, mining families could associate among their own kind, free to talk about their common concerns without worrying about the eyes and ears of the coal company.

Thus, the institutional church, not to say Christianity itself, seems to have had surprisingly small influence upon mining families in coal towns. Nevertheless, nonchurchgoing miners still might describe themselves as religious and express their belief in God. Mae Prater is a good example of one who retained traditional religious values outside the institutional church. She recalled the "bad things" about coal-town life as drinking, playing cards, and gambling as well as the worry she had about the influence of these activities upon her children. She and her family eventually moved to a small farm in order to keep her children from being exposed to these influences:

> I always tried to make myself satisfied and felt like I had a lot to be thankful for anywhere I lived. I've felt like that most all my life. I think we got plenty. We get down, you know, low, then I'll think about our homes and our families and everything and I'll think we got a lot. We've got a *lot* to be thankful for, and we need to live just as close as we can live to the Lord, because sometime or another we're going to leave here and we're going somewhere, going for eternity, eternity, it says forever and ever.[33]

Why did miners support the church at all? Even though many mining families distrusted pastors and felt uncomfortable worshiping in the same congregation with company men, small numbers accepted the operators' support as a means to an end. SC&C, for example, would make wage deductions from a miner's pay to facilitate the formation of congregations and permit them to budget their expenses. When asked about deductions from his wages to support the church, L. F. Minor, formerly from the Stonega Company's town of Imboden, replied that a miner could contribute in this way or personally, "either way you wanted it." Miners at Stonega often chose their own pastor without company interference. Once the company had assisted in the building of the church, SC&C would often deed the building and plot to the congregation.

Interviewer: Did they try and control who preached?

L. F. Minor: Nothing like that went on in our place. Our pastors come, and they stayed their time. Some'd stay three year and some four. Some'd stay one—just whatever the, the church had wanted to change him or send somebody else to you.

Also, according to Minor, foremen and miners attended church together. He concluded: "No, there's nothing wrong about the church, the company didn't fool with the church at all."[34] Fred Gaddis from Stonega, a church deacon for twenty years, reported that the company never attempted to interfere in church life.[35] Melba Kizzire and D. B. Oglestree of Docena both emphasized the independence of their congregations from company interference and control.[36] To an interviewer's freighted question of whether TCI fomented anti-union feeling through the pastor of her church, Edith Shoemaker of Docena answered, "No."[37]

Miners approached matters of religion and church in the same rational ways they dealt with other spheres of life in a company town. Some accepted the assistance of mining companies in building churches, forming congregations, and hiring pastors. The coal company could do things for them that they could not accomplish by themselves. From the miners' perspective, the operators made churches possible. But even their support of the "company" church was grounded in a belief of noninterference from the company. Had the operators sought more extensively to control and manipulate miners through the company church, the miners would have been quick to react to the use of the church as an instrument of social control. Coal companies prohibited the use of the church for labor agitation, but it is doubtful that miners were troubled by that to any great extent. The reasons are uncertain: whether due to fatalism, an otherworldly faith, religious indifference to labor problems, or the existence of the union to channel dissent, labor and religion just did not seem to mix. Many would have viewed the church as simply an inappropriate place for labor agitation.

The church was another part of the Stonega's Company paternalism during World War I, one more hope for stabilizing the supply of labor, even though the numbers of those interested were small. The company donated building sites, lent a hand to congregations in securing ministers, contributed to ministers' salaries until congregations got on their financial feet, made annual donations to Sunday Schools and organizations, and offered the bookkeeping services of the company to congregations and to members who desired to have deductions made from their pay to support the church.

After World War I and the end of the coal boom, however, when labor was no longer in short supply, the incentive of the company to support the church for reasons of labor stability was no longer there. In the 1920s and thereafter, until the closing of the coal towns in the 1950s, the operators left churches to fend for themselves. By this time, most miners had found alternative ways to meet their social and religious needs.

Forces of Change, 1930–1960

The years between the peak of company-town growth in the mid-1920s, and the 1950s – when coal companies began to dismantle their towns – were years of change and decline in company towns. The pioneer and paternalistic phases lasted a generation or two. During the latter period the company town moved quickly from a primitive camp to a self-sufficient town complete with a wide range of social and recreational activities. The years of decline extended over an equal period of time, but the changes were far more drastic. The bust in the coal industry and the end of the era of labor shortages placed labor in a much more vulnerable position than ever before. Operators no longer needed to be as concerned about the quality of life in company towns. The practice of bringing workers in "on transportation" ceased. The collieries had enough labor to meet production demands, at least until World War II, which caused a temporary labor boom. The rise of alternative fuel sources, the Great Depression, the automobile, mechanization in the mines, unionization, and World War II were the forces of change that reshaped the company towns and ultimately caused their closing.

Economic troubles in the coal industry began as early as 1919, with the effects of diminished postwar coal demand, and worsened throughout the 1920s. Shifts by the railroads and the iron and steel industry to using oil, gas, and electricity for fuel caused a sharp decline in bituminous coal production. The high price of coal, together with labor strife, which made coal an unstable industrial fuel, encouraged the nations's plants to convert to fuel oil. Between 1917 and 1927, the use of hydroelectric power doubled, causing additional inroads into coal demand. Technological advances, including more efficient industrial boilers, electric generators, and better locomotive fireboxes cut consumption needs. The coal slump forced marginal operators into bankruptcy or sale, produced wage cuts for miners in the nonunion fields, and weakened the trade union movement. Long before the stock market crash in 1929, the coal industry had already tasted the effects of the Great Depression.[1]

The Great Depression caused a deepening economic crisis in the coalfields as it swept over the rest of the country. Hilton Garrett recalled the change from a nice town at Wheelwright until the Depression came, when times got "tight" and the company "no longer seemed to care if you stayed or left." Miners took note of signs of depression, such as an increase of hoboes riding the rails. According to Marvin Gullett, after 1929 machinery rusted, tipples and houses rotted, people drifted like vagrants begging for work, and mines slipped into receivership. Ernest B. Fishburn, the treasurer of Borderland, reported in 1931 that the Number One store, the manager's house, and numerous other dwellings needed repairs to the roofs, new gutters, new porch floors, and "practically all need painting badly." The neglecting of repairs and painting was the least drastic of measures taken to adjust to slack coal demand.[2]

SC&C resorted to a variety of strategies in order to adjust, some designed to buy time and weather the storm of the Depression, others fashioned to cushion its effects upon the miners, and still others pursued as a means of addressing some of the company's vexing personnel problems. In 1931 the company hired not a single new employee. To meet short-range production demands, "it was thought best to increase the working time of old employees." The company reported that this practice – actually a version of the textile industry's "stretch out" where fewer employees are asked to produce more – was accepted by laborers content just to be working and taking home a paycheck when many in the hard-pressed industry were out of work. Their major complaint was the problem of sustaining continuous employment, which the company had increasing difficulty guaranteeing. The following year, as the Depression deepened, Stonega slashed wages 12 percent, the first reduction it had made since the 1927 wage scale. Some collieries were operated on a restricted tonnage basis; others, like Dunbar and Exeter, were closed completely.[3]

The closing of collieries, of course, brought an end to some company towns. The Depression also added to the numbers of miners who did not live in the company town in which they worked. Already by the 1930s, at Stonega's collieries, the automobile and the expansion of passable roads had made the separation of work and residence possible for the small number of employees who could afford this means of transportation. When Dunbar and Exeter were closed, SC&C "scrutinized very carefully" its list of nonresident employees, mostly older miners "who were living away from the collieries in the surrounding towns and on their small farms." SC&C established a priority order for the miners it released. The first to be released were single men, followed by nonresident miners, and then 1 son of employees with 2 working sons. Married men who had worked for the company for "a good many years" were retained. All were told that they would be reinstated as soon as possible, but the priority of rehires would be those of good records and long service. Altogether, 232 men were laid off (Arno 3, Derby 53, Dunbar 84, Exeter 20, Imboden 42, Roda 30, Stonega 0) and 177 reassigned (from Dunbar, 60 men to Derby and 50 to Roda; from Exeter, 59 men to Imboden, 6 to Arno, and 2 to Derby). Not all Exeter and Dunbar miners could find sufficient housing at their new places of work and so continued to live in their old locations and commute to their respective collieries. Of the 53 men laid off at Derby, 5 were black and 48 were native whites. Most (30) were loaders. The company described them as good (23), fair (26), and poor (4) workers.[4]

Examples of the miners laid off included R. R. and Roy Dixon, both living on small farms with small families. According to SC&C, they were laid off because somebody had to be released due to the drop in coal demand, and better these men who had some source of income than "men living in our houses with no other source of income than the mines." Cleve Phillips, who owned a small farm and a gristmill near Big Stone Gap, was laid off for the same reason. Charlie Parvin, who married "a rather old woman with two grown sons – they have been loitering around for 2 years, one went to jail for petty thievery – " was laid off because the sons were a "nuisance" and better to cut him off than a man with a small child to support. Roy Blair, of Roda, was discharged for refusing to be searched for matches and cigarettes when he went to work in a gaseous mine where it was routine to search all miners.[5]

SC&C also attempted to help employees weather the Depression by making allowances for house rent during periods of shutdown. In August 1931, R. E. Taggart, vice-president from Philadelphia, wrote to Stonega General Manager J. D. Rogers noting that free house rent had reached $1,465 per month and saying that he believed it proper to grant some allowance because there was little work. But "we do not think that it is the proper thing to make a voluntary contribution of this house rent to our employees as it is a form of paternalism that would not be appreciated in the proper manner and would create the impression that we owe them a living." Instead, he suggested a kind of industrial public-relief program whereby workers would be put to work doing something one day in each half of the month, e.g., cleaning hallways, aligning tracks, surfacing roadways, digging ditches, or doing colliery road work.[6]

At Docena, Claude Crane reported that miners were allowed to live rent-free and that TCI did not try to collect for water or light bills. Similarly, miners were given odd jobs, such as painting houses. One former resident said that flour, meal, and rice were allotted to miners. Another reported an allotment of $10 per month to live on when the mines were shut down. In all cases, however, the company kept records of these advances, and when the mines returned to full production, the miners were expected to repay the company.[7]

Company handouts were insufficient to enable miners to survive the Depression. Miners had to rely upon their own survival strategies, ones they had relied upon before the migration to company towns. Gardening and preserving food became especially popular during these years. In 1900, at age eleven, Wiley Pennington migrated from Smyth County, Virginia, to Pie Pan, West Virginia, to work as a trapper boy. When the Depression hit, he was mining at Ligon, Kentucky. Some weeks the mines would open for a day or two; at other times they might stay shut for two weeks with only a day's work during the period. By now Pennington had a family with ten children. He was able to make it financially only by gardening. SC&C Vice-President Rogers complained of miners cutting trees and clearing company land to plant gardens. Garden strips fenced and planted by the miners suddenly appeared along river branches. "As to what might be going on back in the mountain away from the colliery, I do not know," one Stonega official despaired. At Docena, the company actually made 80 to 140 acres available to miners to clear and farm. TCI supplied the mules and wagons. Robert Hamm, a Kentucky miner, complained of never knowing exactly how many days of work he would get during a week. But when he was not working, "we raised gardens all the time, . . . we had a cow, . . . we always managed to have something to eat. Hamm was able to acquire a small piece of land upon which he built a house and had a small farm.[8]

Poverty was a relative condition for which rural migrants were prepared. Miners like Hamm were familiar with poverty before migrating to the mines. Consequently, they were prepared to take the Depression in stride. When asked if he could live better by farming than by mining, Hamm was quick to answer that he lived better working in the mines. Over and over again, miners stated that they were able to survive the Depression without much real hardship because their gardens and rural traditions of preserving food served them well. According to Celia Chambers of Kaymoor, for example: "It was not so bad for me, because we raised so much stuff you know. A lot of people had it pretty tough. Just for my husband and I we got along pretty good. I had a great long meat box on the porch and kept it locked up. I had plenty meat. Plenty of chickens." Mae Prater expressed the same stoic confidence of always being able to get by, even without money. She also acknowledged, however, that some gave up and left the coal town.[9]

Borrowing upon other traditions, miners passed the additional free time in visiting, playing cards, or potluck suppers. Elizabeth Lambert

recalled men working only on Saturdays, if at all. With little to do, they
played cards at night to amuse themselves. At Docena, neighborhood
houses would pool food and gather on someone's front porch for a covered-
dish supper. Each family would supply a different dish – corn, lima beans,
potatoes, and gingerbread, for example.[10]

Thus the Great Depression signaled the beginnings of a different relationship between miners and operators and a return of miners to greater
reliance upon rural traditions of mutual aid. The slump in coal demand,
which had begun in the 1920s, eased the labor shortage. Company paternalism continued, but, only as a temporary expedient in dealing with an
economic crisis, not as a means to attract and hold labor. Some towns
closed. A few became bedroom towns, where the mines had closed and
the miners commuted to nearby active mines. Increasingly more and
more miners commuted to work from rural areas in the vicinity of the
mines. The coal towns that remained open were not maintained with the
same care and concern that had marked the paternalistic phase. Still,
the pressures on profits mounted, and operators looked toward other
belt-tightening measures. Mechanization was a solution that allowed
operators to lower the costs of production and, when needed, to produce
more coal with less labor.

The mechanization of southern Appalachian mining was an uneven
development, occurring over an extended period and sooner in some
mines than others. Undercutting machines, which relieved the miner of
the difficult and protracted task of notching the coal at the base of the
seam, were an early form of mechanization. In 1891 only 2 percent of
West Virginia's coal was undercut by machine. By 1915, undercutters
were used to mine 60 percent of West Virginia's coal compared to 55 percent in the United States as a whole. Using a pick, the undercut might
take up to three hours of a miner's day. The electric cutter could cut a
six-foot-deep wedge across a thirty-foot room in thirty minutes. The productivity of the average bituminous miner rose from three to four and
one-half tons per day as a result of the electric cutter. By the 1920s most
companies were using them. About the same time, mules began to be
replaced with locomotives. In 1930 SC&C eliminated its last mule team
from the mines. TCI, on the other hand, did not completely eliminate
mules until 1950.[11]

Eliminating the handloading of coal was probably the most dramatic
change. With some exceptions, machine loading swept over the industry
in the late 1930s and early 1940s. Island Creek (Wheelwright) launched
a full mechanization program in the earlier decade, financed out of the
profits of the 1920s. But SC&C first began to employ mobile loaders or

conveyors in the 1940s (Roda and Dunbar, 1941; Derby and Stonega, 1945). The use of trackless loaders mounted on wheel-driven cars and capable of moving anywhere in the mines without the need of steel rails was a great advance in mining technology in the 1940s and 1950s. In 1933 less than 1 percent of the coal in southern Appalachia was machine loaded. Within seven years, 75 percent of the coal in West Virginia and Kentucky, and two-thirds of it in Virginia, was machine loaded. Tennessee and Alabama lagged behind the rest of the region with two-thirds of Alabama's coal and 90 percent of Tennessee's still being handloaded in 1940. Finally, the process of cutting and loading coal in a single operation came with the Joy continuous miner, a twenty-six-foot-long, eight-foot-wide giant of a machine consisting of a ripper bar to tear coal from the face and discharge it onto a conveyor which fed a central hopper. TCI first experimented with one in 1949; SC&C first tried one in 1952. A continuous miner and ten men could produce the output of eighty-six handloaders at one-third the labor costs. On 11 June 1952, SC&C reported its three most recently opened mines to be 100 percent mechanized: Glenbrook, Crossbrook, and Pine Branch. Derby was 75 percent mechanized, Roda 60 percent, and Imboden 32 percent. In the forty-year period since incorporation in 1910, the company had gone from pick-and-shovel mining to the most modern techniques in mining technology. Equally significant, none of its new facilities were company towns; they were commuter mines.[12]

The continuous miner's impact upon mining can hardly be overstated. For example, the mechanical loader resulted in a 20 percent rise in productivity between 1930 and 1950, from 5.1 to 6.2 tons per man-day. In the decade of the 1950s, however, productivity in southern Appalachia rose nearly 100 percent due to the continuous miner, from 6.2 to 12 tons per man-day. The impact is more easily grasped by examining the case of Primus Prude, a black miner from West Virginia. Prude exceeded the national record for tons of coal loaded in a lifetime in 1948, after fifty years of backbreaking toil in which he had loaded 90,000 tons. This "staggering human achievement" seemed insignificant beside the capacity of the continuous miner to break Prude's record in a scant three hundred days. Miners like Prude could scarcely compete with such machinery, and thousands were laid off or let go entirely after the introduction of the continuous miner. Between 1950 and 1970, white employment dropped from about 484,000 to 128,000, or by nearly 75 percent. The effects on blacks were even more devastating. Their numbers dropped from 30,000 to 3,700, or nearly 90 percent.[13]

The consequences of mechanization in the workplace were extensive but can be given only brief mention here. The heavy use of machinery in cramped underground quarters escalated the dangers to miners and brought elevated levels of coal dust, which began to manifest itself in an increased incidence of black-lung cases in the 1940s and 1950s. Mine fatalities increased with the first generation of machinery. For example, fatalities averaged 2.6 per 1,000 miners from 1880 to 1889, when few machines were in use. The figures for 1900 to 1909 and 1910 to 1919 were 3.6 and 3.4 respectively, when additional machinery was introduced into the mines.[14] Warning shouts of impending roof falls and other sounds of danger could not be heard over the din of machinery. Acceleration of the pace of work brought other risks. Mules moved slowly enough to give men a second chance when they made a mistake; machinery was unforgiving. A moment's inattention might result in mashed hands and fingers or being "rolled" between the roof and the top of the mine car.

Mechanization reduced the social fraternity of miners considerably. It divided men into smaller crews with more specialized tasks. Cutting, repair, and maintenance crews worked at night; timbermen, trackmen, and their helpers also worked separately from the loaders. Loaders, once the craftsmen of the industry, became machine tenders. Given the noise, dust, and danger created by mining machines, only the machine operator was likely to work in the immediate vicinity, and casual conversation became more difficult and less frequent. Jobs formerly performed by boys – slate picker, pumper, oil boy, spragger, trapper, or mule driver – disappeared, and mining as a father-son activity became less common.

Mechanization sharply curtailed the freedom and independence of miners, according to the most recent study, by Keith Dix. In the hand-loading era, roughly 1880 to 1930, miners were skilled craftsmen who worked independently with men of their own choosing on schedules of their own making. They rarely saw a foreman (see chapter 5). According to U. G. Jordan, who began mining in 1926: "In hand loading you were your own boss, you worked as hard as you wanted to work." Jordan averaged six to eight two-ton cars a day and frequently completed his workday by two o'clock in the afternoon. With the coming of the Joy loader, the company "started to plan for mechanical mining," to organize men into crews around the machinery, and to work full shifts under the constant scrutiny of a foreman.[15] Gradually, de-skilling and routinization of mine labor robbed miners of their previous capacity to control their schedules, pace of work, and wages.

Mechanization brought sharply reduced levels of employment at the collieries, and black miners suffered the most. According to one estimate, 46 men with mobile loaders could do the work of 100 handloaders. At the Docena mine, loaders were able to load more coal in an hour than 40 men could handload in a month. Between 1920 and 1970 coal employment fell by 80 percent as 146,000 miners produced nearly as much coal in 1970 as 785,000 had in the earlier decade. In the same years, the number of tons of coal produced per worker each day jumped from 4 to 16 while labor costs per ton fell by 80 percent. Black miners were the hardest hit. In 1930, 44,266 blacks mined coal in the southern Appalachians, a figure which comprised about one-fifth of all mine labor. In 1960, 8,807 black miners – 6.5 percent of all mine labor – made up the labor force. Total mine labor during this period dropped from about 197,000 to 136,000 miners, with only Virginia recording an increase among the coal-producing states of the region. World War I brought sharp reductions in immigrant labor, and mechanization thinned the ranks of black labor so that in 1960 close to 90 percent of mine labor was composed of native-born whites.[16]

As war and mechanization "whitened" the mines, the automobile and improved roads allowed miners to travel to and from the mechanized mines or to leave the company towns and live in rural areas. A six-hundred-dollar Ford appeared in Wheelwright in 1925 but was mostly confined to the town due to the lack of roads. Autos were not plentiful in the 1920s anywhere in Appalachia. According to one estimate, only about a hundred could be found in the city of Charleston, West Virginia. But as early as 1922, the U.S. Coal Commission noted that the coming of the auto was beginning to increase the mobility of miners; it noted a tendency of miners to desert the smaller towns for the cities, contributing to the demise of less-desirable company towns. In 1940 Stonega Company Vice-President J. D. Rogers, complained to a mine superintendent about miners constructing garages without permission. Rogers stated that he was under strict orders not to allow outbuildings at any of the company's collieries and that the company could not construct individual garages for everyone. The auto also replaced the train as a source of entertainment and temporary escape. In 1947, the Boone Report noted that the growth of good roads, public transportation, and the auto had caused inevitable changes in the status of company towns: remote areas became more accessible, and travel time from urban centers and other communities to the mines diminished. According to the report, some operators hung on, but most closed their camps. Regardless, the miner now had a choice – assuming he could afford a separate residence and the commute. The spread of the national interstate system in the late 1950s accelerated the demise of company towns until finally the auto became a necessity.[17]

World War II brought back the problem of the labor shortage, but it was not nearly so intense as during the previous war. Mechanization had increased the ability of coal companies to increase production with fewer miners. The growing use of oil and gas for for industrial fuel provided alternatives to coal and relieved the pressures on coal production.

Still the collieries experienced shortages. In 1942, SC&C employed 3,456 men and 46 women. It reported "critical shortages" of 200 loaders and 50 coke puller-loaders. In the sixty days prior to the report, Stonega had hired 357 workers; 263 of these were new, and 94 were rehires. It estimated a need for 250 loaders, 50 coke pullers, and 25 company men (motormen, brakemen, machinemen, and trackmen). E. B. Leisenring, Jr., the SC&C president, stated in September: "We are at the start of a real labor shortage." Once again the competition for labor increased. The Tennessee Valley Authority and Holston Ordnance Works in Kingsport, Tennessee, became the subject of Stonega's concern as small numbers of men left for these companies.[18]

Meanwhile the War Manpower Commission reported a surplus of labor in Danville, Lynchburg, Richmond, and Roanoke in Virginia; Chattanooga, Knoxville, and Nashville in Tennessee; and Owensboro and Paducah in Kentucky. Stonega's problem was exacerbated by losses of men to the military. In December 1942, 72 employees entered the armed forces, and as of 26 March 1943 about 540 Stonega employees had joined the military. E. P. Humphrey, a Philadelphia vice-president, inquired of his Big Stone Gap vice-president, H. W. Meador:

Are you doing all you can to interest our employees to stay at work? Would it be wise to send someone to nearby towns to see if they could interest some men to move to Exeter or any other town with empty houses to work in the mines? We might even get a bus load, drive them to Exeter and offer to pay moving expenses. I don't want to antagonize other coal companies. I also recall difficulty in getting [miners] from another state.

Before the war ended, the Island Creek operators relaxed physical requirements to take men with one good eye, a hernia "if not too bad," and high blood pressure "if not over 165 systolic." Then in 1945 the war ended and the labor crisis abated.[19]

After 1933 the trade union became a major influence on the working and living conditions of the individual miner and his family. According to the provisions of the first wage agreement with the "smokeless" operators in West Virginia, miners got a seven-hour day, thirty-five-hour week, two hours of pay for going to and from the mine, six holidays, a checkweighman of their choosing, a wage rate based upon a 2,000-pound ton as opposed to the British or long ton of 2,240 pounds, twice-a-month paydays, an age restriction of no person under seventeen in the mine, a mine committee of three elected persons to settle disputes, and the day off when a miner was killed. Higher wages, improved benefits, safer mines, and greater autonomy were the advantages of unionization mentioned by former miners.

According to Mae Prater, before unionization her children did not see their father much because they would not be out of bed when he left in the morning and they would already be in bed when he arrived at night. When the union came, however, he made a good wage and worked shorter hours. Lloyd Vick Minor pointed out that before the union the miner got nothing for the long walk to the mine and his workplace. The union, on the other hand, brought "portal to portal" pay. Lula Lall Jones said the union meant going to the company store and getting anything you wanted, with higher wages. It also ended the practice of the miner having to purchase his own tools. Instead, they were provided by the company. Ada Wilson Jackson, a black miner's wife, spoke of being "freer to speak," equal treatment of blacks (not altogether the case, as we shall see below), shorter hours, and better wages. Hilton Garrett felt that vacations with pay were the major benefit of unionization. Sid Atkins of Wheelwright said "the union was the greatest thing that ever happened for safety." He also pointed out the greater leverage it gave the miners. Hours and wages continued to improve over the years of union contracts. In the 1940s and 1950s, unionism began to offer miners insurance plans, retirement benefits, and health and hospital care.[20]

Between 1947 and 1955, ninety-seven thousand disabled miners received medical and rehabilitation help, with twenty-three thousand of them able to reenter the workforce, some in mining. The UMWA Welfare and Retirement Fund began operation in 1949 when it was estimated that fifty thousand disabled miners and their families needed immediate medical care. Word of the assistance plan spread in coal-mining communities. Union miners were issued a UMWA health card which entitled them to hospital care, treatment by a physician, drugs and medicine, and any required appliances or prostheses. For three decades, until 1977, the UMWA Health and Retirement Fund laid claim to being the primary health and welfare system for miners. In Kentucky, Virginia, and West Virginia, ten hospitals opened in 1955–56; they were called Miners' Memorial Hospitals. The UMWA also developed and financed many health clinics. Miners' union dues and company contributions together helped finance the health and retirement system. Union benefits replaced both the voluntary associations of miners – which in some cases the UMWA absorbed – and the paternalism of the operators.[21]

Unionism was not without its drawbacks. Its major failings were: outlaw strikes, which idled the mines over petty grievances and cost the miners in fines and time lost; abuses in the health and retirement system, which led to its replacement in 1977; corruption in the union leadership along with its growing isolation from the rank and file; and the failure of the union to support miners where they needed it, such as demanding minimum standards of housing or community facilities as the towns deteriorated or supporting miners displaced by the effects of mechanization – especially black miners.

Outlaw strikes became nettlesome and impossible to control, even though they meant penalties for the miner – in 1930 a dollar per day, with fifty cents going to the company and fifty cents to the UMWA – in addition to the days of lost pay. A few examples will serve to indicate the reasons for outlaw strikes. The following such strikes occurred at Stonega in 1934: a five-man crew struck at Derby Number Three after a discussion of their pay for work done the day before; twenty-nine miners refused to carry powder to their working places, even though this was customary; two coal loaders went home after being given other jobs to do when an undercut had not been made. In 1938: five men set up a conveyor and then quit because someone did not come immediately with the key to the explosives box; four men at Dunbar refused to work the 7:30 shift, which idled the entire shift; four men at Dunbar refused to set timbers and left the mine; thirty men at Derby refused to report to work after hearing that the previous shift had struck because of water in places. According to W. B. Turner, Sr., when the union was first organized, there were more wildcat strikes than there were later, and neither side knew what was going on. However petty the grievance, miners would not go to work – some for fear of being assaulted. A history of violence around the issue of scab labor was intimidating to any miner who wished to challenge a strike, regardless of how insignificant the cause. James Edwards of Wise County recalled working only 215 days in two years during the 1930s due to strikes. Each strike set in motion an elaborate grievance-and-arbitration procedure. Regardless of Turner's recollections, wildcatting at Stonega did not decline. In 1952 the company experienced thirty-three unauthorized strikes. Together with a general strike of twelve days, the miners lost sixty-seven workdays during the year to strikes. In the words of Chan Forren, a former miner, "we let the minority rule the majority" at times. He believed that strikes gave foreign competitors an advantage while Americans lost business and jobs.[22]

Wildcat strikes depressed coal production, which in turn reduced the flow of royalties into the pension and welfare fund. The union's near-crimminal neglect of mine health safety practices after 1960 under President W. A. "Tony" Boyle, John L. Lewis's successor, and gross abuse of the pension system invited the fund's collapse. Miners and health officials took advantage of the bureaucratic red tape and inefficiency, weakening the fund further: miners loaned their health cards to friends and relatives; doctors and hospitals exaggerated costs, gave unnecessary treatment, charged for visits not made, and performed needless surgery.

Abuses bankrupted the system; finally it had to be replaced in 1977, when miners began to pay on a fee basis for a percentage of their medical care costs. Company doctors, nurses, and hospitals arguably provided equivalent care at less cost to the miner and his family.[23]

The greatest failure of unionism, however, was the impoverishment of thousands of black and white miners who were thrust into the maw of mechanization. Between 1950 and 1965, an estimated 300,000 miners lost their jobs to the continuous miner alone. John L. Lewis never fought mechanization, advocating it as early as 1925 and supporting it vigorously until his retirement in 1960. He never fully grasped the consequences of "technological unemployment," believing that displaced miners would be absorbed into other industries. Thousands of miners were forced to leave the coalfields to find work. An "exodus" began, especially from the central Appalachian fields "where mines were located in small isolated towns with few alternatives for other employment." Mining coal continued to provide a good living for the remaining miners and their families. Park of this reality was the visible result of unionization. The invisible costs were the thousands of mining families who had to leave because "The L&N Don't Stop Here Anymore" as the words of a familiar mining song written in the 1950s put it.[24]

In October, 1953, SC&C officials at Big Stone Gap received permission from their Philadelphia headquarters to sell the now mostly empty dwellings at Osaka, Roda, Arno, and Stonega. The inventory of buildings in itself told a historical saga about the nature of housing; the clustering of miners by race, class, and ethnicity; and the social world of mining settlements. At Osaka, for example, the company inventoried five three-room houses in "Slabtown," a ten-room boarding house for "colored," the servant's house for the superintendent, an amusement hall, and a garage near the company store. Above the coke ovens, it wanted to sell four four-room structures, four six-room structures, and one two-room structure. In the "trot section," it had seven two-room and eleven three-room structures. Also for sale: a barn and garage at the "white" church, another servant's house, a coop, and another garage. "Hunktown" and "Happy Hollow" identified the locations of housing at Roda. The mixture of barns and garages revealed another slice of history about the transformation of the company towns from horse-and-buggy days to the automobile. The selling and dismantling continued through 1958: the Roda "Colored" School was sold; one Osaka house was given to the Andover Methodist Church, another was dismantled for a scout cabin; a few occupants of the buildings, "none of whom are present employed or pay rent," were given notice to vacate; at the "colored" church at Osaka, all the furniture and equipment were removed and the "rest" reverted to SC&C. At Dunbar, where the empty houses had deteriorated, Stonega set a book value of $230 per dwelling. And so on it went until the once-flourishing company towns of the Stonega Company vanished like the coal.[25]

At Docena, the mines closed on 8 February 1961. About five or six miners out of an unknown total mining population were fortunate enough to find mine work elsewhere. Some received black-lung disability; others retired. Unlike Stonega's towns, which were more isolated, Docena was situated close to Birmingham, and TCI managed to sell the little houses to the mining families. In fact, miners got first choice at the houses, and Melba Kizzire said the majority bought them. According to Christine Cochran, many miners enlarged the houses, which are still occupied by former miners. Reuben Barnes bought one of the standard four-room box houses, to which a room sixteen by fifteen feet had been added, for $3,680 in July 1950. "It no longer feels like a mining camp," Cochran told her interviewer in 1979. Docena had two modern churches, a community center in an old school building, a civic league, and a voluntary fire department. A grocery store had been made from the old company store. Many had cars in spite of a city bus system that served the town.[26]

At Kaymoor, demolition of company houses began in 1954 and continued for the next two years. By 1958, everyone in Kaymoor Bottom had moved out. About fifty-four houses still stood; most were eventually destroyed by fires and vandalism. Today only the foundations of a few dwellings and a shell or two which somehow survived the vandals mark the spot of the New River Gorge town.[27]

Hilton Garrett underscored the extraordinary changes in the coal town in the brief space of two decades when he contrasted the differences at Wheelwright between the 1930s and the 1950s. He described Wheelwright in the 1930s as crowded with "a good bunch of people" and "a bunch of youngsters." By the 1950s, there were few people left except the old. Gone too were the filling stations, shoe shops, a soda fountain, and the bathhouse. The trains no longer came through. Even the train station disappeared. Garrett concluded:

A youngster grows up here, has got to go somewhere. There's nothing left. Whenever they pulled that railroad out, they pulled that railroad track out, and when they moved that tipple and when they converted, changed this mine, handed over to this machine work, it's been going down ever since. Just like them other coal camps down here, like them on Right Beaver, Wayland, and Garrett, you know.[28]

What had passed was a way of life, but miners recognized that, when stripped of everything except what could not be replaced, it was not the way of life that counted. Indeed, they had proven that rural culture was malleable. In the migration from farm to mine, they had adjusted to life in the industrial village, assimilating themselves to new conditions of life and labor while relying upon former traditions in making the transition and confronting crises. When necessary, they had created modern forms of association and stood up to the operators collectively, relinquishing some of their cherished freedom in the interest of even greater independence. A laboring people's culture arose out of this blend of inherited tradition and the environmental conditions of industrial labor.

Paradoxically, the miners' hour of triumph in the late 1930s was also the moment of their greatest loss. The paternalism of the coal operators had provided miners with benefits and concessions of cultural space in the interest of placating and controlling them. Additional freedom had come from the labor union, which miners used to force further concessions out of their employers. But, under legal protection, the union achieved power over the miners in the 1930s. Coal operators combined with labor leaders in the interest of labor harmony, and together they denied to substantial numbers of miners the freedom of choice miners had struggled to preserve. The convergence of the interests of capital and organized labor, both dedicated to self preservation, proved ominous. The labor movement threw its support to mechanization and accepted technological unemployment. In one way or another, thousands of miners lost the one thing that counted most: their jobs.

Notes

Abbreviations

AOHP, Alice – Appalachian Oral History Project, Alice Lloyd College, Pippa Passes, Kentucky

AOHP, Emory – Appalachian Oral History Project, Emory and Henry University

BCC – Borderland Coal Company Collection, University of Virginia, Charlottesville

JCP – Justus Collins Papers, West Virginia University Library, Morgantown

LMIC – Low Moor Iron Company Collection, University of Virginia, Charlottesville

NRGC – New River Gorge Collection, Glen Jean, West Virginia

SC&C – Stonega Coke and Coal Company

SOHC – Samford Oral History Collection, Samford University, Birmingham, Alabama

WCCR – Westmoreland Coal Company Records, Hagley Museum and Library, Wilmington, Delaware

Preface

1. Ronald L. Lewis, *Black Coal Miners in America: Race, Class, and Community Conflict 1780–1980* (Lexington: University Press of Kentucky, 1987), 191–93.

2. Ibid.

3. For a stimulating discussion of these relationships, see Robert Darnton, *The Great Cat Massacre and Other Episodes in French Cultural History* (New York: Vintage Books, 1985), 3–7, 257–63. Darnton succinctly sums up the *Annales* historiographical tradition, "a blend of French Marxists and revisionists [whose views are] inscribed in the title of France's most influential historical journal, *Annales: Économies, sociétés, civilisations*," as one that has conceived of the past in three levels: economics and demography, social structure, and culture:

> "the third level (culture) somehow derives from the first two (economics and demography, and social structure); and . . . third level phenomena can be understood in the same way as those on the deeper levels (by means of statistical analysis, the play of structure and conjuncture, and considerations of long-term change rather than of events)." (257)

4. See especially Eugene Genovese, *Roll, Jordon, Roll: The World the Slaves Made* (New York, Pantheon, 1974); also Jacquelyn Dowd Hall, et al., *Like a Family: The Making of a Southern Cotton Mill World* (Chapel Hill: University of North Carolina Press, 1987), esp. 139–72; and Peter Kolchin, *Unfree Labor: American Slavery and Russian Serfdom* (Cambridge, Mass.: The Belknap Press of Harvard University Press, 1987), chap. 2.

Introduction

1. David Alan Corbin, *Life, Work, and Rebellion in the Coal Fields: The Southern West Virginia Miners, 1880-1922* (Urbana: University of Illinois Press, 1981), 61 (first quotation) and 77 (second quotation).

2. Richard M. Simon, "Uneven Development and the Case of West Virginia," *Appalachian Journal* 8 (Spring 1981): 172 (first quotation) and 170 (second quotation).

3. Ronald D. Eller, *Miners, Millhands, and Mountaineers: Industrialization of the Appalachian South, 1880-1930* (Knoxville: University of Tennessee Press, 1982), 198 (all but last quotation) and 194 (last quotation).

4. Quoted on cover of Herbert Gutman, *Work, Culture and Society in Industrializing America* (New York: Vintage Books, 1977).

5. See M. I. A. Bulmer, "Sociological Models of the Mining Community, *Sociological Review* 23 (Feb. 1975): 61-92, for a survey of the theoretical models for examining European mining settlements.

6. Lewis, *Black Coal Miners*, xii.

7. Ibid.

8. Ibid. This is a curious statement since the system of legal segregation commonly referred to as "Jim Crow" did exist already, indeed was nearly universal in the South from the 1890s until the 1950s. See C. Vann Woodward, *The Strange Career of Jim Crow.* (New York: Oxford University Press, 1974).

9. Lewis, *Black Coal Miners*, xii.

10. Ibid.

11. Ibid., xiii.

12. Corbin, *Life, Work, and Rebellion*, xviii.

13. In 1922 the U.S. Coal Commission produced a five-volume study of the industry. In 1947 the U.S. Coal Mines Administration produced *A Medical Survey of the Bituminous-Coal Industry*, under the direction of Rear Admiral Joel T. Boone. In 1980 a presidential commission under John D. Rockefeller IV produced *The American Coal Miner: A Report on Community and Living Conditions in the Coalfields*. In notes as well as in the text these are referred to as, respectively, the U.S. Coal Commission, Boone, and Rockefeller reports.

14. Eller, *Miners*, 161.

15. Eric Wolf, *Europe and the People without History* (Berkeley: University of California Press, 1982).

16. Mary Beth Pudup, "The Boundaries of Class in Preindustrial Appalachia," *Journal of Historical Geography* 15(1989): 139-62. See also her unpublished Ph.D. thesis, "Land before Coal: Class and Regional Development in Southeastern Kentucky" (University of California, Berkeley, 1987). Pudup's study appeared when my work was virtually complete. Uncannily, we reached nearly identical conclusions (discussed later in text).

17. Eller, *Miners*, 3.

18. Pudup, "The Boundaries of Class," 140.

19. Helen Lewis, Linda Johnson, and Donald Askins, eds., *Colonialism in Modern America: The Appalachian Case.* (Boone, N.C.: Appalachian Consortium Press, 1978). On the coal barons, see Eller, *Miners*, chap. 6; John Gaventa, *Power and Powerless-*

ness: Quiescence and Rebellion in an Appalachian Valley. (Urbana: University of Illinois Press, 1980). Gaventa elaborates a political theory on "quiescence and rebellion" and the stages of colonization of the "victims of industrialization." His study is especially useful for its discussion of local politics and the trade union movement after the 1950s.

20. Pudup, "The Boundaries of Class," 142.

21. C. Vann Woodward, *Origins of the New South, 1877-1913* (Baton Rouge: Louisiana State University Press, 1951); Paul M. Gaston, *The New South Creed: A Study in Southern Mythmaking* (New York: Vintage Books, 1973); Phillip Shaw Paludan, *Victims: A True Story of the Civil War* (Knoxville: University of Tennessee Press, 1981), chap. 3.

22. As Pudup notes, even when the existence of a preindustrial elite is acknowledged and class distinctions are recognized, the "bandwagon consensus" of an egalitarian society under assault from the outside remains stubbornly entrenched. Local individuals who become tycoons and occupy centers of power and influence in the county seats remain "exceptions to the rule" rather than "pioneering entrepreneurs." Pudup analyzes family lineages to trace the emergence of a commercial and professional middle class in the Kentucky counties of Floyd, Perry, and Harlan. See Pudup, "The Boundaries of Class," 143 (quotation), 152-59.

23. On Kentucky, see James C. Cobb, *Industrialization and Southern Society, 1877-1984* (Chicago: Dorsey Press, 1984), and Harry M. Caudill, *Night Comes to the Cumberlands: A Biography of a Depressed Area* (Boston: Little, Brown, 1962). On West Virginia, see Eller, *Miners,* 47 (quotation), and chap. 2.

24. The same outlook prevailed among the textile-mill workers in the company town of Amoskeag in Manchester, New Hampshire, as described by Tamara K. Hareven and Randolph Langenbach:

> Most of these people preferred the industrial city to the "lost," mythical, rural community which, today, is often idealized for its harmonious and wholesome way of life. They had a realistic view of industrial life, with all its difficulties and exploitation; and they accepted the modern world into which they had been swept. In adapting themselves to it, they also modified it, wherever possible, to fit their own needs and traditions. *Amoskeag: Life and Work in an American Factory-City* (New York: Pantheon, 1978) 12.

25. Gutman, *Work, Culture and Society.*

26. Ibid.

27. Mintz, quoted in Gutman, *Work, Culture and Society,* 16.

28. Bauman quoted in Gutman, *Work, Culture and Society,* 16. See the work of Mintz, Bauman, and Eric Wolf cited in Gutman, 16-17. See also Wolf, *Europe and the People without History.*

29. Gutman, *Work, Culture and Society,* 18.

Chapter 1

A shorter version of this chapter was presented in San Francisco at the 104th annual meeting of the AHA, 27-30 December 1989.

1. Rowland Berthoff, *An Unsettled People: Social Order and Disorder in American History* (New York: Harper & Row, 1971).

2. Ibid. 179 (quotation), 329.

3. For the purposes of this essay, the southern Appalachians include the mountain portions of the states of Virginia, West Virginia, Kentucky, Tennessee, Georgia, and North Carolina. Exemplary of these studies are Eller, *Miners*, 28-38; and Paludan, *Victims*, chap. 1. Traditional Appalachia is also captured by the following authors whose valuable community studies, too numerous to list here, are cited in the bibliography: George L. Hicks, Elmora Messer Matthews, Horace Kephart, John B. Stephenson, Marion Pearsall, William Lynwood Montell, Jack Weller, John C. Campbell, Mandel Sherman and Thomas P. Henry, Laurel Shackelford and Bill Weinberg, and John Fetterman. On folk Appalachia, see Gene Wilhelm, Jr., "Folk Settlements in the Blue Ridge Mountains," *Appalachian Journal* 5 (Winter 1978): 204-45.

4. See Eller, *Miners*. See also Gordon B. McKinney, "Industrialization and Violence in Appalachia in the 1890s," in *An Appalachian Symposium*, ed. Joel W. Williamson (Boone, N.C.: Appalachian Consortium Press, 1978), 131-44. Helen Matthews Lewis, Sue Easterling Kobak, and Linda Johnson, "Family, Religion and Colonialism in Central Appalachia; or Bury My Rifle at Big Stone Gap," in Lewis, et al., ed., *Colonialism in Modern America* (Boone, N.C. Appalachian Consortium Press, 1978), 249; John Alexander Williams, *West Virginia: A History* (New York: Norton, 1984); Gaventa, *Power and Powerlessness*; Richard M. Simon, "Uneven Development;" Altina L. Waller, *Feud: Hatfields, McCoys, and Social Change in Appalachia, 1860-1900.* (Chapel Hill: University of North Carolina Press, 1988), esp. 6-10 for a survey of the social history; Hall, et al., *Like a Family*, chap 1. For a study of the intellectual and economic "discoveries" of Appalachia and the pernicious effects of simultaneous discovery, see Henry D. Shapiro, *Appalachia on Our Mind: The Southern Mountains and Mountaineers in the American Consciousness, 1870-1920* (Chapel Hill: University of North Carolina Press, 1978).

5. For the theoretical argument that mobility may actually facilitate community or reveal family and community in the process of transformation rather than destruction, see Thomas Bender, *Community and Social Change in America* (Baltimore: Johns Hopkins University Press, 1978), 92-93, 122-23, 143-50. James Henretta has persuasively argued that mobility need not necessarily be connected with the desires of a cultural, racial, or class group to improve its material condition. See Henretta, "The Study of Social Mobility: Ideological Assumptions and Conceptual Bias," *Labor History* 18, no. 2 (Spring 1977): 165-78.

6. Gaps in the study of Appalachian history may have thwarted efforts to reach a comprehensive theory of change and continuity beyond the model of modernization. For a treatment of the gaps in the region's history, see Ronald D. Eller, "Towards a New History of the Appalachian South," *Appalachian Journal* 5, no. 1 (Autumn 1977): 74-81; in fact, the entire Autumn 1977 issue of the *Appalachian Journal* was devoted to a guide to Appalachian studies, ed. Stephen L. Fisher, J. W. Williamson, and Juanita Lewis. See also Charlotte Ross, ed., *Bibliography of Southern Appalachia* (Boone, N.C. Appalachian Consortium Press, 1976).

7. For the background of this movement, see James G. Leyburn, *The Scotch-Irish: A Social History* (Chapel Hill: University of North Carolina Press, 1962), 179-83. The

"five great waves of emigration" came in 1717-18, 1725-29, 1740-41, 1754-55, and 1771-75 (Leyburn, 169). According to best estimates, a total of 200,000 Scotch-Irish emigrated to America in the eighteenth century. The Germans averaged 2,000 per year between 1727 and 1754 and diminished thereafter. See also James T. Lemon, *The Best Poor Man's Country: A Geographical Study of Early Southeastern Pennsylvania.* (Baltimore: Johns Hopkins University Press, 1972), 3-24; John C. Campbell, *The Southern Highlander* and His Homeland (Lexington: University of Kentucky Press, 1969); and A.B. Faust, *The German Element in the United States* (New York: Houghton Mifflin, 1927).

8. Avery O. Craven, *Soil Exhaustion as a Factor in the Agricultural History of Virginia and Maryland* (Urbana: University of Illinois Press, 1922). Livestock drovers were other sources of traffic through the region as they urged giant herds of up to 5000 hogs at once through parts of Ohio, Tennessee, Virginia, and the Carolinas. Mules, horses, and cattle passed through the Cumberland Gap into the Tennessee Valley and on southward to southern plantations. See Campbell, *The Southern Highlander,* 47-48; Gene Wilhelm, Jr., "Animal Driver in the Southern Highlands," *Mountain Life and Work* 42 (1966): 6-11; and Gene Wilhelm, "Animal Driver: A Case Study in Historical Geography," *Journal of Geography* 66 (1967): 327-34; Ronald D. Eller, "Land and Family: An Historical View of Preindustrial Appalachia," *Appalachian Journal* 6 (Winter 1979): 94. A number of county histories of southwest Virginia mention the livestock driver and the spectacle of massive herds moving through the mountains to the calls and shouts of anxious drovers.

9. Robert V. Wells, *Uncle Sam's Family: Issues in and Perspectives on American Demographic History* (Albany: State University of New York Press, 1985), esp. chap. 2, "Revolutions in Childbearing in Nineteenth-Century America." Ethnic and racial differences, urbanization, land scarcity, economic conditions, occupation and income, and attitudes and values have all been suggested as answers regarding motives for the control of childbearing. Of these, attitudes and values seem most influential. The total fertility rate (TFR) is an estimate of the number of children a cohort of a thousand women would bear if they were subject to the age-specific fertility rates that prevailed at the time of their childbearing years. Demographers consider the TFR as the best available cross-sectional measure of fertility.

10. Completed family size is the number of children a woman had during her childbearing years and is therefore a better measure of fertility. Although the total sample was 363 women, the number of completed families upon which this median could be calculated was only seventy-eight. Not large enough to guarantee statistical accuracy, the results nevertheless coincide with the general trends in the region, and a larger sample would probably produce similar figures. The Upper Cumberland includes eleven counties in northeast Tennessee: Clay, Cumberland, DeKalb, Fentress, Jackson, Macon, Overton, Pickett, Putnam, Smith, and White. I am indebted to Jeanette Keith for sharing her research with me and to Don H. Doyle for making it known to me. See Jeanette Keith, "The Hill-Country of Zion: Community, Church and Society in Tennessee's Upper Cumberland, 1890-1929," Ph.D. thesis in progress, Vanderbilt University, Nashville, Tenn.

11. Durwood Dunn, *Cades Cove: The Life and Death of a Southern Appalachian Community* (Knoxville: University of Tennessee Press, 1988), 79.

12. Waller, *Feud.*

13. Ibid., 38-39.

14. Ibid., 96, 276n.

15. William H. Turner, "The Demography of Black Appalachia: Past and Present," in William H. Turner and Edward J. Cabbell, eds., *Blacks in Appalachia* (Lexington: University of Kentucky Press, 1985), 241. These figures were derived from averaging the decennial percentage increases between 1820 and 1930.

16. Thomas R. Ford and Gordon F. DeJong, "The Decline of Fertility in the Southern Appalachian Mountain Region," *Social Forces* 42, no. 1 (Oct. 1963): 89-96.

17. Paludan, *Victims,* 8 and 8n.

18. Hal Seth Barron, "A Case for Appalachian Demographic History," *Appalachian Journal.* 4 (Spring-Summer 1977), 212.

19. George A. Hillery, Jr., *Population Growth in Kentucky, 1820-1960,* University of Kentucky Agricultural Experiment Station *Bulletin* 705 (Feb. 1966): 25-26.

20. *Economic and Social Problems and Conditions of the Southern Appalachians,* U.S. Department of Agriculture Miscellaneous Publication No. 205 (Washington, D.C., 1935), 124-25. Hereafter cited as USDA Report.

21. Eller, *Miners,* 16, 18.

22. Jack Temple Kirby, *Rural Worlds Lost: The American South, 1920-1960* (Baton Rouge: Louisiana State University Press, 1987), 276-79, analyzes itinerancy in the twentieth century.

23. Ibid., chap. 8.

24. In Cades Cove, economic decline after the Civil War altered emigration patterns. Prior to to the war, Cove residents had the means to move to new lands on the frontier. Afterwards, they moved to neighborhoods usually no more than fifty miles away. Dunn, *Cades Cove,* 74.

25. Campbell, *The Southern Highlander,* 47-48; Gene Wilhelm, Jr., "Animal Driver in the Southern Highlands," 6-11; Wilhelm, "Animal Driver: A Case Study in 327-34; Hall, et al., *Like a Family,* 14; Pete Daniel, "The Crossroads of Change: Cotton, Tobacco, and Rice Cultures in the Twentieth Century," *Journal of Southern History* 50 (Aug. 1984): 429-56; and Daniel, *Standing at the Crossroads: Southern Life in the Twentieth Century* (New York: Hill and Wang, 1986), 14-19.

26. Gavin Wright, *The Political Economy of the Cotton South: Households, Markets and Wealth in the Nineteenth Century* (New York: W. W. Norton, 1978).

27. Dunn, *Cades Cove,* chap. 3.

28. See Daniel, *Standing at the Crossroads,* 14-16.

29. Hall, et al., *Like a Family,* 14.

30. My own father's education ended in the third grade when he was old enough to stand on a box and put the harness on a horse. According to him, this was customary for boys in the Blue Ridge Mountains of Virginia where he grew up helping his father sharecrop in the 1920s.

31. Hall, et al., *Like a Family,* 14-15.

32. Frederick A. Bode and Donald E. Ginter, *Farm Tenancy and the Census in Antebellum Georgia* (Athens: University of Georgia Press, 1986), 183; Durwood Dunn, *Cades Cove,* esp. chap. 3. Mountain agriculture, its evolution, and the "capitalist transformation" which swept across the Piedmont South in the nineteenth century has yet

to find its historian. For stimulating essays on rural change, see Steven Hahn and Jonathan Prude, eds., *The Countryside in the Age of Capitalist Transformation* (Chapel Hill: University of North Carolina Press, 1985), especially the essay by Hahn, "The 'Unmaking' of the Southern Yeomanry: The Transformation of the Georgia Upcountry, 1860 and 1890," 179–203; see also Hahn's larger study, *The Roots of Southern Populism: Yeoman Farmers and the Transformation of the Georgia Upcountry, 1850–1890* (New York: Oxford University Press, 1983). See Hall, et al., *Like a Family*, 24–31, on the impact of the market economy in the Georgia and Carolina piedmonts. See also the fine surveys of Gilbert C. Fite, *Cotton Fields No More: Southern Agriculture 1865–1980* (Lexington: University Press of Kentucky, 1984); and Kirby, *Rural Worlds Lost*, both of which show that the modernization of southern agriculture did not come until the 1940s.

33. Waller, *Feud*, 70.

34. Daniel, *Standing at the Crossroads*, 52.

35. See Dunn, *Cades Cove*, 73, 180–82.

36. *Soil Survey, Wise County, Virginia*, U.S. Department of Agriculture Soil Conservation Service Series 1940, no. 12 (Washington, D.C.: Government Printing Office, 1954), 4, 44.

37. U.S. Department of Commerce, Bureau of the Census, *Twelfth Census of the United States: 1900* (Washington, D.C., 1901–2) *Population*, vol. 1: 44.

38. USDA Report, 131; *Twelfth Census*, 1:44; James A. Henretta, *The Evolution of American Society, 1700–1815* (Lexington, Mass.: D. C. Heath, 1973), chap. 1.

39. Other factors may account for population growth in Wise during this period. For example, in Knox County, a nearby coal-mining county of eastern Kentucky, a population surge in the 1930s resulted from the "return . . . of working-age adults who had lost their industrial jobs elsewhere." Kirby, *Rural Worlds Lost*, 100.

40. In 1983, the natural increases were as follows: India, 20; Ethiopia, 24; Mexico, 26; and Egypt, 28. U.S. Bureau of the Census, *World Population 1983: Recent Demographic Estimates for the Countries and Regions of the World* (Washington, D.C.: U.S. Government Printing Office, 1983).

41. Hal Seth Barron, "A Case for Appalachian Demographic History," *Appalachian Journal* 4 (Spring-Summer) 212; Carl N. Degler, *At Odds: Women and the Family in America from the Revolution to the Present* (New York: Oxford University Press, 1980), 178–209; Wells, *Uncle Sam's Family*, chap. 2.

42. Barron, "A Case," 211.

43. Kirby, *Rural Worlds Lost*, 99.

44. Ibid.

45. For a good study of the consequences of population growth and lack of opportunity, see Michael J. McDonald and John Muldowny, *TVA and the Dispossessed* (Knoxville: University of Tennessee Press, 1982). Although not in Appalachia as conventionally defined, the Ozark Mountains of Arkansas and Missouri did suffer from similar problems of population growth, land scarcity, and limited alternatives.

46. Dunn, *Cades Cove*, 45.

47. Ibid.

48. John Egerton, "Boom or Bust in the Hollows," *New York Times Magazine*, 18 Oct. 1981. Martin County is also a good example of the exploitation that accompanied

industrialization. Unfortunately, two-thirds of the coal was surface mined, causing extensive damage to local streams and water supplies. Surface mining also provided fewer jobs than deep mining. In addition, state and local officials at first failed to tax adequately some of the enormous wealth generated from coal production and channel it back into county needs for schools, housing, sanitation, and roads. In 1981 the state treasury promised to return $1.6 million in coal-severance tax funds out of about $18 million collected.

49. Interestingly, similar patterns affected South African mining areas. See George Fredrickson, *White Supremacy: A Comparative Study in American and South African History* (Oxford: Oxford University Press, 1981), 230. See the works of Eller and Shapiro cited above on the background and meaning of the discovery. The phrase "selective perception" was used by Dunn, *Cades Cove,* chap. 6, to refer to writers and travelers who came to the cove and found what they came in search of.

50. In 1924, Lee County, Virginia, had forty-three sawmills, eight businesses, and thirty-five coal mines with miners who farmed "on the side" in the summer. "Personal travel was difficult. There was a macadam road from Pennington to St. Charles, and a dirt road from Keokee to Appalachia. Otherwise the wagon roads were rocky and steep. Eighty five percent of the county was covered with forests, and slopes were frequently too steep to till." In 1925, 57 percent of the population was living on farms. Besides the mines, Lee farmers worked part-time or in the off-season in lumber camps; fruit growing was a major source of income. Walter R. Hibbard, Jr., "The Coalfields of Virginia: An History of People, Machinery, and Natural Resources," unpublished manuscript, Virginia Center for Coal and Energy Research, Virginia Polytechnic Institute and State University, Blacksburg, 45.

51. L. F. Minor interview, SOHC, 18. A complete listing of all interviews in the book is contained in the bibliography under the collection of record. In the notes, they will be referred to with the informant's name, abbreviation of collection of record, and page number when available.

52. Ernest Carico interview, AOHP, Emory, 2–6.

53. Ernest Meade Interview, AOHP, Emory, 4–5.

54. USDA Report, 124–25.

55. Sidney Pollard, *Peaceful Conquest: The Industrialization of Europe, 1760–1970* (New York: Oxford University Press, 1981), vii, 6 (quotation), 77. Cf. T. S. Ashton, *The Industrial Revolution, 1760–1830* (London: Oxford University Press, 1964), 25.

56. Stonega Coke and Coal Company, Annual Report, 1917, Westmoreland Coal Company Records, Hagley Library, Wilmington, Del., 3. Collection hereafter cited as WCCR.

57. Lloyd V. Minor interview, 21, SOHC; also Marvin Gullet interview, 11 AOHP, Alice.

58. George Wickes to Frank Lyman, 21 April 1906, Low Moor Iron Company Papers, Alderman Library, University of Virginia (hereafter cites as LMIC).

59. The textile mill experience has been examined most recently in Hall, et al., *Like a Family,* 43 (quotations). See also David Carlton, *Mill and Town in South Carolina* (Baton Rouge: Louisiana State University Press, 1982).

60. Cf. Josef J. Barton, *Peasants and Strangers: Italians, Rumanians and Slovaks in an American City* (Cambridge, Mass.: Harvard University Press, 1975), 48–58.

61. Melvin Profitt interview, 2, 5, 15–19, AOHP, Alice. On similar patterns in the textile mills, see Hall, et al., *Like A Family,* 33–34, 37–38.

62. Rev. Stuart Frazier interview, 22.11–12, 22.13, New River Gorge Oral History Collection, Glen Jean, W.Va. (hereafter cited as NRGC). References to this collection include the number assigned to the interview, followed by the page number of the transcript.

63. Hilton Garrett interview, 2 (quotation), AOHP, Alice.

64. Tony Dunbar, *Our Land Too* (New York: Pantheon, 1971), 115.

65. Ibid., 116–17. See also G. C. Jones, *Growing Up Hard in Harlan County* (Lexington: University Press of Kentucky, 1985).

66. Michael Kline, "The Coon Dog Truth: Charlie Blevins at the Red Robin Inn," *Goldenseal* 8, no. 4 (Winter 1982): 37.

67. For a stimulating discussion of the relationship between culture and the social order and the elusive quest for the history of mentalities, see Darnton, *The Great Cat Massacre,* esp. 3–7, 257–63.

68. Waller, *Feud,* 100–101, 141–50.

69. Cf. Edward L. Ayers, *Vengeance and Justice: Crime and Punishment in the Nineteenth-Century South* (New York: Oxford University Press, 1984), and Bertram Wyatt-Brown, *Southern Honor: Ethics and Behavior in the Old South* (New York: Oxford University Press, 1982). Dunn, *Cades Cove,* 149–50, 195–200.

70. Elliott J. Gorn, "'Gouge and Bite, Pull Hair and Scratch': The Social Significance of Fighting in the Southern Backcountry," *American Historical Review* 90, no. 1 (February 1985): 35.

71. David Potter has noted that the historian's advantage of hindsight "is really a disadvantage in understanding how a situation seemed to the participants." For Potter, the most difficult job of the historian is to "see the past through the imperfect eyes of those who lived it." Potter, *The South and the Sectional Conflict* (Baton Rouge: Louisiana State University Press, 1968), 245–46.

Chapter 2

1. For the estimate of coal reserves, see Eller, *Miners,* 128; for an analysis of the consequences of these discoveries for the people of Appalachia, see Shapiro, *Appalachia on Our Mind,* and Gaventa, *Power and Powerlessness.*

2. Eller, *Miners,* 48–52, 69–70.

3. Ibid., chaps. 2 and 4, contains a thorough treatment of railroad developments in the region.

4. Lewis, *Black Coal Miners,* 121–22; Caudill, *Night Comes to the Cumberlands,* chap. 9; Eller, *Miners,* 128–30, 132–33, 149–53; Walter R. Hibbard, Jr., "An Abridged History of the Southwest Virginia Coal Industry," unpublished manuscript, Virginia Center for Coal and Energy Research, Virginia Polytechnic Institute and State University, Blacksburg, Va., July 1987, 1–2.

5. Donald L. Miller and Richard E. Sharpless, *The Kingdom of Coal: Work, Enterprise, and Ethnic Communities in the Mine Fields* (Philadelphia: University of Pennsylvania Press, 1985), 5, 287; W. P. Tams, Jr., *The Smokeless Coal Fields of West Vir-*

ginia (Morgantown: West Virginia University Press, 1983), 15-17; Lewis, *Black Coal Miners*, 122.

6. Eller, *Miners*, 49. See also Hibbard, "An Abridged History," 23-24.

7. Paul M. Gaston, *The New South Creed*, 17-42; Hibbard, "An Abridged History, 23; Eller, *Miners*, 49.

8. John Leggett Pultz, "The Big Stone Gap Coal-Field of Virginia and Kentucky," *Engineering Magazine* (27 (Oct. 1904): 71-85; Hibbard, "An Abridged History," 23-24; Eller, *Miners*, 49.

9. Pultz, "The Big Stone Gap Coal Field," 72, 75; Hibbard, "An Abridged History," 24-25.

Chapter 3

1. *Report of the U.S. Coal Commission*, part 3, table 14, p. 1467; Eller, *Miners*, 162-63.

2. Tams, *Smokeless Coal Fields*, 100-106.

3. Margaret Ripley Wolfe, "Putting Them in Their Places: Industrial Housing in Southern Appalachia, 1900-1930," *Appalachian Heritage* 7 (Summer 1979): 28-29; see also Wolfe's "Aliens in Appalachia: The Construction of the Clinchfield Railroad and the Italian Experience," in Emmett M. Essin, ed., *Appalachia: Family Traditions in Transition* (Johnson City: East Tennessee State University Press, 1975).

4. Wolfe, "Putting Them in Their Places," 28.

5. "Stonega Coke and Coal Company: Company History," compiled at the Hagley Museum and Library, Wilmington, Del.; see also E. J. Prescott, compiler, *The Story of the Virginia Coal and Iron Company, 1882-1945*, Big Stone Gap, Va.: n.p. 1945. For the percentage of Virginia miners employed by SC&C, see H. W. Meador to E. P. Humphrey, 4 March 1943, WCCR.

6. These years, which show when the collieries went into production, have been gleaned from the records of the Stonega Company at Hagley Museum and Library. On the company's employment, see V. P. to Mr. Remsen, c/o *Coalfield Progress*, 3 July 1935, WCCR.

7. Gino Speranza, "Getting Evidence in the Labor Camps of West Virginia," Gino Speranza Papers, microfilm, New York Public Library, and in Immigration and History Research Center, University of Minnesota. (Speranza was an Italian-American investigator for the Society for the Protection of Italian Immigrants).

8. Margaret Ripley Wolfe, "Changing the Face of Southern Appalachia: Urban Planning in Southwest Virginia and East Tennessee, 1890-1929," *Journal of the American Planning Association* 47 (1981): 245-55.

9. The quotations and early description of Stonega are provided in Wolfe, "Putting Them in Their Places," 27-36, 30.

10. Wolfe, "Changing the Face," 254-55.

11. Lou Athey, *Kaymoor: A New River Community* (Eastern National Park and Monument Association, 1986), 2, 6, 8-9; see also Matthew P. Marowitz, et al., compilers, "A History of the Low Moor Iron Company," in the Low Moor Iron Company Records, Alderman Library, University of Virginia, Charlottesville, hereafter referred to as LMIC.

12. Athey, *Kaymoor,* 2–4, 31–32.

13. "A History of the Borderland Coal Company," Matthew P. Marowitz, et. al., compiler, in Edward L. Stone–Borderland Coal Company Papers, Alderman Library, University of Virginia. Hereafter referred to as BCC.

14. Ibid.; Matthew P. Marowitz, et al., compilers, "Biography of Edward L. Stone," 4–8, BCC.

15. Stonega Annual Report, 1918, WCCR, 40–43.

16. Ibid.

17. Eller, *Miners,* 71; Hibbard, "An Abridged History," 19–21 (quotation, 20).

18. Chapter 5 examines the risks and uncertainties of mining.

19. Birmingham *News,* 31 May 1904; Birmingham *Post,* 30 Dec. 1944; Robert Gregg, "Origin and Development of the Tennessee Coal, Iron and Railroad Company," n.d., all in a scrapbook, Birmingham Public Library. Gregg was president of TCI at some point. According to the *Post,* 20 Sept. 1963, Tennessee Coal, Iron and Railroad moved to Birmingham in 1886, although its earlier account above gave 1944 as the date of the company headquarters being moved to Birmingham.

20. Christine Cochran interview, 1; Melba Kizzire interview, 30–32, both in SOHC.

21. Melba Kizzire interview, 30–32, SOHC, Lewis M. Williams, "The Transformation of a Coal Mining Town," Wheelwright Coal Camp Collection, 1930–78, unpublished manuscript, Special Collections, Margaret I. King Library, University of Kentucky, Lexington, Ky., 5, 10; Wood Cooley interview, 6–9; 22–23, 25 (quotation, 6), AOHP, Alice.

22. In chapter 4, I examine the recruitment of foreign and black labor.

23. T. B. Pugh interview, 4.6, NRGC.

24. Lloyd Vick Minor interview, 8, SOHC.

25. Letter of Edward Stone in response to critics of Representative James P. Woods, 25 Oct. 1920, BCC.

26. A. H. Reeder to D. B. Wentz, 19 Nov. 1913, WCCR.

27. T. B. Pugh interview, 4.20, NRGC.

28. Athey, *Kaymoor,* 39–40.

29. Interview by Arnell Oden and Clara Higgins, 5 Sept. 1971, McRoberts, Kentucky, 6 AOHP, Alice.

30. Stonega Annual Report, 1916, p. 15. In the same year, the Low Moor Iron Company gave children a box of candy, single men a box of cigars, and married men one hen and one bag of flour. See J. W. Monteith to G. K. Anderson, Jr., Madison Hepler, and R. A. Lipscomb, 5 Dec. 1916. LMIC.

31. Stonega Annual Report, 1916, 61.

32. Gregg, "Origin and Development," 15, 20–21 (quotation).

33. Stonega Annual Reports, 1920, 229 (first quotation); 1915, 51 (second, third, and fourth quotations); 1916, 51 (fifth quotation); 1918, 152 (last two quotations).

34. Athey, *Kaymoor,* 38.

35. Stonega annual Report, 1916, 5; Margaret Ripley Wolfe, "Changing the Face," 255, 264, 31n.

36. E. R. Price to Dr. Don J. Schleissmann, Public Health Service, series 7, box 17, Wheelwright Collection, King Library, University of Kentucky, Lexington; Stonega Annual Reports, 1924 (4,434 total cases) and 1940 (3,025 total cases). It is not possible to tell if these case totals include only new cases or also include repeat visits.

37. Stonega Annual Reports, 1924 and 1940.

38. A. G. Kramer to Clarence B. Randal, 20 Oct. 1941; Medical Report, 30 Jan. 1943, series 7, box 17; Medical Report, 6 Feb. 1951, series 7, box 16, all in Wheelwright Collection.

39. George Wolfe to Justus Collins, 7 Aug. 1916 and 19 Sept. 1918, both in Justus Collins Papers, West Virginia University Library, Morgantown, hereafter cited as JCP; Stonega Annual Report, 1915, 82.

40. J. D. Rogers to D. B. Wentz, 20 Sept. 1938, "Personal and Confidential," WCCR. This letter reveals that "for the last few years" SC&C had been quietly denying requests for free house rent, telling requesters that the policy had been withdrawn. Although worried about "someone taking us to court" for being in violation of contract, the company planned to continue to phase out the program in this way. Stonega Annual Reports, 1922 (quotations) and 1940, WCCR.

41. Christine Cochran interview, 18, and Frank Bonds interview, n.p., both in SOHC; Athey, *Kaymoor,* 32–33; L. E. Armentrout to Edward L. Stone, 9 June 1922, BCC.

42. Ronald L. Filippelli, *Labor in the United States,* (New York: Random House, 1984), 186; Lewis M. Williams, "The Transformation of a Coal Mining Town," 5, 10, and 18.

43. Ibid., 14, 17–18; Wood Cooley interview, 21–22, AOHP, Alice.

44. Williams, "The Transformation of a Coal Mining Town," 10–12, 21 (quotation).

45. Wood Cooley interview, 22; Everett Hall interview, 12, both in AOHP, Alice.

46. For the argument that West Virginia's towns were integrated, see Corbin, *Life, Work, and Rebellion,* 66–68. Cf. Lewis, *Black Coal Miners,* esp. 143–56, which argues that West Virginia's miners were segregated but had equal facilities. On the Jim Crow system in the South, see Woodward, *The Strange Career of Jim Crow.*

47. L. R. Anderson to Justus Collins, 13 Aug. 1923, JCP. Anderson was a black newspaper publisher who moved among black miners at Goodwill and reported to Collins; Wolfe to Collins, 31 Mar. 1917, JCP; Tams, *Smokeless Coal Fields* 67–68; Athey, *Kaymoor,* 33.

48. Stone letter of 25 Oct. 1920 on newspaper attacks upon James P. Woods, BCC.

49. Ada Wilson Jackson interview, 26.30; Annie Kelly interview, 15.10, both in NRGC.

50. Wolfe to Collins, 7, 8, and 9 June 1916, JCP.

51. Hilton Garrett interview, 8–13; Marvin Gullet interview, 3–34, 37, 39–41, 44, both in AOHP, Alice.

52. Everett Hall interview, 7–8, AOHP, Alice. E. R. Price to J. T. Parker, 22 Apr. 1942. Wheelwright Collection, series 7, box 16.

53. The inventories are contained in H. W. Meador to G. B. Taylor, 12 Oct. 1953 and 17 May 1954; Stonega Annual Reports, 1916 (remodeling), 118; 1915 (new commissary), 125; 1915 (first aid teams), 2; 1924 (Andover contest), 149–50; C. G. Duffy to A. H. Reeder, 3 Mar. 1913 (barbershop); R. E. Taggart to E. Drenon, 5 Nov. 1914 (cemetery), all in WCCR.

54. Reuben Barnes interview, 4, gives for the 1930s 437 houses and a population of 500 whites, 2,700 blacks. William H. Walker interview, 11, SOHC. Walker was a foreman at Docena who said that 85 percent of his 396 men were black. Mary P. Gray interview, 3 (layout of Docena), SOHC; Belinda Mardis interview, 2–3, 13 (quotation); Claude

Crane interview, 5 (separate churches); also Reuben Barnes interview on other facilities, 1,4; Christine Cochran interview, 12 (mail call); Mary P. Gray interview, 3, 18
(blacks in white homes); D. B. Oglestree interview, 12 (work in mines); Luther V. Smith
interview, 2-3; Edith Shoemaker interview, 2-3, 10, 11; and William H. Walker interview, 11. Smith, Shoemaker, and Walker all comment on the discrimination against
black miners underground. All of these interviews in SOHC.

55. Wolfe, "Changing the Face of Southern Appalachia," 262.

56. Ibid., 262.

Chapter 4

1. Report of the U.S. Coal Commission, part 3, 1412, 1414-15.

2. Ibid., 1414-15.

3. For the 1907 figures, see James T. Laing, "The Negro Miner in West Virginia,"
71-72; for 1909-17, see Kenneth R. Bailey, "A Judicious Mixture: Negroes and Immigrants in the West Virginia Mines, 1880-1917," 119; for 1930, 1940, and 1950, see William
H. Turner, "The Demography of Black Appalachia," all in Turner and Cabbell, eds.,
Blacks in Appalachia.

4. Superintendent Duffy to A. H. Reeder, Oct. 1913, LMIC.

5. John Leonard to Edward L. Stone, 19 Aug. 1913, BCC.

6. Athey, *Kaymoor,* 20.

7. George Wickes to Menotti Bank, 20 May 1907; Menotti to Wickes, 21 May 1907;
Wickes to Menotti, 29 May, 9 June, and 22 June 1907, all in LMIC.

8. Stonega Annual Report, 1920, p. 5, WCCR.

9. Stonega Annual Report, 1920, p. 5, WCCR.

10. R. A. Lipscomb to S. G. Cargill, 8 Apr. 1904; Moore Lime Company to S. E.
Cogill, May 1906, both in LMIC.

11. George Wickes to E. C. Means, 31 July 1906, LMIC.

12. George Wickes to E. C. Means, 11 July 1906, LMIC.

13. E. D. Wickes to E. C. Means, 11 Jan. 1906, LMIC.

14. A. H. Reeder to Superintendent Duffy, 9 Oct. 1913, WCCR.

15. E. C. Berkeley to Justus Collins, 30 Aug. 1916, JCP.

16. Blank Atwood Employment Agency form, LMIC.

17. W. L. Alley to Atwood's Employment Office, 27 May 1907, LMIC.

18. Atwood to Alley, 28 May 1907, LMIC.

19. E. D. Wickes to E. C. Means, LMIC.

20. *The American Coal Miner: A Report on Community and Living Conditions in
the Coalfields,* President's Commission on Coal, John D. Rockefeller IV, Chairman
(Washington, D.C., 1980), 18-19, hereafter cited as Rockefeller Report; Eller, *Miners,*
174.

21. George Wickes to Frank Lyman, 21 Apr. 1906. LMIC.

22. George Wickes to E. C. Means, 10 Mar. 1906, LMIC.

23. Miller and Sharpless, *The Kingdom of Coal,* 172. For a sobering account of the
population crisis in Europe and the emigration it propelled, see Philip J. Taylor, *The
Distant Magnet: European Emigration to the U.S.A.* (New York: Harper & Row, 1971).

24. Steve Tomko interview, 1–3, 12, 27 (quotation), AOHP, Alice.

25. John Sokira interview, 1, SOHC.

26. Athey, *Kaymoor*, 46.

27. George Wickes to Lynchburg Labor Agency, 20 May 1907, LMIC. In the letter, he offers to hire Italians at the same wage rate.

28. American National Bank to George Wickes, 21 May 1907, LMIC.

29. W. M. Dues to George Wickes, 22 May 1907; Wickes to Dues, 24 May 1907, both in LMIC.

30. Laing. "The Negro Miner," 72.

31. Steve Tomko interview, 24, AOHP, Alice.

32. L. F. Minor interview, 6, SOHC.

33. Lula Lall Jones interview, 27.11, NRGC.

34. Lloyd Vick Minor interview, 9, SOHC.

35. Russell D. Parker, "The Black Community in a Company Town: Alcoa, Tennessee, 1919–1939," in Turner and Cabbell, eds., *Blacks in Appalachia*, 127.

36. Bailey, "A Judicious Mixture," 127

37. For an examination of race and class in the southern fields, see Lewis, *Black Coal Miners,* esp. part 4.

38. E. E. Hartsook to George Wolfe, 21 Sept. 1916, JCP.

39. Athey, *Kaymoor*, 46.

40. Virgil W. Burgess interview, 47.13, NRGC.

41. William H. Walker interview, 13, SOHC.

42. Irene Hicks interview, Skaggs, NRGC; T. B. Pugh interview, 4.21, NRGC; Dewey Osborne interview, 14, AOHP, Alice.

43. L. F. Minor interview, SOHC, 21.

44. E. D. Wickes to E. C. Means, 2 May 1907, LMIC.

45. Lee Armentrout to Edward L. Stone, 10 June, 13 June, and 2 October 1916; Stone to Armentrout, 11 June 1916, all in BCC.

46. E. C. Means to George Wickes, April 1907, LMIC.

47. Stonega Annual Reports, 1905–16, WCCR.

48. 1916, Stonega Annual Report, WCCR.

49. U.S. Dept. of Labor, Women's Bureau, *Home Environment and Employment Opportunities of Women in Coal-Mine Workers' Families,* Bulletin 45, 1925), 3. The source of data for this report was the U.S. Coal Commission study of 1925.

50. Eller, *Miners,* 197.

51. Athey, *Kaymoor*, 9.

52. Lewis, *Black Coal Miners,* 147.

53. Job applications, 1929, WCCR, box 538; Joseph Tony interview, 13, AOHP, Emory.

54. George Wolfe to Justus Collins, 23 Sept. 1916, JCP.

55. Lee Armentrout to Edward L. Stone, 17 Apr. 1917, BCC.

56. Edward L. Stone to Dr. M. D. Thomas, 10 Mar. 1918.

57. A. H. Reeder to Dr. C. B. Boyer, 5 Jan. 1931, WCCR.

58. George Wolfe to Justus Collins, 25 Aug. 1917, JCP.

59. George Wolfe to Justus Collins, 6 June 1917, JCP. The total number of miners is unknown.

60. Stonega Annual Report, 1917, WCCR.

61. Vice-President to D. B. Wentz, 19 May 1917, WCCR.

62. George Wolfe to Justus Collins, Aug. 1917, JCP.

63. Stonega Annual Report, 1917, WCCR.

64. James Woods to Edward L. Stone, 22 Aug. 1917. BCC.

65. Edward L. Stone to Dr. M. D. Thomas, 10 Mar. 1918, BCC.

66. Stonega Annual Report, 1917, WCCR.

67. Ibid.

68. George Wolfe to Justus Collins, 23 Sept. 1916, JCP.

69. Stonega Annual Report, 1917, WCCR.

Chapter 5

1. John Benson, *British Coalminers in the Nineteenth Century: A Social History* (Dublin: Gill and Macmillan, 1980), 31. For a description of the 1842 act and the sketches that accompanied the investigation, see George Rosen, *The History of Miners' Diseases: A Medical and Social Interpretation* (New York: Shuman's, 1943), 430-33.

2. Rockefeller Report, 191.

3. "Virginia Manufacturer's Report for the Virginia World War II History Commission," 1945, in WCCR.

4. Annie Kelley interview, 15.20, NRGC.

5. *Home Environment and Employment Opportunities of Women,* 7.

6. Ibid., 37-39.

7. Lula Lall Jones Interview, 27.12-27.13, NRGC.

8. *Home Environment and Employment Opportunities of Women,* 7.

9. Ibid.

10. Christine Cochran interview, 8, SOHC.

11. For a patronizing picture of the work of coal miners' wives, see U.S. Coal Mines Administration, "The Coal Miner and His Family," 22-31, a supplement to *A Medical Survey of the Bituminous-Coal Industry,* report of the Coal Mines Administration, 1947, commonly referred to as "the Boone Report" after Rear Admiral Joel T. Boone, who directed the study (I have followed this convention in later notes).

12. Annie Kelly interview, 15.36, NRGC.

13. Chan Forren interview, 17.40, NRGC.

14. Annie Kelly interview, 15.36, NRGC.

15. Ada Wilson Jackson interview, 26.39, NRGC.

16. "Opinion Survey" and profile from *The Stonegazette,* May 1951 box 535, WCCR.

17. See Gutman, *Work, Culture and Society,* chap. 1.

18. Michael W. Flinn, *The History of the British Coal Industry,* vol. 2, *1700-1830: The Industrial Revolution* (Oxford: Clarendon Press, 1984), 82; Benson, *British Coalminers,* 54. In contrast, the longwall system involved mining the broad length of a seam of coal without leaving supporting pillars, the roof being supported by props and waste. Flinn found the longwall system in use in some fields as early as the opening of the eighteenth century, and Benson pointed out that it had replaced the "bord and pillar" method by the late nineteenth century.

19. For this description I have relied upon Carter Goodrich, *The Miner's Freedom:*

A Study of the Working Life in a Changing Industry (New York: Arno Press, 1977), 19–22; Keith Dix, *Work Relations in the Coal Industry: The Hand-Loading Era, 1880–1930* (Morgantown, W.Va.: Institute for Labor Studies, West Virginia University, 1977), 4–8; Tams, *Smokeless Coal Fields*, 36–40.

20. Athey, *Kaymoor,* 11.

21. W. T. Williams to W. W. Coe, 23 Apr. 1907, BCC.

22. "Report on Physical Conditions of Mines No. 1 and 2," by W. R. Dudley, 18 July 1930, BCC.

23. Stonega Annual Report, 1916, WCCR.

24. Tams, *Smokeless Coal Fields,* 35. Dewey Osborne interview, 21, AOHP, Alice. Cf. Alvin W. Gouldner, *Patterns of Industrial Bureaucracy: A Case Study of Factory Administration* (New York: Free Press, 1954), 136.

25. For the fascinating discography of this and other miners' songs, see Archie Green, *Only a Miner: Studies in Recorded Coal-Mining Songs* (Urbana: University of Illinois Press, 1972); Green's chap. 2 examines the Travis legacy.

26. A miner's day is detailed in "The American Coalminer and his Family," a supplement to the Boone Report.

27. Descriptions of the process of mining coal may be found in Dix, *Work Relations,* 8–14; Steve Tomko interview, 18, AOHP, Alice; and L. F. Minor interview, 4–5, SOHC.

28. L. F. Minor interview, 4–5; John Sokira interview, 9, both in SOCH.

29. Green, *Only a Miner,* 311–12 (Ames quoted on 310).

30. Edward L. Stone to Lee Armentrout, 6 Dec. 1922, BCC.

31. Armentrout to Stone, 11 Dec. 1922, BCC.

32. R. E. Taggert to A. H. Reeder, 23 May 1913, WCCR.

33. C. G. Duffy to J. L. Salyers, 31 Jan. 1913 WCCR.

34. Goodrich, *The Miner's Freedom,* 55.

35. James B. "Buck" Jones interview, 14.20; and Charlie Crawford interview, 2.15, both in NRGC.

36. D. B. Oglestree interview, 11, SOHC.

37. Athey, *Kaymoor,* 15.

38. Ibid.

39. C. G. Duffy to M. H. Duffy, 1913, WCCR.

40. Stonega Annual Report, 1915, WCCR.

41. This generalization is based upon tonnage figures given in tabular form in the company's records.

42. Melvin Profitt interview, 1, AOHP, Alice.

43. Russell Matthew interview, NRGC.

44. John Luther "Bud" Whittington interview, NRGC.

45. Quoted in Michael Kline, "The Coon Dog Truth: Charlie Blevins at the Red Robin Inn," *Goldenseal* 8 (Winter 1982): *38.*

46. Ralph Sanders interview, NRGC.

47. Elbert Salmons interview, 10, AOHP, Alice.

48. Quoted in Kline, "Coon Dog Truth," 38.

49. Irene Skaggs interview, 4, NRGC.

50. Chan Forren interview, 17.44, NRGC.

51. R. E. Taggert to C. G. Duffy, 25 July 1914, WCCR.

52. W. C. Skunk to H. H. Ingles, 22 Oct. 1929, WCCR.

53. Russell Matthew interview, 36.8–36.10, NRGC.

54. A similar pattern characterized British mining; see Benson, *British Coalminers,* 48–54.

55. Gouldner, *Patterns of Industrial Bureaucracy,* 127–36. Gouldner first noted the importance of spatial factors and common danger to worker solidarity among underground gypsum miners.

56. Listed in the Stonega Division records of the WCCR for 1948. A coal seam carried the name of a company engineer or the person who discovered the seam, such as the Imboden seam, named after John D. Imboden.

57. Stonega Annual Report, 1920, 162–75, WCCR.

58. Tams, *Smokeless Coal Fields,* 48–49; for the quotation, see 49.

59. Ibid., 103.

60. This account was taken from a feature article by Roland Lazenby in the Roanoke *Times and World News,* 11 Mar. 1984, on the one-hundredth anniversary of the explosion.

61. Rockefeller Report, 109.

62. Eller, *Miners,* 180.

63. *Ibid.,* 181.

64. Rockefeller, Report, 110.

65. Stonega Annual Report, 1924, WCCR; U.S. Department of Commerce, Bureau of the Census, *Historical Statistics of the United States: A Supplement to the Statistical Abstract of the United States* (Washington, D.C.: Government Printing Office, 1949), series G, 144–58. The figures for Stonega and Great Britain come from the Stonega Annual Report. The company's figures, however, nearly match the census figures. For example, SC&C reported a figure of 3.73 fatalities per million tons mined for 1914–23 in the bituminous fields of the United States. The census average for the period was 3.68

66. D. J. Jones, N. M. Wilder, and John F. Maurice, "Mountain Bumps in the Coal Fields of Harlan County, Kentucky," Kentucky Department of Mines and Minerals, series 8, *Bulletin* 1 (1 Dec. 1934): 16. Found in WCCR.

67. Ibid., 3–4, 16–18.

68. Ibid., 17–19.

69. Ibid., 3.

70. Stonega Annual Report, 1934, 123, WCCR.

71. Stonega Annual Report, 1940, 123, WCCR.

72. Stonega Annual Report, 1935, 58, WCCR.

73. Ibid.

74. Stonega Annual Reports, 1915–20, 110; 1940, 2; 1952, 3, WCCR. In nineteenth-century British mines, the figure was virtually identical: 98.9 nonfatal accidents for every fatality; see Benson, *British Coalminers,* 39–40.

75. Stonega Annual Report, 1952.

76. Ibid. 1920 is used as the typical year.

77. Stonega Annual Report, 1934, 58–60, WCCR.

78. This paragraph is drawn from the discussion of workmen's compensation laws below.

79. See Rosen, *History of Miners' Diseases*. See also Martin Cherniack, *The Hawk's Nest Incident: America's Worst Industrial Disaster* (New Haven: Yale University Press, 1986). At least seven hundred men are said to have died from silicosis at Hawk's Nest, many of them black migrant laborers from the South, in boring a three-mile tunnel through Gauley Mountain during the Great Depression. Company officials, with the help of physicians, newspaper editors, lawyers, and state regulatory officials, managed to cover up the incident. In the 1960s, reformers used the incident to galvanize the public into the recognition of occupational disease. See also Mark Rowh, "The Hawk's Nest Tragedy: Fifty Years Later," 31–34, and David Orr and Jon Dragan, "'A Dirty Messy Place to Work,' B. H. Metheney Remembers Hawk's Nest Tunnel," 34–41, both in *Goldenseal* 7, no. 1 (Jan.–Mar. 1981).

80. William Graebner, *Coal Mining Safety in the Progressive Period: The Political Economy of Reform* (Lexington: University Press of Kentucky, 1976).

81. Anthony F. C. Wallace, *St. Clair: A Nineteenth-Century Coal Town's Experience with a Disaster-Prone Industry* (New York: Alfred A. Knopf, 1987), 446–56, 448 (first quotation), 452 (second quotation).

82. Cf. Gaventa, *Power and Powerlessness*.

83. Tams, *Smokeless Coal Fields*, 41.

84. R. E. Taggart to A. H. Reeder, 23 May 1913; Taggart to C. G. Duffy, 23 May 1913, both in WCCR.

85. Stonega Annual Report, 1915, 48, WCCR.

86. Superintendent of Mines to P. W. McNulty, 1911, and 4 April 1912, LMIC.

87. D. B. Oglestree interview, 2, SOHC.

88. Ermine Hall interview, 2, AOHP, Alice.

89. Wood Cooley interview, 2–3, AOHP, Alice.

90. James T. Laing, "The Negro Miner in West Virginia," in Turner and Cabbell, eds., *Blacks in Appalachia*, 73.

91. Ermine Hall interview, 5, AOHP, Alice.

92. Rev. Stuart Frazier Sr., interview, 22.21. NRGC.

93. Enoch Hatfield interview, 6, AOHP, Alice.

94. Hilton Garrett interview, 2, AOHP, Alice.

95. Stonega Annual Report, 1934, 124, WCCR.

96. Ibid., 161.

97. Gabe Newsome interview, 4, AOHP, Alice.

98. U.S. Bureau of the Census, *Statistical Abstract of the United States, 1982–1983*. See p. 452 for the consumer price index and p. 714 for average hourly earnings of coal miners in 1970.

99. Mae Prater interview, 31 (first quotation), 30 (second quotation), AOHC, Alice.

100. Ibid., 36.

101. Ibid., 29.

Chapter 6

1. By-Laws of Derby Burial Fund, box 473, WCCR.
2. By-Laws of Dunbar Relief Fund, box 360, WCCR.

3. C. G. Duffy to A. H. Reeder, 14 Nov. 1913. WCCR.

4. U.S. Works Progress Administration, Social and Ethnic Studies, A760, Manuscripts Division, Library of Congress.

5. C. G. Duffy to A. H. Reeder, 14 Nov. 1913, WCCR.

6. J. D. Rogers to R. E. Taggart, 10 May 1934, WCCR.

7. Cf. Benson, *British Coalminers,* 205.

8. Lewis, *Black Coal Miners,* 139.

9. Justus Collins to Thomas L. Felts, 20 Mar. 1914 and Felts to Collins, 30 Mar. 1914, JCP.

10. Corbin, *Life, Work, and Rebellion,* 87.

11. Daniel P. Jordan, "The Mingo War: Labor Violence in the Southern West Virginia Coal Fields, 1919-1922," in Gary M. Fink and Merle E. Reed, eds., *Selected Papers, Southern Labor History Conference,* 1976 (Westport, Conn.: Greenwood Press, 1977), 102-43.

12. Corbin, *Life, Work, and Rebellion,* viii (first quotation); Eller, *Miners,* 197 (second quotation).

13. Eller, *Miners,* 156-60. The six Kentucky counties were Bell, Harlan, Perry, Letcher, Floyd, and Pike.

14. Edward Stone letter on the newspaper attacks on Woods, 22 Oct. 1920, BCC. In this lengthy diatribe to an unknown recipient, Stone is responding to what he calls "press attacks" on his vice-president, James P. Woods, who is also U.S. representative of Virginia's Sixth District.

15. Ibid.

16. Edward L. Stone to Lee Armentrout, 30 Sept. 1911, 14 Apr. 1915; Armentrout to Stone, 14 Dec. 1916, all in BCC.

17. Baldwin-Felts agents' reports, 10 Mar., 22 Mar., 28 Mar., and 13 May, 1915, all from Hatfield, West Virginia; Armentrout to Stone, 13 Apr. 1915, all in BCC.

18. For an account of these events, see Jordan, "The Mingo War."

19. "Notice to Borderland Employees," 5 May 1920; Armentrout to Stone, 11 Sept. 1922, both in BCC.

20. Telegram, Lee Armentrout to J. J. Moore, Attorney, 22 Oct. 1920; clipping from *Manufacturer's Record,* 3 Apr. 1924, both in BCC.

21. Secret-service reports, 15 May 1915; J. E. Meadows to Edward L. Stone, n.d. but about 1921 (quotation), all in BCC.

22. Lee Armentrout to Edward L. Stone, 28 June 1920; Stone to Armentrout, 7 July 1920. Telegrams from Armentrout to Stone, 8 July and 14 July 1920. Armentrout to Stone 15, 26, and 29 July 1920. Telegrams from Armentrout to Stone, 22 Aug. 1920; Stone to Borderland, 23 Aug. 1920. Borderland to Stone, 22 Aug. 1920; Stone to Armentrout, 23 Aug. 1920; Armentrout to Stone, 23 Aug. 1920. Telegram, Armentrout to Stone, 17 Dec. 1920. Armentrout to Stone, 30 Oct. 1922. All in BCC.

23. Stone to Armentrout, 31 Dec. 1921; Armentrout to Stone, 3 Jan. 1922, both in BCC.

24. Affidavit signed by L. E. Armentrout, 22 Oct. 1920, BCC.

25. James Woods to Stone, 26 Aug. 1924; J. E. Meadows to Stone, 6 March 1925; Armentrout to Stone, 22 Sept. 1925; letter in folder entitled "Correspondence," no signature, 27 Jan. 1930, all in BCC. A yellow-dog contract was the union's term for a contract between employer and worker affirming that the worker did not belong to a labor union and would not join one so long as employed with the contracting firm.

26. Stone to Armentrout, 22 July 1920.

27. Southern Auto-Ordnance to Ernest B. Fishburne, 6 Apr. 1921; Stone to Southern Auto-Ordnance, 12 and 26 May 1921, and 1 June 1921; Armentrout to Stone, 9 Mar. 1922; Stone to Armentrout, 24 Mar. 1922, all in BCC.

28. Copy of text of decree, *Gasaway and Van Horn v. Borderland Coal Corporation*, BCC.

29. Copy of the appeal, BCC.

30. Armentrout to Stone, 29 Nov. 1921, 30 Oct. 1922, 4 Nov. 1922; Stone to Armentrout, 3 Nov. 1922; James P. Woods to Stone, 27 Feb. 1922, all in BCC.

31. Stone to Armentrout, 23 Feb., 24 Feb., and 22 May 1922; Armentrout to Stone, 1 Mar. 1922, all in BCC. Stone corresponded with several other organizations similar to the league which subscribed to "law and order," such as the American Plan Association of Cleveland and the Corporations' Auxiliary Company of Cincinnati.

32. Armentrout to Borderland Sales Company, 3 Oct. 1923; Stone to NAM, 23 July 1925, both in BCC.

33. Stone to L. Franklin Moore, 22 June 1933, BCC.

34. L. F. Minor interview, 12–14, SOHC.

35. Fred Gaddis interview, 3, SOHC.

36. Lloyd Vick Minor interview, 4–6, SOHC.

37. Legal section of the 1933 Stonega Annual Report.

38. General Supt. to J. D. Rogers, 21 May 1934; Stonega Annual Report, 1934, 4, both in WCCR.

39. John Saxton to J. D. Rogers, 23 Mar. and 9 Apr. 1936; Rogers to Saxton, 25 Mar. 1936, both in WCCR.

40. J. L. Camblos to T. J. Reach, 19 May 1936

41. J. D. Rogers to all mine superintendents, 8 Apr. 1936; "Request for Injunction, 3 Jun. 1936, all in WCCR.

42. Stonega Annual Report, 1937, 161, WCCR.

43. Hailed as labor's New Deal when it became law on 5 July 1935, the Wagner act (the National Labor Relations Act) made no concessions to management. Instead, every unfair labor practice it banned applied to management, and the act explicitly acknowledged that only government help could bring equality into the relationship between labor and manangement.

44. Stonega Annual Reports, 1937, 161, and 1938, 6, WCCR.

45. Stonega Annual Report, 1939, 6, WCCR. The percentages unionized varied with each colliery: Arno, 98 percent; Derby, 67 percent; Dunbar, 98 percent; Imboden, 93 percent; Roda, 66 percent; and Stonega, 38 percent; see Vice-President Rogers to E. P. Humphrey, 20 Jan. 1939, WCCR.

46. John Showmaker, Local 8771, to C.H. Hagy, Supt., 11 Oct. 1950, WCCR.

47. John Howard to J. D. Rodgers, 26 Nov. 1932, WCCR.

48. "Final Statement of Roda Relief Society," 10 Mar. 1947; "Dissolution–Dunbar Relief Society," 12 July 1949, both in WCCR.

49. "Constitution and By-Laws of the Exeter Village Organization," 3 May 1950, WCCR.

50. W. B. Turner Sr., interview, 7–8; Fred O. Gaddis interview, 5; D. B. Oglestree interview, 9–12, all in SOHC.

51. The last quotation is Junior Oliver's. From a story by Douglas Pardue, Roanoke *Times and World News,* 3 Sept. 1989, on the strike against the Pittston Coal Company in southwestern Virginia.

52. John Luther interview, 6.21, NRGC.

53. "Coal Strike: Armageddon for U.M.W. and Leader?" New York *Times,* 15 Aug. 1989.

54. Ibid. Less than 17 percent of all miners are now represented by a union.

Chapter 7

1. Shirley Young Campbell, "Coal Towns," *Goldenseal* 13, no. 2 (Summer 1987): 53.

2. Boone Report, 20; Rockefeller Report, 5–6. Betram-Wyatt Brown has noted the "infatuation" of historians "with the notion that alienation is a modern ordeal growing from capitalistic and industrial societies" in his *Southern Honor: Ethics and Behavior in the Old South* (New York: Oxford University Press, 1982), 273;

3. *Report of the U.S. Coal Commission,* part 3, 1482. Actual weights in percentage terms were: housing, 19; water supply and distribution, 25; sewage and waste disposal, 19; community layout and general upkeep, 8; food and merchandise supply, 10; medical and health provisions, 8; education, 6; and religion and recreation, 5.

4. Boone Report, 14.

5. Melba Kizzire interview, 3–4. SOHC.

6. *Rockefeller Report, 6* (first quotation); Martin Bulmer, ed., *Mining and Social Change: Durham County in the Twentieth Century* (London: Croom Helm, 1978), 23 (second quotation), esp. "Social Structure and Social Change in the Twentieth Century," 15–48, and app. B, "The Study of Coal Mining Settlements and Theories of 'Community,'" 297–301.

7. Cf. Michael Anderson, *Family Structure in Nineteenth Century Lancashire* (Cambridge: Cambridge University Press, 1971); also, Norman E. Whitten, Jr., and John F. Szwed, eds., intro. to *Afro-American Anthropology* (New York: Free Press, 1970), 23–53.

8. *Boone Report,* 198 (first, second, and third quotations), 218 (fourth quotation), 202 (fifth quotation).

9. Winthrop D. Lane, *Civil War in West Virginia* (New York: Arno and New York Times, 1969), 36–37. Lane's chapter 3 is entitled "Some Good Mining Camps," and chapter 4, "Some Bad Mining Camps." In both cases, the physical appearance and sanitation were determinative.

10. The perspective of the labor historian is best seen in Corbin, *Life, Work, and Rebellion,* esp. 61–86; see also Gaventa, *Power and Powerlessness,* and Simon, "Uneven Development," 165–86. For older descriptions of coal towns, see Homer Lawrence Morris, *the Plight of the Bituminous Coal Miner* (Philadelphia, 1934), 85–97, and Raymond E. Densmore, *The Coal Miner of Appalachia* (Parsons, W.Va.: McClain Printing Co., 1977), 10–11. Gaventa, Corbin, and Eller emphasize the alienating effects of the Industrial Revolution in their work.

11. Lula Lall Jones interview, 27.44, NRGC.

12. See Eller, *Miners,* 190–91 for this estimate. Mae Prater interview, 36, AOHC, Alice. Historians have adopted the term "model town" to refer loosely to those towns,

by one estimate roughly 2 percent of all coal towns, which operators sometimes built as standards of excellence. For writers who want to stress the alienation of miners, it has become a convenient means of dismissing any town about which former residents have said anything positive as "a model town," and therefore "atypical." According to Eller, the town of Jenkins, Kentucky, is an example. Built by Consolidated Coal Company, it "provided garbage and rubbish collection, a complete sewer system, and a company-owned dairy in its community plan." Other model towns, like Holden, West Virginia, had "a modern theater building and a clubhouse which included showers, a library, a reading room, two bowling alleys, and even 'an up-to-date squash court.'" Eller, *Miners,* 190. A theory akin to the theme of alienation is that of Appalachia as a colony of eastern capitalists. For an introduction to this literature, see Lewis, et al. eds., *Colonialism in Modern America.*

13. Christine Cochran interview, 1; D. B. Oglestree interview, 4; Melba Kizzire interview, 1-2, 33-34, all in SOHC.

14. Celia Chambers interview, 6 and 12 (quotations), NRGC.

15. Dometrius Woodsen interview, 20.37 (quotation), both in NRGC.

16. Thelma Rotenberry to Crandall Shifflett, 23 Feb. 1985 (in author's possession).

17. Jane Taylor to Crandall Shifflett, 12 Dec. 1984 (in author's possession).

18. Interviews by author 18 and 28 Aug. 1986, Blacksburg, Virginia (in author's possession).

19. Cora Frazier interview, 12-14; and Marvin Gullet interview, 12, both in AOHP, Alice. Rockefeller Report, 33; the statements of this miner's wife directly contradict the "accurate" image of company mining towns proclaimed elsewhere in the report.

20. Stonega "Opinion Survey," 1951, box 535, WCCR. Of the 137 interviews, seven were mail-ins, and the rest were personal interviews. The total number represents about 4 percent of Stonega's workforce. The following list gives first to (to the left of the slash) the number who lived in the coal town, then (to the right of the slash) the total who worked there that were interviewed: Roda 14/40, Imboden 7/24, Stonega 15/23, Derby 12/16, Glenbrook 0/16, and Pine Branch 0/11. These figures show that, by 1951, company towns had already begun to empty out.

21. Stonega "Opinion Survey," questions 2, 4-6, 9-13, 15. Responses to some questions total less than 137 because some respondents gave no opinion.

22. Ibid., questions 32-37.

23. Ibid., questions 14-16.

24. Ibid., questions 28-29.

25. Ibid., questions 21-22, 30.

26. Potter, *The South and the Sectional Conflict,* 245-46.

27. Bulmer, *Mining and Social Change,* 299 (for the term "analytical primacy"), Cf. Daniel J. Walkowitz, *Worker City, Company Town: Iron and Cotton-Worker Protest in Troy and Cohoes, New York, 1855-1884* (Urbana: University of Illinois Press, 1978), 68-70.

28. Corbin, *Life, Work, and Rebellion.* See also John Hevener, *Which Side Are You On? The Harlan County Coal Miners, 1931-1939* (Urbana: University of Illinois Press, 1978).

Chapter 8

1. John Benson, *British Coalminers*, 163; Mae Prater interview, 7, AOHP, Alice.
2. Paul J. Nyden, "Coal Town Baseball," in *Goldenseal* 6, no. 4 (Oct.-Dec. 1980): 31-39.
3. Ibid., 31.
4. Ibid., 31-32.
5. Hilton Garrett interview, 17 (first quotation), 18 (second quotation); Everett Hall interview, 11, both in AOHP, Alice. Clippings in file, "Tennessee Coal, Iron, and Railroad Company, TCI," Birmingham, Ala., Public Library.
6. Dometrius Woodsen interview 20.19-20, NRGC; also Nyden, "Coal Town Baseball," 36.
7. Stonega "Facilities Survey," 1916, box 461, WCCR. Virgil W. Burgess interview, 47.14; Stewart Frazier interview, 17.18; Ada Wilson Jackson interview, 35.10; Chan Forren interview, 17. 27-28 (last quotation), all in NRGC. See also Nyden, "Coal Town Baseball," 36.
8. Nyden, "Coal Town Baseball," 38-39.
9. U.S. Department of Interior, Bureau of Mines *Report*, 2 Feb. 1916, Stonega, Box 533, WCCR. Lloyd Vick Minor interview, 9; and Reuben Barnes interview, 15, both in SOHC.
10. Marvin Gullet interview, AOHP, Alice; 7, Joseph Tony interview, 7, AOHP, Emery.
11. T. B. Pugh interview, 4.5, NRGC.
12. Stonega "Opinion Survey," 1951, questions 24, 25, and 26, elicited the following preferences. "For radio programs: "Amos 'n' Andy," "Jack Benny," "Beulah," "Mr. Chameleon," "Gang Busters," "Mr. Keen," "Charlie McCarthy," "Red Skelton," "Mr. and Mrs. North," "Farm and Home," "Hopalong Cassidy," "Lowell Thomas," "Sam Spade," "Cisco Kid," "Inner Sanctum," "Boston Blackie," and "Our Miss Brooks"; for entertainers: John Wayne, Alan Ladd, Rod Brasfield, Minnie Pearl, Little Jimmy Dickens, Roy Acuff, Red Foley, Cowboy Copas, Ernest Tubb, Randolph Scott, Gary Cooper, Roy Rogers, Gene Autry, and Hopalong Cassidy; for movies: *Steel Helmet, Halls of Montezuma, Thirty Seconds over Tokyo, Great Missouri Raid, Return of Jesse James, Robin Hood, Sands of Iwo Jima, Little Women*, and *China*; for magazines: *Saturday Evening Post, Reader's Digest, UMW Journal, Popular Mechanics, Good Housekeeping, Southern Farmer, Pathfinder, Collier's, True Detective, True Confessions*, and *Field and Stream*. See also *The Stonegazette* 1, no. 1 (May 1951).

It is interesting to note that a Norton, Virginia, radio station (WNVA) sent out a questionnaire in 1946 to ask what kind of Sunday programming sponsored by the Virginia Coal Operators' Association would be of most interest. In order of importance, the response was popular music, news, "hillbilly" music, and sacred music. The slight variation in preference may be due to the inclusion of more foremen than miners in this survey. E. P. Humphrey to George H. Esser, President, Virginia Coal Operators Association, 6 Nov. 1946, WCCR.

13. Lloyd Vick Minor interview, 9, SOHC; J. W. Monteith to J. A. Hibbert, 7 Feb. 1923, LMIC; Edith Shoemaker interview, 8, SOHC; Harry Sydenstricker interview, 12.15-12.18, NRGC.
14. Athey, *Kaymoor*, 2, 44-45; T. B. Pugh interview, 4.22, NRGC. .
15. T. B. Pugh interview, 17.18, 4.28-30, 4.24; Stewart Frazier interview, 22.32 (first quotation), 22.35 (second quotation), 22.39, 22.42-43, both in NRGC.

16. Chan Forren interview, 17.20–21; Celia Chambers interview, 21, both in NRGC.

17. Justus Collins to Issac T. Mann, Bramwell, W.Va., 16 July 1909; E. C. Payne to T. L. Felts, Bluefield, W.Va., 11 Apr. 1912; and P. J. Riley to Collins, 3 June 1907, all in JCP.

18. Reuben Barnes interview, 11, 16 (quotation), SOHC.

19. Edith Shoemaker interview, 13 (first quotation); Belinda Mardis interview, 3, (last quotation), both in SOHC.

20. L. F. Minor interview, 6, (first quotation), SOHC. Stonega Annual Reports, 1915, 6, 85 (second quotation); 1917, 3 (last quotation); 1921, 25, for list of towns and the facilities in them, all in WCCR.

21. Stonega "Facilities Survey," 1916, box 461, WCCR. For church activities in Docena, see Melba Kizzire interview, 20, SOHC; on Kaymoor, see Dometrius Woodsen interview, 20.1–37, NRGC.

Chapter 9

1. Annie Kelly interview, 15.35, NRGC; Christine Cochran interview, 11, SOHC.

2. Boone Report, 215.

3. Harry Sydenstricker interview, 12.22, NRGC.

4. Stonega Annual Report, 1915, 4–5.

5. Edith Shoemaker interview, 3; Christine Cochran interview, 5, both in SOHC; Gordon Dodrill, comp., *20,000 Coal Company Stores in the Unived States, Mexico, and Canada* (Pittsburgh, 1971).

6. Corbin, *Life, Work, and Rebellion*, 10 (first and last two quotations); Simon, "Uneven Development," 170 (remaining quotations). See also Curtis Seltzer, *Fire in the Hole: Miners and Managers in the American Coal Industry* (Lexington: University Press of Kentucky, 1985), 19; Anna Rochester, *Labor and Coal* (New York, International Publishers, 1931).

7. Birdie Kyle, "Growing Up in the Coalfields," *Goldenseal* 6 (Apr.–June 1980): 7.

8. Christine Cochran interview, 3; L. F. Minor interview, 7; Lloyd Vick Minor interview, 10, all in SOHC; Elizabeth Lambert interview, 32.19, NRGC; Carry Mae Marcum interview, 18 Aug. 1986 in author's possession.

9. H. A. Alexander to J. D. Rogers, 1933, WCCR; Irene Hicks Skaggs interview, 6, NRGC; A. H. Reeder to General Manager, Stonega, 8 Feb. 1913, WCCR; H. W. Meador to W. L. Long, 16 Aug. 1950, WCCR; Annie Kelly interview, 15.18–19, NRGC; Meador to Alexander, 1938, WCCR; George Wolfe to Justus Collins, 25 Sept. 1918, JCP (quotation).

10. Price V. Fishback, "Did Coal Miners 'Owe Their Souls to the Company Store'? Theory and Evidence from the Early 1900s," *Journal of Economic History* 46 (Dec. 1986): 1011–29. The companies upon which Fishback based these findings included nine mines of the Cabin Creek Consolidated Coal Company in the first six months of 1912, Keystone Mines for half months from Nov. to Jan. 1907, Keystone Mines for half months from Nov. to Jan. 1907, Empire Mines for half months from Oct. to Jan. 1907, Acme Mines from Dec. 1895 to Oct. 1897, all in West Virginia, and all mines of the Stonega Company from 1925 to 1947.

11. For ethnic and racial differences, see James T. Laing, "The Negro Miner in West Virginia," in Turner and Cabbell, eds., *Blacks in Appalachia*, 73–74.

12. Fenwick Mines Payroll Book, Oct. 1902, LMIC.

13. Records of the Eastern Regional Coal Archives, Craft Memorial Library, Bluefield, W.Va.

14. As early as 1887, a law had been passed in Virginia making it unlawful to pay labor in paper unless it was redeemable in "lawful money." Companies apparently evaded this law with metal coins or tokens, or they ignored it. H. W. Goodwin to D. S. Cook, 14 June 1887, LMIC; Stonega Annual Reports, 1917 and 1918, WCCR; L. Epperley to Justus Collins, 21 July 1925, JCP.

15. Margaret Dorsett interview, 13 SOHC. Elizabeth Lambert interview, 32.1–22, NRGC. Athey, *Kaymoor*, 36–37. Boone Report, 215. Dewey Osborne interview, 5; Wiley Pennington interview, 12; Robert Hicks interview, 13–14, all in AOHP, Alice. Ada Wilson interview, 35.9, NRGC.

16. George Wolfe to Justus Collins, 4 Oct. 1913 and 8 Feb. 1915; Collins to Wolfe, 9 Feb. 1915; Wolfe to Collins, 25 Dec. 1915; Collins to Wolfe, 27 Dec. 1915, all in JCP.

17. The Raleigh Coal Company store was located near Beckley, West Virginia, and was frequented by Beckley residents as well as company employees.

18. Wolfe to Collins, 28 Dec. 1915.

19. Fishback, "Did Coal Miners 'Owe Their Souls'" 1015–16.

20. Elizabeth Lambert interview; Dometrius Woodsen interview, 20.1–37; Virgil W. Burgess interview, 47.13; and Ada Wilson interview, 26.35–36, all in NRGC. Wiley Pennington interview; Dewey Osborne interview, 17–18; Ermine Hall interview, 6, 9, 11, all in AOHP, Alice.

21. D. B. Oglestree interview, 9; Frank Bonds interview, 14, both in SOHC. Harry Sydenstricker interview, 12.36; Celia Chambers interview, 11, both in NRGC.

22. For the anaylsis of price differentials and store profits, see Fishback, "Did Coal Miners 'Owe Their Souls'" 1016–1021.

23. "The Village of Keokee," undated newspaper clipping from company records, WCCR.

Chapter 10

1. Elizabeth R. Hooker, *Religion in the Highlands: Native Churches and Missionary Enterprises in the Southern Appalachian Area* (New York: Home Mission Council, 1933), 100.

2. Ibid., 100–101.

3. George Wolfe to Justus Collins, 7 Aug. 1916, JCP.

4. Anonymous miner to Justus Collins, 11 Mar. 1907, JCP.

5. U.S. Dept. of Agriculture, *Economic and Social Problems of the Southern Appalachians*, Miscellaneous Pub. no. 205 (Washington, D.C., 1935), 168–69; 175.

6. Ibid., 172.

7. Laing, "The Negro Miner," in Turner and Cabbell, eds., *Blacks in Appalachia*, 76,

8. Ermine Hall interview, 9, AOHP, Alice.

9. T. B. Pugh interview, 4.23, NRGC. Pugh noted the absence of Catholic churches

in the New River Gorge area except in the larger towns of Fayetteville, Oak Hill, and Mt. Hope. He recalled Saswa, a Polish boy, who attended school in Scarbro where they must have had a Catholic church "because they taught in Polish a half day and English a half day."

10. USDA, *Economic and Social Problems*, 172.

11. Steve Tomko interview, 21, AOHP, Alice.

12. A. H. Reeder to Rev. George H. Gilmer, 9 Dec. 1904; General Manager to W. M. Polly, 24 Feb. 1905, both in WCCR.

13. J. Wayne Flynt, "The Southern Church as Reformer," in Paul D. Escott and David R. Goldfield, eds., *Major Problems in the History of the American South 2, The New South* (Lexington, Mass.: D. C. Health, 1990), 311.

14. Flynt, "The Southern Church as Reformer," 311.

15. USDA, *Economic and Social Problems*, 173.

16. Traffic and Sales Manager to Rev. W. E. Patton, 26 July 1906, WCCR.

17. Members of the Hungarian Reformed Congregation to Executives of Stonega, 27 Mar. 1905, WCCR.

18. T. B. Pugh interview, 4.23, NRGC.

19. Rev. C. R. W. Kegley to SC&C, 7 Oct. 1909, WCCR.

20. Christine Cochran interview, 12, SOHC.

21. Daniel B. Wentz to A. H. Reeder, 23 Feb., WCCR.

22. Stonega Annual Report, 1938, 143, WCCR.

23. Stonega Annual Report, 1918, 62, WCCR.

24. General Manager to E. J. Prescott, 28 Aug. 1906, WCCR.

25. General Manager to R. R. Casper, 26 Sept. 1905; Assistant Superintendent, Stonega, to A. H. Reeder, 22 Dec. 1905, both in WCCR.

26. General Manager to W. B. Edwards, 17 Dec. 1908, contains a long list of such donations as well as other letters scattered throughout the correspondence of the company over the years, WCCR.

27. J. C. Blume interview, NRGC. Some miners found a social outlet through church activities; others who, like Blume, did not, participated in a range of activity that placed them in a social circle different from that of the churchgoers.

28. Wiley Pennington interview, 20, AOHP, Alice.

29. Mae Prater interview, 28, AOHP, Alice.

30. Dr. E. L. McFee interview, 1–4, SOHC.

31. Quoted in Flynt, "The Southern Church as Reformer," 320.

32. Hall, et al., *Like a Family*, 20.

33. Mae Prater interview, 34–35, AOHP, Alice.

34. L. F. Minor interview, 8–10, 9 (first quotation), 10 (second quotation), SOHC.

35. Fred Gaddis interview, 8, SOHC.

36. Melba Kizzire interview, 22–4; D. B. Oglestree interview, 8, both in SOHC.

37. Edith Shoemaker interview, 10, SOHC.

Conclusion

1. Miller and Sharpless, *The Kingdom of Coal*, 288–89; Eller, *Miners*, 159.

2. Hilton Garrett interview, 3; Marvin Gullet interview, 14, both in AOHP, Alice. J. C. Blume interview, NRGC, Ernest B. Fishburn to Edward L. Stone, 12 Feb. 1931, BCC.

3. Stonega Annual Reports, 1931, 3; 1932, 4, both in WCCR.

4. Stonega Annual Report, 1932, 4 (quotations); J. D. Reeder to R. E. Taggart, 12 July 1932; A. H. Reeder to J. D. Rogers, 12 July 1932, all in WCCR.

5. Arno Superintendent to A. H. Reeder, 11 July 1933; Stonega Annual Report, 1932, 4, both in WCCR.

6. R. E. Taggart to J. D. Rogers, Aug. 1931, WCCR.

7. Claude Crane interview, 9; Belinda Mardis interview, 5; and Frank Bonds interview, 15, all in SOHC.

8. Wiley Pennington interview, 5, AOHP, Alice; H. A. Alexander to J. D. Rogers, 12 May 1932, WCCR (first quotation); Robert Hamm interview, 6–9, AOHP, Emory; Reuben Barnes interview, 16, SOHC; Russell Matthew interview, 36.18, NRGC.

9. Celia Chambers interview, 18 NRGC; Mae Prater interview, 36, AOHP, Alice.

10. Elizabeth Lambert interview, 32.17. NRGC; Reuben Barnes interview, 16, SOHC.

11. Dix, *Work Relations*, 20; Seltzer, *Fire in the Hole*, 12.

12. Herbert R. Northrup, "The Coal Mines," in Turner and Cabbell, eds., *Blacks in Appalachia*, 168; Seltzer, *Fire in the Hole*, 65; Stonega Annual Report, WCCR.

13. Lewis, *Black Coal Miners*. 178–180; 180 (quotation).

14. *Historical Abstract*, series M: 259–74, 372; Seltzer, *Fire in the Hole*, 224n.

15. Dix, *What's a Coal Miner to Do*, 88–92, 90.

16. Herbert R. Northrup, "The Coal Mines," in Turner and Campbell, eds., *Blacks in Appalachia*, 168; Belinda Mardis interview, 11, SOHC; Seltzer, *Fire in the Hole*, 36; Lewis, *Black Coal Miners*, app., 191–93.

17. Dewey Osborne interview, 26, AOHP, Alice. Harry Sydenstricker interview, 12.9, NRGC. Rockefeller Report, 1980, 133–37. J. D. Rogers to H. A. Alexander, 27 Mar. 1940, WCCR.

18. Report to U. S. Employment Service, 17 June 1942; Leisenring to R. E. Taggart, 9 Sept. 1942; Rogers to Humphrey, 19 Sept. 1942, all in WCCR.

19. Absenteeism folder, 1942–43; E. P. Humphrey to H. W. Meador, 31 Dec. 1942, both in WCCR. E. R. Price memo, 27 July 1943, Wheelwright Collection.

20. Smokeless Wage Agreement with UMWA, 2 Apr. 1934, JCP. Mae Prater interview, 9, AOHP, Alice. Lloyd Vick Minor interview, 3, SOHC. Lula Lall Jones interview, 27.36, 27.31; Ada Wilson Jackson interview, 26.15, both in NRGC. Hilton Garrett interview, 18; Sid Adkins interview, 5, both in AOHP, Alice.

21. Rockefeller Report, 80, 100–101.

22. J. D. Rogers to E. J. Prescott, 7 July 1936 (on sorting of fines); Stonega Annual Report, 1934, 4–6; Rogers to Prescott, 26 July 1934; notice of A. H. Reeder, 22 Oct. 1934; H. A. Alexander to A. H. Reeder, 5 June 1934; A. H. Reeder to R. H. Knode, 21 Mar. 1934; General Superintendent to D. B. Wentz, 27 Feb. 1934; Stonega Annual Report, 1938, 143–44; all in WCCR. W. B. Turner, Sr., interview, 10, SOHC. James Harlan Edwards interview, 8, AOHP, Emory. Stonega Annual Report, 1952, WCCR. Chan Forren interview, 17.37–38, NRGC.

23. Rockefeller Report, 83-83.

24. Lewis, *Black Coal Miners*, 178-79. On John L. Lewis, see Melvyn Dubofsky and Warren Van Tyne, *John L. Lewis: A Biography* (New York: Quadrangle/New York Times Co., 1977). Seltzer, *Fire in the Hole*, chap. 5.

25. H. W. Meador to G. B. Taylor, 12 Oct. 1953; 19 Oct., 11 Nov., and 18 Nov. 1953; 17 May 1954, and 17 Feb. 1955. W. C. Shott to Meador, 5 Apr. 1955. C. H. Hagy to Schott, 11 Dec. 1956, and 11 Mar. 1957. All in WCCR.

26. Melba Kizzire interview, 26; Christine Cochran interview, 3-4; and Reuben Barnes interview, 6, all in SOHC.

27. Virgil W. Burgess interview, 47.15, NRGC; Athey, *Kaymoor*, 33, 50-51.

28. Hilton Garrett interview, 15-16, AOHP, Alice.

Bibliography

Manuscript Collections

Collins, Justus. Papers. West Virginia University Library, Morgantown.
Eastern Regional Coal Archives, Craft Memorial Library, Bluefield, West Virginia.
Library of Congress, Manuscripts Division. Social and Ethnic Studies, A760.
Low Moor Iron Company. Papers. Manuscripts Division, Special Collections Department, University of Virginia Library.
Stone, Edward L., and Borderland Coal Company. Papers. Manuscripts Division, Special Collections Department, University of Virginia Library, Charlottesville.
Westmoreland Coal Company Records. Hagley Library, Wilmington, Delaware.
Wheelwright Coal Camp Collection. Special Collections, Margaret I. King Library, University of Kentucky, Lexington.

Oral History Collection

Appalachian Oral History Project

Alice Lloyd College Oral History Collection

Adkins, Sid. By Timothy Mullins. Dorton, Ky., 12 June 1974.
Cooley, Wood. By Patti Rose. Bypro. Ky., 16 June 1971.
Frazier, Cora. By Don and Laurel Anderson. N.p., 19 Dec. 1971.
Garrett, Hilton. By Luther Frazier. Wheelwright, Ky., 8 Aug. 1973.
Gullet, Marvin. By Ron Daley. N.p., 2 Jan. 1975.
Hall, Ermine. By Patti Rose. Wheelwright, Ky., 2 July 1971.
Hall, Everett. By Patti Rose. Wheelwright, Ky., 15 June 1971.
Hatfield, Enoch. By Eldo Hall. N.p., 19 July 1973.
Hicks, Robert. By Joey Elswick. Wayland, Ky., 3 July 1975.
Newsome, Gabe. By unknown interviewer. Myra, Ky., 1 June 1971.
Osborne, Dewey. By Patti Rose. Wheelwright, Ky., 29 June 1971.
Pennington, Wiley. By Jimmy Bumphrey. Ligon, Ky., n.d.
Prater, Mae. By Ron Daley. N.p., 21 Aug. 1975.
Profitt, Melvin. By Will Weinberg. N.p., 11 Aug. 1975.
Salmons, Elbert. By Lou Mosley. Mousie, Ky., 13 Aug. 1974.
Tomko, Steve. By Laurel S. Anderson. Wise, Va., 19 Mar. 1975.

Emory and Henry University Oral History Collection:

Carico, Ernest. By Ray Ringley. Wise, Va., Dec. 1973.
Edwards, James Harlan. By Ray Ringley, Wise, Va., 1 Oct. 1973.
Hamm, Robert. By Ray Ringley. Sandy Ridge, Va., 30 Sept. 1973.
Meade, Ernest. By Ray Ringely. Wise, Va., Nov. 1973.
Tony, Joseph. By George G. Smith. Big Stone Gap, Va., 18 Dec. 1972.

New River Gorge Oral History Collection, Glen Jean, West Virginia

Blume, J. C. By Joseph Kanopsis. N.p., 15 Aug. 1983.
Burgess, Virgil W. By Paul J. Nyden. Oak Hill, W.Va., 22 Jan. 1983.
Chambers, Celia. By Jim Worsham. Minden, W.Va., 16 Apr. 1984.
Crawford, Charlie. By Paul J. Nyden. N.p., 5 Aug. 1974.
Forren, Chan. By Paul J. Nyden. Beckley, W.Va., 1 Nov. 1980.
Frazier, Rev. Stewart, Sr. By Paul J. Nyden. Harvey, W.Va., 12 Nov. 1980.
Jackson, Ada Wilson. by Paul J. Nyden. Scarbro, W.Va., 13 Dec. 1980.
Jones, James B. "Buck." By Paul J. Nyden. Edmond, W.Va., 23 Oct. 1980.
Jones, Lula Lall. By Paul J. Nyden. Scarbro, W.Va., 1 Dec. 1980.
Kelly, Annie. By Paul J. Nyden. Lansing, W.Va., 23 Oct. 1980.
Lambert, Elizabeth. By William E. Cox. N.p., 18 Aug. 1986.
Luther, John. By Paul J. Nyden. Beckley, W.Va., 20 Sept. 1980.
Matthew, Russell. By William E. Cox. Oak Hill, W.Va., 10 Aug. 1981.
Pugh, T. B. By Paul J. Nyden. Beckley, W.Va., 6 Sept. 1980.
Sanders, Ralph. By William E. Cox. Beckley, W.Va., June 1981.
Skaggs, Irene Hicks. By Jim Worsham. Fayetteville, W.Va., 13 Mar. 1984.
Skaggs, Carl. By Jim Worsham. South Caperton, W.Va., 13 Mar. 1984.
Sydenstricker, Harry. By Paul J. Nyden. Beckley, W.Va., 16 Oct. 1980.
Whittington, John Luther "Bud." By Paul J. Nyden. Beckley, W.Va., 20 Sept. 1980.
Wilson, Ada. By Paul J. Nyden. Scarbro, W.Va., 13 Dec. 1980.
Woodsen, Dometrius. By Paul J. Nyden. Beckley, W.Va., 7 Nov. 1980.

Samford University Oral History Collection, Birmingham, Alabama

Barnes, Reuben. By Randy Barnes. Docena, Ala., Mar. 1979.
Bonds, Frank. By Patty McDonald. Birmingham, Ala., Mar. 1979.
Cochran, Christine. By Jerry Tapley. Docena, Ala., 1979.
Crane, Claude. By Jim Nogalski. Warrior, Ala., Mar. 1979.
Dorsett, Margaret. By Nancy Barbee. Docena, Ala., Mar. 1979.
Gray, Mary P. by Dana Norman. Docena, Ala., Feb. 1979.
Gaddis, Fred. By Wayne Flynt. Stonega, Va., Aug. 1974.
Kizzire, Melba. By Joy Richardson. Docena, Ala., 1979.
Mardis, Belinda. By Mr. Kelley. Docena, Ala., Mar. 1979
McFee, Dr. E. L. By Jim Nogalski. Birmingham, Ala., Mar. 1979.
Minor, L. F. By Wayne Flynt. Big Stone Gap, Va., Aug. 1974.
Minor, Lloyd Vick. By Wayne Flynt and James Brown. Pennington Gap, Va., Aug. 1974.

Oglestree, D. B. By Ronnie Boulware. Docena, Ala., 28 Feb. 1979.
Shoemaker, Edith. By Kenny Headley. Docena, Ala., Mar. 1979.
Smith, Luther V. By Benny Hendrix. Quinton, Ala., 27 Nov. 1974.
Sokira, John. By Selena Cason. Brookside, Ala., 7 Aug., 1975.
Turner, W. B., Sr. By Don Sullivan. Docena, Ala., Mar. 1979.
Walker, William H. By David Massey. Birmingham, Ala., 1979.

Oral History and Private Correspondence in Author's Collection

Marcum, Carry Mae. By author. Blacksburg, Va., 18 and 28 Aug. 1986.
Thelma Rotenberry, Bristol, Tenn., to author, 23 Feb. 1985.
Mrs. Ernest W. Stone, Elk Creek, Va., to author, 10 Dec. 1984.
Jane Ford Taylor, Fincastle, Va., to author, 12 Dec. 1984.

Unpublished

Cantry, William S., III. "Derby Goes Union: The Decline of Welfare Capitalism and the Rise of Labor Unionism in a Southern Appalachian Coal Town, 1922–1933." Unpublished paper. Yale University, October 1974. Located in WCCR.
Gregg, Robert. "Origin and Development of the Tennessee Coal, Iron and Railroad Company." N.d. Scrapbook. Birmingham Public Library.
Hagley Museum and Library. "Stonega Coke and Coal Company: Company History." Wilmington, Del., n.d.
Hibbard, Walter R., Jr. "The Coalfields of Virginia: An History of People, Machinery, and Natural Resources." Unpublished manuscript. Virginia Center for Coal and Energy Research, Virginia Polytechnic Institute and State University, Blacksburg, Va., 1989.
———. "An Abridged History of the Southwest Virginia Coal Industry." Unpublished manuscript to Virginia Center for Coal and Energy Research, Virginia Polytechnic Institute and State University, Blacksburg, Va., July 1987.
Keith, Jeanette. "The Hill Country of Zion: Community, Church, and Society in Tennessee's Upper Cumberland, 1890–1929." Ph.D. thesis in progress. Vanderbilt University, Nashville, Tenn.
Marowitz, Matthew P., et. al., compilers. "A History of the Borderland Coal Company." Alderman Library, Charlottesville, Va.
———. "A History of the Low Moor Iron Company." Alderman Library, Charlottesville, Va.
Pudup, Mary Beth. "Land before Coal: Class and Regional Development in Southeastern Kentucky." Ph.D. thesis. University of California, Berkeley, 1987.
Williams, Lewis M. "The Transformation of a Coal Mining Town." Wheelwright Collection, Margaret I. King Library, University of Kentucky, Lexington, Ky.

Printed Documents

Hillery, George A., Jr. *Population Growth in Kentucky, 1820–1960*. University of Kentucky Agricultural Experiment Station *Bulletin* 705 (February 1966).

Jones, D. J., N. M. Wilder and John F. Maurice. "Mountain Bumps in the Coal Fields of Harlan County, Kentucky." Kentucky Department of Mines and Minerals. Series 8, *Bulletin* 1 (1 Dec. 1934).

Prescott, E. J., compiler. *The Story of the Virginia Coal and Iron Company, 1882–1945*. Big Stone Gap, Va., 1945.

President's Commission on Coal, John D. Rockefeller IV, chairman. *The American Coal Miner: A Report on Community and Living Conditions*. Washington, D.C., 1980.

Speranza, Gino. "Getting Evidence in the Labor Camps of West Virginia." Microfilm. Gino Speranza Papers, New York Public Library.

U.S. Coal Mines Administration. *A Medical Survey of the Bituminous-Coal Industry*. Directed by Rear Admiral Joel Boone. Washington, D.C., 1947.

U.S. Congress, Senate. *Report of the U. S. Coal Commission*. Senate Document 195, 68th Congress, 2d sess. Washington, D.C., 1925.

U.S. Department of Agriculture. *Economic and Social Problems of the Southern Appalachians*. Miscellaneous Publication no. 205. Washington, D.C., 1935.

———. *Soil Survey, Wise County, Virginia*. Soil Conservation Service Series 1940, no. 12. Washington, D.C., 1954.

U.S. Department of Commerce, Bureau of the Census. *Ninth Census of the United States: 1870*. Washington, D.C., 1872.

———. *Tenth Census of the United States: 1880*. Washington, D.C., 1883.

———. *Eleventh Census of the United States: 1890*. Washington, D.C., 1895.

———. *Twelfth Census of the United States: 1900*. Washington, D.C., 1901–02.

———. *Thirteenth Census of the United States:* 1910. Washington, D.C., 1911..

U.S. Department of Commerce, Bureau of the Census. *World Population 1983; Recent Demographic Estimates for the Countries and Regions of the World*. Washington, D.C., 1983.

U.S. Department of Labor, Women's Bureau. *Home Environment and Employment Opportunities of Women in Coal-Mine Workers' Families*.

Bulletin 45, 1925. Virginia Polytechnic Institute, Engineering Extension Division. *Industrial Survey for Southwestern Virginia, Inc., Wise County, Virginia*. June 1929, Blacksburg, Va.

Books

Anderson, Michael. *Family Structure in Nineteenth Century Lancashire*. Cambridge: Cambridge University Press, 1971.

Ashton, T. S. *The Industrial Revolution, 1760–1830*. London: Oxford University Press, 1964.

Athey, Lou. *Kaymoor: A New River Community*. W.Va.: Eastern National Park and Monument Association, 1986.

Ayers, Edward L. *Vengeance and Justice: Crime and Punishment in the Nineteenth-Century American South*. New York: Oxford University Press, 1984.

Barton, Josef J. *Peasants and Strangers: Italians, Rumanians, and Slovaks in an American City*. Cambridge, Mass.: Harvard University Press, 1975.

Barton, W. B. *An Appalachian Doctor and His Patients*. New York: n.p., n.d.

Beebe, Gilbert Wheeler. *Contraception and Fertility in the Southern Appalachians*. Baltimore: Williams and Wilkins, 1942.

Bender, Thomas. *Community and Social Change in America*. Baltimore: Johns Hopkins University Press, 1978.

Benson, John. *British Coalminers in the Nineteenth Century: A Social History*. Dublin: Gill and Macmillan, 1980.

Berthoff, Rowland. *An Unsettled People: Social Order and Disorder in American History*. New York: Harper & Row, 1971.

Bode, Frederick A., and Donald E. Ginter. *Farm Tenancy and the Census in Antebellum Georgia*. Athens: University of Georgia Press, 1986.

Bulmer, Martin. *Mining and Social Chage: Durham County in the Twentieth Century*. London: Croom Helm, 1978.

Campbell, John C. *The Southern Highlander and His Homeland*. Lexington: University of Kentucky Press, 1969.

Carlton, David. *Mill and Town in South Carolina*. Baton rouge: Louisiana State University Press, 1982.

Caudill, Harry M. *Night Comes to the Cumberlands: A Biography of a Depressed Area*. Boston: Little, Brown, 1962.

Cherniack, Martin. *The Hawk's Nest Incident: America's Worst Industrial Disaster*. New Haven, Conn.: Yale University Press, 1986.

Cobb, James C. *Industrialization and Southern Society, 1877–1984*. Chicago: Dorsey Press, 1984.

Conley, Philip Mallory. *History of the West Virginia Coal Industry*. Charleston, W. Va.: Education Foundation, 1960.

Corbin, David Alan. *Life, Work, and Rebellion in the Coal Fields: The Southern West Virginia Miners, 1880–1922*. Urbana: University of Illinois Press, 1981.

Craven, Avery O. *Soil Exhaustion as a Factor in the Agricultural History of Virginia and Maryland*. Urbana: University of Illinois Press, 1922.

Daniel, Pete. *Standing at the Crossroads: Southern Life in the Twentieth Century*. New York: Hill and Wang, 1986.

Darnton, Robert. *The Great Cat Massacre and Other Episodes in French Cultural History*. New York: Vintage Books: 1985.

Degler, Carl N. *At Odds: Women and the Family in America from the Revolution to the Present*. New York: Oxford University Press, 1980.

DeJong, Gordon F. *Appalachian Fertility Decline, A Demographic and Sociological Analysis*. Lexington: University Press of Kentucky, 1968.

Densmore, Raymond E. *The Coal Miner of Appalachia*. Parsons, W.Va.: McClain Printing Co., 1977.

Dix, Keith. *Work Relations in the Coal Industry: The Hand-Loading Era, 1880–1930*. Morgantown, W.Va.: Institute for Labor Studies, West Virginia University, 1977.

————. *What's a Coal Miner to Do? The Mechanization of Coal Mining*. Pittsburgh: University of Pittsburgh Press, 1989.

Dodrill, Gordon, comp. *20,000 Coal Company Stores in the United States, Mexico, and Canada*. Pittsburgh, 1971.

Doyle, Don H. *New Men, New Cities, New South: Atlanta, Nashville, Charleston, Mobile, 1860–1910*. Chapel Hill: University of North Carolina Press, 1990.

Dubofsky, Melvyn, and Warren Van Tyne. *John L. Lewis: A Biography*. New York: Quadrangle/New York Times Co., 1977.

Dunbar, Tony. *Our Land Too*. New York: Pantheon 1971.

Dunn, Durwood. *Cades Cove: The Life and Death of a Southern Appalachian Community, 1818–1937*. Knoxville: University of Tennessee Press, 1988.

Eller, Ronald D. *Miners, Millhands, and Mountaineers: Industrialization of the Appalachian South, 1880–1930*. Knoxville: University of Tennessee Press, 1982.

Faust, A. B. *The German Element in the United States*. New York: Houghton Mifflin, 1927.

Fetterman, John. *Stinking Creek: The Portrait of a Small Mountain Community in Appalachia*. New York: Dutton, 1970.

Filippelli, Ronald L. *Labor in the United States*. New York: Random House, 1984.

Fite, Gilbert C. *Cotton Fields No More: Southern Agriculture 1865–1980*. Lexington: University Press of Kentucky, 1984.

Flinn, Michael W. *The History of the British Coal Industry*. Vol. 2, *1700–1830 The Industrial Revolution*. Oxford: Clarendon Press, 1984.

Flynt, Wayne. *Poor But Proud: Alabama's Poor Whites*. Tuscaloosa, Ala., 1989.

Fredrickson, George. *White Supremacy: A Comparative Study in American and South African History*. Oxford: Oxford University Press, 1981.

Gaston, Paul M. *The New South Creed: A Study in Southern Mythmaking*. New York: Vintage Books, 1973.

Gaventa, John. *Power and Powerlessness: Quiescence and Rebellion in an Appalachian Valley*. Urbana: University of Illinois Press, 1980.

Genovese, Eugene. *Roll, Jordon, Roll: The World the Slaves Made*. New York: Pantheon, 1974.

Goodrich, Carter. *The Miner's Freedom: A Study of the Working Life in a Changing Industry*. New York: Arno Press, 1977.

Gouldner, Alvin W. *Patterns of Industrial Bureaucracy: A Case Study of Factory Administration*. New York: Free Press, 1954.

Graebner, William. *Coal Mining Safety in the Progressive Period: The Political Economy of Reform*. Lexington: University Press of Kentucky, 1976.

Green, Archie. *Only a Miner: Studies in Recorded Coal-Mining Songs*. Urbana: University of Illinois Press, 1972.

Gutman, Herbert G. *Work, Culture and Society in Industrializing America: Essays in American Working-Class and Social History*. New York: Vintage Books, 1977.

Hahn, Steven. *The Roots of Southern Populism: Yeoman Farmers and the Transformation of the Georgia Upcountry, 1850–1890*. New York: Oxford University Press, 1983.

Hahn, Steven and Jonathan Prude, eds. *The Countryside in the Age of Capitalist Transformation*. Chapel Hill: University of North Carolina Press, 1985.

Haines, Michael. *Fertility and Occupation: Population Patterns in Industrialization.* New York: Academic Press, 1979.

Hall, Jacquelyn Dowd, James Leloudis, Robert Korstad, Mary Murphy, Lu Ann Jones, and Christopher B. Daly. *Like a Family: The Making of a Southern Cotton Mill World.* Chapel Hill: University of North Carolina Press, 1987.

Hall, Robert L. and Carol B. Stack, eds. *Holding on to the Land and the Lord: Kinship, Ritual, Land Tenure, and Social Policy in the Rural South.* Athens: University of Georgia Press, 1982.

Hareven, Tamara K. and Randolph Langenbach. *Amoskeag: Life and Work in an American Factory-City.* New York: Pantheon, 1978.

Henretta, James A. *The Evolution of American Society, 1700–1815.* Lexington, Mass. D. C. Heath, 1973.

Hevener, John W. *Which Side Are You On? The Harlan County Coal Miners, 1931–1939.* Urbana: University of Illinois Press, 1978.

Hibbard, Walter R., Jr. *Virginia Coal: An Abridged History and Complete Data Manual of Virginia Coal Production / Consumption from 1748 to 1988.* Blacksburg, Va.: Virginia Center for Coal and Energy Research, Virginia Polytechnic Institute and State University, 1990.

Hicks, George L. *Appalachian Valley.* New York: Holt, Rinehart and Winston, 1976.

Hooker, Elizabeth R. *Religion in the Highlands: Native Churches and Missionary Enterprises in the Southern Appalachian Area.* New York: Home Mission Council, 1933.

Jones, G. C. *Growing Up Hard in Harlan County.* Lexington: University Press of Kentucky, 1985.

Kephart, Horace. *Our Southern Highlanders.* New York: Outing Publishing Co., 1913.

Kirby, Jack Temple. *Rural Worlds Lost: The American South 1920–1960.* Baton Rouge: Louisiana State University Press, 1987.

Kolchin, Peter. *Unfree Labor: American Slavery and Russian Serfdom.* Cambridge, Mass.: Belknap Press, 1987.

Lane, Winthrop D. *Civil War in West Virginia.* New York: Arno and New York Times, 1969.

Lemon, James T. *The Best Poor Man's Country: A Geographical Study of Southeastern Pennsylvania.* Baltimore: Johns Hopkins University Press, 1972.

Lewis, Helen Matthew, Linda Johnson, and Donald Askins, eds. *Colonialism in Modern America: The Appalachian Case.* Boone, N.C.: Appalachian Consortium Press, 1978.

Lewis, Ronald L. *Black Coal Miners in America: Race, Class, and Community Conflict.* Lexington: University Press of Kentucky: 1987.

Leyburn, James G. *The Scotch-Irish: A Social History.* Chapel Hill: University of North Carolina Press, 1962.

Matthews, Elmora Messer. *Neighbor and Kin: Life in a Tennessee Ridge Community.* Nashville: Vanderbilt University Press, 1965.

McDonald, Michael J., and John Muldowny. *TVA and the Dispossessed.* Knoxville: University of Tennessee Press, 1982.

Miller, Donald L., and Richard E. Sharpless. *The Kingdom of Coal: Work, Enterprise, and Ethnic Communities in the Mine Fields.* Philadelphia: University of Pennsylvania Press, 1985.

Montell, William Lynwood. *The Saga of Coe Ridge: A Study in Oral History.* Knoxville: University of Tennessee Press, 1971.

Morris, Homer Lawrence. *The Plight of the Bituminous Coal Miner.* Philadelphia: University of Pennsylvania Press, 1934.

Paludan, Phillip Shaw. *Victims: A True Story of the Civil War,* Knoxville: University of Tennessee Press, 1981.

Parkinson, George. *Guide to Coal Mining Collections in the United States.* Morgantown, W.Va., 1978.

Pearsall, Marion. *Little Smokey Ridge: The Natural History of a Southern Appalachian Neighborhood.* University: University of Alabama Press, 1959.

Petersen, Bill. *Coaltown Revisited: An Appalachian Notebook.* Chicago, 1972.

Pollard, Sidney. *Peaceful Conquest: The Industrialization of Europe, 1760–1970.* New York: Oxford University Press, 1981.

Potter, David. *The South and the Sectional Conflict.* Baton Rouge: Louisiana State University Press, 1968.

Reid, Donald. *The Miners of Decazeville: A Genealogy of Deindustrialization.* Cambridge, Mass.: Harvard University Press, 1985.

Rochester, Anna. *Labor and Coal.* New York: International Publishers, 1931.

Rosen, George. *The History of Miners' Diseases: A Medical and Social Interpretation.* New York: Shuman's, 1943.

Ross, Charlotte, ed. *Bibliography of Southern Appalachia.* Boone, N.C.: Appalachian Consortium Press, 1976.

Seltzer, Curtis. *Fire in the Hole: Miners and Managers in the American Coal Industry.* Lexington: University Press of Kentucky, 1985.

Shackelford, Laurel, and Bill Weinberg. *Our Appalachia.* New York: Hill and Wang, 1977.

Shapiro, Henry D. *Appalachia on Our Mind: The Southern Mountains and Mountaineers in the American Consciousness, 1870–1920.* Chapel Hill: University of North Carolina Press, 1978.

Sherman, Mandel and Thomas R. Henry. *Hollow Folk.* Berryville, Va.: Thomas Y. Crowell, 1933.

Shifflett, Crandall A. *Patronage and Poverty in the Tobacco South: Louisa County, Virginia, 1860–1900.* Knoxville: University of Tennessee Press, 1982.

Stephenson, John B. *Shiloh: A Mountain Community.* Lexington: University Press of Kentucky, 1968.

Tams, W. P., Jr. *The Smokeless Coal Fields of West Virginia.* Morgantown: West Virginia University Press, 1983.

Taylor, Philip J. *The Distant Magnet: European Emigration to the U.S.A.* New York: Harper & Row, 1971.

Turner, William H., and Edward J. Cabbell, eds. *Blacks in Appalachia.* Lexington: University of Kentucky Press, 1985.

Vance, Rupert B. *Human Geography of the South: A Study in Regional Resources and Human Adequacy.* Chapel Hill: University of North Carolina Press, 1932.

Verhoeff, Mary. *Kentucky Mountain Transportation and Commerce, 1750–1911.* Louisville, Ky., 1911.

Walkowitz, Daniel J. *Worker City, Company Town: Iron and Cotton-Worker Protest in Troy and Cohoes, New York, 1855–1884.* Urbana: University of Illinois Press, 1978.

Wallace, Anthony F. C. *St. Clair: A Nineteenth-Century Coal Town's Experience with a Disaster-Prone Industry.* New York: Alfred A. Knopf, 1987.

Waller, Altina L. *Feud: Hatfields, McCoys, and Social Change in Appalachia, 1860–1900.* Chapel Hill: University of North Carolina Press, 1988.

Weller, Jack. *Yesterday's People: Life in Contemporary Appalachia.* Lexington: University Press of Kentucky, 1965.

Wells, Robert V. *Uncle Sam's Family: Issues in and Perspectives on American Demographic History.* Albany: State University of New York Press, 1985.

Whisnant, David E. *All That is Native and Fine: The Politics of Culture in an American Region.* Chapel Hill: University of North Carolina Press, 1983.

White, Marjorie Longenecker. *The Birmingham District: An Industrial History and Guide.* Birmingham, Ala.: Birmingham Historical Society, 1981.

Williams, John Alexander. *West Virginia: A History.* New York: Norton, 1984.

Williamson, Joel W. *An Appalachian Symposium.* Boone, N.C.: Appalachian Consortium Press, 1978.

Wolf, Eric. *Europe and the People without History.* Berkeley: University of California Press, 1982.

Woodward, C. Vann. *Origins of the New South, 1877–1913.* Baton Rouge: Louisiana State University Press, 1951.

———. *The Strange Career of Jim Crow.* New York: Oxford University Press, 1974.

Wrigley, E. A. *Industrial Growth and Population Change: A Regional Study of the Coalfield Areas of Northwest Europe in the Later Nineteenth Century.* Cambridge: Cambridge University Press, 1961.

Wright, Gavin. *The Political Economy of the Cotton South: Households, Markets and Wealth in the Nineteenth Century.* New York: W. W. Norton, 1978.

Wyatt-Brown, Bertram. *Southern Honor: Ethics and Behavior in the Old South.* New York: Oxford University Press, 1982.

Articles

Bailey, Kenneth R. "A Judicious Mixture: Negroes and Immigrants in the West Virginia Mines, 1880–1917." In *Blacks in Appalachia*, ed. Turner and Cabbell.

Barron, Hal Seth. "A Case For Appalachian Demographic History." *Appalachian Journal* 4 (Spring–Summer 1977): 208–15.

Brown, James S. and Harry K. Schwarzweller. "The Appalachian Family." In *Appalachia: Its People, Heritage, and Problems*, ed. Frank S. Riddel. (Dubuque: Kendall/Hunt Publishing, 1974).

Bulmer, M. I. A. "Sociological Models of the Mining Community." *Sociological Review* 23 (Feb. 1975): 61–92.

Campbell, Shirley Young. "Coal Towns." *Goldenseal* 13 (Summer 1987): 53.

Daniel, Pete. "The Crossroads of Change: Cotton, Tobacco, and Rice Cultures in the Twentieth Century." *Journal of Southern History* 50 (Aug. 1984): 429–56.

Egerton, John. "Boom or Bust in the Hollows," *New York Times Magazine.* 18 Oct. 1981.

Eller, Ronald D. "Industrialization and Social Change in Appalachia, 1880–1930: A Look at the Static Image." In *Colonialism in Modern America*, ed. Lewis, et al.

———. "Land and Family: An Historical View of Preindustrial Appalachia." *Appalachian Journal* 6 (Winter 1979): 83–109.

———. "Towards a New History of the Appalachian South." *Appalachian Journal* 5 (Autumn 1977): 74–81.

Fishback, Price V. "Did Coal Miners 'Owe Their Souls to the Company Store'? Theory and Evidence from the Early 1900s." *Journal of Economic History* 46 (Dec. 1986): 1011–29.

Fisher, Stephen L., J. W. Williamson, and Juanita Lewis, eds. *A Guide to Appalachian Studies.* Special issue of *Appalachian Journal* 5 (Autumn 1977).

Flynt, J. Wayne. "The Southern Church as Reformer." In *Major Problems in the History of the American South* 2, *The New South*, ed. Paul D. Escott and David R. Goldfield. Lexington, Mass.: D. C. Heath, 1990.

Ford, Thomas R., and Gordon F. DeJong. "The Decline of Fertility in the Southern Appalachian Mountain Region." *Social Forces* 42 (Oct. 1963): 89–96.

Gaventa, John. "Property, Coal, and Theft." In *Colonialism in Modern America*, ed. Lewis et al.

Gorn, Elliott J. "'Gouge and Bite, Pull Hair and Scratch': The Social Significance of Fighting in the Southern Backcountry." *American Historical Review* 90 (Feb. 1985): 18–43.

Henretta, James. "The Study of Social Mobility: Ideological Assumptions and Conceptual Bias." *Labor History* 18 (Spring 1977): 165–78.

Jordon, Daniel P. "The Mingo War: Labor Violence in the Southern West Virginia Coal Fields, 1919–1922." in *Selected Papers, Southern Labor History Conference, 1976*, ed. Gary M. Fink and Merle E. Reed. Westport, Conn.: Greenwood Press, 1977.

Kline, Michael. "The Coon Dog Truth: Charlie Blevins at the Red Robin Inn." *Goldenseal* 8 (Winter 1982): 35–42.

Kyle, Birdie. "Growing Up in the Coalfields." *Goldenseal* 6 (Apr.–June 1980): 6.

Laing, James T. "The Negro Miner in West Virginia." In *Blacks in Appalachia*, ed. Turner and Cabbell.

Lewis, Helen M., and Edward E. Knipe. "The Colonialism Model: The Appalachian Case." In *Colonialism in Modern America*, ed. Lewis, et. al.

Lewis, Helen M., Sue Easterling Kobak, and Linda Johnson. "Family, Religion, and Colonialism in Central Appalachia; or Bury My Rifle at Big Stone Gap." In *Colonialism in Modern America*, ed. Lewis, et al.

McKinney, Gordon B. "Industrialization and Violence in Appalachia in the 1890s. In *An Appalachian Symposium*, ed. Joel W. Williamson.

Northrup, Herbert R. "The Coal Mines." In *Blacks in Appalachia*, ed. Turner and Cabbell.

Nyden, Paul. "Coal Town Baseball." *Goldenseal* 6 (Oct.–Dec. 1980): 31–39.

Orr, David, and Jon Dragan. "'A Dirty Messy Place to Work,' B. H. Metheney Remembers Hawk's Nest Tunnel," *Goldenseal* 7 (Jan.–Mar. 1981): 34–41.

Parker, Russell D. "The Black Community in a Company Town: Alcoa, Tennessee, 1919–1939." In *Blacks in Appalachia*, ed. Turner and Cabbell.

Pudup, Mary Beth. "The Boundaries of Class in Preindustrial Appalachia." *Journal of Historical Geography* 15 (1989): 139–62.

Pultz, John Leggett. "The Big Stone Gap Coal-Field of Virginia and Kentucky." *Engineering Magazine* 27 (Oct. 1904): 71–85.

Rowh, Mark. "The Hawk's Nest Tragedy: Fifty Years Later." *Goldenseal* 7 (Jan.–Mar. 1981): 31–33.

Simon, Richard M. "Uneven Development and the Case of West Virginia: Going beyond the Colonialism Model." *Appalachian Journal* 8 (Spring 1981): 165–86.

Turner, William H. "The Demography of Black Appalachia: Past and Present." In *Blacks in Appalachia*, ed. Turner and Cabbell.

Whitten, Norman E., Jr. and John Szwed, "Introduction." In *Afro-American Anthropology*, ed. Whitten and Szwed. New York: Free Press, 1970.

Wilhelm, Gene, Jr. "Folk Settlements in the Blue Ridge Mountains." *Appalachian Journal* 5 (Winter 1978): 204–45.

———. "Animal Driver in the Southern Highlands." *Mountain Life and Work* 42 (1966): 6–11.

———. "Animal Driver: A Case Study in Historical Geography." *Journal of Geography* 66 (1967): 327–34.

Wolfe, Margaret Ripley. "Aliens in Appalachia: The Construction of the Clinchfield Railroad and the Italian Experience." In *Appalachia: Family Traditions in Transition*, ed. Emmett M. Essin. Johnson City: East Tennessee State University Press, 1975.

———. "Changing the Face of Southern Appalachia: Urban Planning in Southwest Virginia and East Tennessee, 1890–1929." *Journal of American Planning* 47 (1981): 252–65.

———. "Putting Them in Their Places: Industrial Housing in Southern Appalachia, 1900–1930." *Appalachian Heritage* 7 (Summer 1979): 27–36.

Wyatt-Brown, Bertram. *Southern Honor: Ethics and Behavior in the Old South*. New York: Oxford University Press, 1983.

Index